How Will It All End?

How Will It All End?

End-Time Insights from the Book of Revelation

Dr. Felix J. Rolle II

Library of Congress Control Number:		2021915531
ISBN:	Hardcover	978-1-6641-8750-4
	Softcover	978-1-6641-8749-8
	eBook	978-1-6641-8748-1

Scripture quotations marked KJV are taken from the King James Version of the Bible. Public domain.

Scripture quotations marked NLT are taken from the Holy Bible, New Living Translation, copyright © 1996, 2004, 2007, 2013, 2015 by Tyndale House Foundation. Used by permission of Tyndale House Publishers, Inc., Carol Stream, Illinois 60188. All rights reserved.

Scriptures marked NIV are taken from the New International Version®, NIV®. Copyright © 1973, 1978, 1984, 2011 by Biblica, Inc.™ Used by permission of Zondervan. All rights reserved worldwide, www.zondervan.com. The "NIV" and "New International Version" are trademarks registered in the United States Patent and Trademark Office by Biblica, Inc.™

Scripture quotations marked (TLB) are taken from The Living Bible copyright © 1971. Used by permission of Tyndale House Publishers, Inc., Carol Stream, Illinois 60188. All rights reserved.

Special editing by: One Rib Publications, www.oneribpublications.com, email: oneribpublications@gmail.com.

Cover designed by: Propresenters, www.propresenters.org, email: propresenters@outlook.com.

Photography: Sawyers Studios, www.sawyersstudios.com, email: portraitala@gmail.com.

Dr. Felix J. Rolle II
Nassau, N.P., Bahamas
Telephone: 1 (242) 357-7565
Email: felixjrolle@gmail.com

Print information available on the last page.

Rev. date: 08/06/2021

To order additional copies of this book, contact:
Xlibris
844-714-8691
www.Xlibris.com
Orders@Xlibris.com
829187

CONTENTS

To all the people the Lord has allowed me to minister to
over my many years in the Kingdom of God,
and
to the people who have poured into my life
in positive ways, great and small,
and
to all the people who are searching for and
not afraid of the truth.

God is a loving Father. He is not going to send anyone to hell. You have a free will, so you choose where you want to go when you are done with this world.

PREFACE

THIS BOOK UNVEILS truths that give a clearer picture of Jesus Christ in His fullness—the divine Person, what's important to Him, His mission, His office, and His future administration. Jesus of Nazareth is the Son of God and the Son of Man, and the firstfruits of the resurrection. As you read, do not be distracted by what you do not understand. Instead, focus on what you know is true: Jesus Christ is the only begotten Son of God, and He shall return someday soon.

How Will It All End? also tells of things which must take place. It makes known "the events of the end-times." It speaks to assure you that there is a reckoning day to come for everyone and everything. There is a judgment day. The book of Revelation is documentation and proof that God has set forth and declared a time of reckoning for everything under the sun. He has made this time known so that no one can truthfully say, "I didn't know!"

> The Revelation of Jesus Christ, which God gave Him to show His servants—things which must shortly take place. And He sent and signified it by His angel to His servant John, who bore witness to the word of God, and to the testimony of Jesus Christ, to all things that he saw. Blessed is he who reads and those who hear the words of this prophecy, and keep those things which are written in it; for the time is near, (Revelation 1:1–3, emphasis added)

Even though the book of Revelation is an exposure of Jesus Christ's future ministry, some have described the vast amount of extraterrestrial information contained in it in other ways:

o   Already fulfilled prophecy (thereby downplaying its significance).

o   Symbolism "too deep" to comprehend.

o   Spiritual principles applicable to a certain sect only.

o   Too mysterious for natural understanding because it is written in codes (thereby minimizing its relevance for the common person).

o   A forecast of universal history, like the book of Daniel, which it truly is.

If Revelation is a forecast of universal history, then it would be frightening to deal casually with this book. However, you can find some comfort in the scripture quoted above for it reveals that there is a blessing upon everyone who receives and adheres to the prophecy of this book. Keep in mind that Revelation was written to "His servants" in the various churches and not to spiritual leaders only.

The credibility of the book of Revelation is a topic all by itself. Nevertheless, its contents are in alignment with the rest of the Bible. Old Testament prophets David, Isaiah, Jeremiah, Daniel, and others have recorded similar events of prophecy. Being familiar with and applying the principles and teachings of the other twenty-six books of the New Covenant would enhance your understanding of the significance of this one book. The same thread of Revelation—that the Kingdom of Heaven is now present in the earth and that Jesus the Messiah is the King of this kingdom and the King of kings—runs throughout the New Testament. Therefore, remove your fears and accept the gravity and truthfulness of Revelation so that you do not take it for granted.

ACKNOWLEDGMENTS

I GIVE SPECIAL thanks to my daughter Simone Daley, who helped me in ways I cannot recount because of the number of times and various circumstances, and to my dear friend Lana Ross, who assisted me far beyond my expectations. Their endless patience, generosity, and caring hearts allowed me to complete this work on time, making it possible for you to have it in your hands.

The staff and editor of One Rib Publications deserve my special mention for their professionalism and demands for excellence.

I extend special gratitude to New Birth Ministries International, where I served as pastor for six years and Bible teacher for nineteen years and to Bahamas Faith Ministries International, where I grew up in the Lord as I traveled with the leaders and sat under great ministers of the gospel from around the Caribbean. I must recognize Christian International, where I received hands-on apostolic and prophetic training, and North Carolina Theological Seminary, where I earned my Master of Theology and Doctor of Theology degrees.

The opportunities to serve in these and other ministries kept me on the cutting edge of what God is doing on the earth today. I am a better person because of their involvement in my life. May God bless them all!

INTRODUCTION

A LOT OF people are talking today about how this world will end. Some of them think the world will never end while others believe the end will be according to what they learn from ancient and modern books, archeological findings, and the man-made theories presented by scientists and self-proclaimed prophets of God. These are all good sources of information, and I have referred to them in the writing of this book. However, the primary source of information for *How Will It All End? End-Time Insights from the Book of Revelation* is the New King James Version of the Holy Bible with emphasis on the book of Revelation, which is also known as the last (no more following this) book of the Holy Bible.

As an ardent believer in Christ Jesus for more than thirty-five years and a Bible teacher for most of those years and being filled with the Holy Spirit since seven weeks after accepting Jesus Christ as my personal Lord and Savior, I have seen enough of the things of Jehovah God to know that He is real and that His Word will stand forever. I am led by my personal conviction under the guidance of the Holy Spirit to write this volume so that others might gain a better understanding of the book of Revelation.

Nature and life itself have taught us that all seasons have a beginning and an end. Everything with a time factor has a beginning and an end. Everything changes as nothing natural lasts forever. This age (generation, dispensation, era of life) will come to an end (culmination, entire completion, consummation). According to the Scriptures, it is not a question of if but when this will happen.

The enemy who sowed them is the devil, the harvest is the end of the age, and the reapers are the angels. Therefore as the tares are gathered and burned in the fire, so it will be at the end of this age. (Matthew 13:39–40)

For the sake of time, let us accept the position stated in the above scripture as a truth; verification of it will come later. There is no way you would wish for what's happening now in this world to continue forever. This is a period of lawlessness, open rebellion, shedding of innocent blood, perverseness, sexual immorality, hatred, and rejection of God's Word and His Son Jesus Christ must come to an end for even the biggest dark cloud has a silver lining. Jehovah God knows this, and He has prepared for it. You have a major part to play in securing your future, that is, in determining what happens to you after this age comes to its end. Continue reading to find out if you are in a good position or not.

There are many references where God says that He would not have us ignorant of matters that concern His kingdom. His Word also says that He is still revealing mysteries concerning His kingdom today (1 Corinthians 2:10–12; Ephesians 1:9–10, 3:2–5; Colossians 1:25–26). Amos 3:7 tells us that "surely the Lord GOD does nothing unless He reveals His secrets to His servants the prophets." Therefore, we can count on Him nowadays to reveal more secrets and specific information concerning His future moves on the earth.

While there are certain things the heavenly Father has kept to Himself, there are other matters which He reveals to His apostles and prophets. Our Lord told His disciples, "No longer do I call you servants, for a servant does not know what his master is doing; but I have called you friends, for all things that I heard from My Father I have made known to you" (John 15:15). Jesus wants you to know as much about His kingdom as you are prepared to receive.

I do not purport to know everything about the Kingdom of Heaven nor about the end-time. There will always be more revelations to come simply because the Lord is still revealing secrets. But I truly believe what has been given to me is satisfactory for this publication at this time. *How Will It All End?* is not intended to be the world's final book on the subject but rather a proper exposition based on where the world is at this time. If this world is still around twenty to thirty years from now, it would not mean that the information in this book is untrue; it might just be unfamiliar to you because you will never know everything. Bear in mind that because "the secret things belong to the Lord our God, but those things which are revealed belong to us" (Deuteronomy 29:29), we should make good use of what is made available until we get more refinements. For example, when modern computers came into popular use in the 1980s, they must have made Charles Babbage, the father of programmable computers, look like a caveman. When John the Revelator received his Word about two thousand years ago, there were no guns and airplanes as we know them today. John could write only from his knowledge at that time. And that is what I am doing: writing from the knowledge I have at this time.

As a believer in Christ Jesus, you can also pray and ask the heavenly Father to give you the Spirit of wisdom and revelation in the knowledge of Him. That is what I have done. So help me, Holy Spirit!

> that the God of our Lord Jesus Christ, the Father of glory, may give to you the spirit of wisdom and revelation in the knowledge of Him, the eyes of your understanding being enlightened; that you may know what is the hope of His calling, what are the riches of the glory of His inheritance in the saints, and what is the exceeding greatness of His power toward us who believe, according to the working of His

mighty power which He worked in Christ when He raised Him from the dead and seated Him at His right hand in the heavenly places, far above all principality and power and might and dominion, and every name that is named, not only in this age but also in that which is to come. (Ephesians 1:17–21)

The primary intent of this book is to simplify as much as possible the things which made the book of Revelation seem difficult to understand or too scary to open. Another aim is to help clear up the false doctrines and outright lies propagated by various sects concerning the end-time. Even though Revelation is a prophetic book, the characters, places, and events it describes are real. Bear in mind that every prophecy God has given must be fulfilled; otherwise, God would be fallible and not trustworthy. His every word must come to pass before this world as we know it ends, every word. Therefore, I have chosen to accept the eternal, infallible wisdom of God Jehovah over the best opinions and scientific proofs of men.

We now know more than our fathers did. We are living in the age of information. Whatever we want to know we can find at our fingertips. There is no legitimate excuse for remaining ignorant in this twenty-first century. Yet the Creator is saying:

My people are destroyed for lack of knowledge. Because you have rejected knowledge, I also will reject you from being priest for Me; because you have forgotten the law of your God, I also will forget your children. (Hosea 4:6)

Please have a copy of Revelation and/or the Holy Bible nearby as you read *How Will It All End?* so that you can easily examine scripture references not printed in this book to minimize the size of this volume.

From the completion of the first manuscript to the stage of the final editing of this book a few prophesied global events have taken place or been rumored. At the rate which end-time events are unfolding there is a need for a follow up or revision to this publication in the not too distant future. Stay tuned as the Book of Revelation becomes a reality in this age.

CHAPTER 1

About the Book of Revelation and Its Author

The Author

THE AUTHOR OF Revelation is John the Revelator, a Jewish fisherman from the Sea of Galilee, and the most beloved of the twelve apostles of Jesus Christ (John 13:23–25; Luke 5:9–11). He is the son of Zebedee and Salome and the younger brother of James. Because of their fiery zeal, Jesus called the two brothers "Boanerges," meaning "Sons of Thunder" (Mark 3:17; Luke 9:54). John is a trustworthy eyewitness to the things he wrote, being the one to whom the revelations were shown. He knew the Lord personally as he was one of the favored three of Jesus's inner circle (Matthew 17:1–2; Mark 5:37–38, 14:32–33; John 19:26–27, 21:20–24).

The book of Revelation was written near the end of the first century (about AD 95) and probably while John was on the island of Patmos (Revelation 1:9).[1] Strangely, though a Jew, the author deals very little with Judaism and more with the "new" universal eternal kingdom Jesus constantly spoke about. His purpose in writing Revelation is found in the first three verses of the first chapter of the book. The author states clearly:

> The Revelation of Jesus Christ, which God gave Him to show His servants—things which must <u>shortly</u> take place. And He sent and signified it by His angel to His servant

John, who bore witness to the word of God, and to the testimony of Jesus Christ, to all things that he saw. Blessed is he who reads and those who hear the words of this prophecy, and keep those things which are written in it; for the time is near. (Revelation 1:1–3, emphasis added)

The Book

The book of Revelation was written from two perspectives— prophecies soon to come and prophecies for the distant future. It is the only prophetical book in the New Testament. It is not historical, poetic, or an epistle, and it is definitely not a narrative. Because this book deals specifically with the future, it is placed last in the canon of the Christian church.

In reading Revelation, you will find that

- the number seven—meaning "completion," "totality," or "perfection"—is the dominant number in the book.[2]
- the number twelve—referring to "unity and completeness"—is used numerous times also.[3]
- the closing chapters of the book mirror in reverse order the opening chapters of Genesis, the first book of the Bible. The effect of this mirroring is to show that as it was in the beginning with Adam and the Creator, so it will be in the end with mankind and the Creator. The Creator's purpose will be fulfilled in the earth. Mankind, not Satan and his cohorts, will have full dominion over the earth to subdue it and be fruitful in it.
- there are many visions to be examined. Explore them in chronological order to get a better understanding of the entire revelation. Because they are visions, some clarification and prior knowledge will be necessary to

get the proper meaning; the same applies to dreams. Do not take all the visions literally.

- the angelic staff of Heaven will conduct many tours throughout the place.

- some events will take place in the different heavens (the plural means that there is more than one heaven) and some on earth.

- it dramatizes that a spiritual war is now going on with drastic persecution against the church, that there is a real enemy who wars against the Kingdom of God, and that there will be deceptions and schemes to cause the inhabitants of the earth to lose focus. However, the Lamb, who is the main character in the book, is victorious over evil. Thus, overcomers are praised and rewarded.

- it tells graphically and explicitly what the end-time will be like. The end was revealed; now we are living out what was said would lead up to the end. If you can appreciate the value and purpose of an architect's plans, then you can easily accept the Creator giving mankind a blueprint (the book of Revelation) of what the earth looks like as it comes to its end. Remember that this is God's earth and He will get what He wants (Exodus 9:29; Psalms 24:1–2).

- At the time of its writing, the entire book was prophecy (Revelation 22:19). Today, some of the events have taken place before our time, some are unfolding now, and the rest is still to come.

Guidelines for Understanding the Book

Here are some guidelines for understanding the book of Revelation.

o   Keep events in chronological order. The entire book was prophecy when it was written. It is not a history book.
o   Bear in mind that an individual might be portrayed as a group, an organization, or a nation.
o   Times and dates are not easily understood and therefore should not be taken at face value (Psalms 90:4; 2 Peter 3:8).
o   Some events might be symbolic and some literal.
o   Do not change a character's role or name unless the Scriptures expressly say to do so.

Why the Book of Revelation?

The hunger to understand what will happen in the end or to answer the question "Have I made the right decision in living by the Word of God?" was so intense that a field of study called eschatology—the study of the last things—developed over the centuries and is still growing today. The book of Revelation is an apocalypse, true revelations of end-time prophecies. It gives revelations on the final kingdom of the Messiah when life as we know it will be brought to fulfillment, an end.

Prophet Amos talks about "the day of the Lord," the day when God will visit His wrath on the enemies of Israel when those who are unrighteous and disobedient to God will be judged—Israelites and Gentiles alike (Amos 5:16–20). The book of Revelation along with other New Testament writings gives much light on how, where, and when this judgment will happen.

Here are what other Old and New Testament writers have to say about the end-time:

But the Lord shall endure forever; He has prepared His throne for judgment. He shall judge the world in righteousness, and

He shall administer judgment for the peoples in uprightness.
(Psalms 9:7–8, 96:11–13)
"He has appointed a day on which He will judge the world
in righteousness by the Man whom He has ordained. He has
given assurance of this to all by raising Him from the dead."
(Acts 17:31)
See also Romans 2:15–16 and 2 Peter 3:7.

The Mayans (an ancient civilization of the Western world
that is known for its advanced art, architecture, mathematics,
calendar, and astronomy) also believed that the world would end
somehow. According to one of their calendars and calculations,
2012 was the predicted year.[4]

Who Is Able to Reveal Secrets and Mysteries?

Daniel tells how he was able to understand mysteries:

Daniel answered and said:
"Blessed be the name of God forever and ever,
For wisdom and might are His.
And He changes the times and the seasons;
He removes kings and raises up kings;
He gives wisdom to the wise
And knowledge to those who have understanding.
He reveals deep and secret things;
He knows what is in the darkness,
And light dwells with Him.
"I thank You and praise You,
O God of my fathers;
You have given me wisdom and might,
And have now made known to me what we asked of You,
For You have made known to us the king's demand."

The king answered and said to Daniel, whose name was Belteshazzar, "Are you able to make known to me the dream which I have seen, and its interpretation?" Daniel answered in the presence of the king, and said, "<u>The secret which the king has demanded, the wise men, the astrologers, the magicians, and the soothsayers cannot declare to the king</u>. But there is a God in heaven who reveals secrets, and He has made known to King Nebuchadnezzar what will be in the latter days. (Daniel 2:20–23, 26–28a, emphasis added)

The God about whom Daniel was talking is *'elohiym* (el-o-heem'). This Hebrew word in its ordinary sense means gods, but when specifically used in the plural and with the article, it refers to the Supreme God.[5]

Prophet Jeremiah received this from the Lord:

"Thus says the LORD who made it, the LORD who formed it to establish it (the LORD is His name): 'Call to Me, and I will answer you, and show you great and mighty things, which you do not know.'" (Jeremiah 33:2–3)

Prophet Amos tells how he got his revelations:

Surely the Lord GOD does nothing, unless He reveals His secret to His servants the prophets. (Amos 3:7)

The Hebrew name for God is *Yehovah* (yeh-ho-vaw'). It denotes the Self-Existent or Eternal. Jehovah is the Jewish national name of God.[6] There are many gods out there, but there is only one Creator of all things—Jehovah.

Apostle Paul explains:

But as it is written:
"Eye has not seen, nor ear heard,

Nor have entered into the heart of man
The things which God has prepared for those who love Him."
But God has revealed them to us through His Spirit. For the
Spirit searches all things, yes, the deep things of God. For
what man knows the things of a man except the spirit of the
man which is in him? Even so no one knows the things of
God except the Spirit of God. Now we have received, not the
spirit of the world, but the Spirit who is from God, that we
might know the things that have been freely given to us by
God. (1 Corinthians 2:9–12)
See also Romans 16:25–27 and Ephesians 1:7–10.

Ignorance is associated with darkness and the unknown.
Jesus, who is the "Light of the world," had a say in the matter
also. He said:

"For nothing is secret that will not be revealed, nor anything
hidden that will not be known and come to light." (Luke
8:17)

If you want accurate revelations and understanding of
mysteries, you have to go to that same God Daniel went to.
Otherwise, you will have to use satanic means, like the slave
girl did who encountered Apostle Paul at Philippi. Other spirits
can give revelations too, but these spirits are limited and can be
silenced (Acts 16:16–18).

"The secret things belong to the LORD our God, but
those things which are revealed belong to us and to our
children forever, that we may do all the words of this law."
(Deuteronomy 29:29)
Remember the former things of old, For I am God, and there
is no other; I am God, and there is none like Me, Declaring
the end from the beginning, And from ancient times things
that are not yet done, Saying, 'My counsel shall stand, And
I will do all My pleasure . . .'
(Isaiah 46:9–10)

The Holy Spirit's Intervention

The book of Revelation is amazing. It is awesome how Apostle John wrote this book of prophecies while exiled on the island of Patmos. At that time Patmos was a small deserted place in the Aegean Sea, ten miles by six miles, which was used as a prison camp by the Romans. John was a political prisoner there, where the hills were used as a quarry and the caves sheltered the occupants.[7]

The specific details John records are precisely what writers of other books either vaguely or distinctly penned decades and centuries before. His writings are in agreement with the other books of the Old and New Testaments, beginning with Genesis. Some of these writers he quotes verbatim. There were no libraries, scrolls, or research materials at this prison camp. If John had access to this material before he was incarcerated, then he had an excellent memory to recall all these details from so many sources. John had to have been led by the Holy Spirit (supernatural intervention) in order for his writings to achieve a high level of agreement with other writers across multiple subjects and eras.

CHAPTER 2

Revelation 1—the Certainty of Christ's Coming Again

JUST AS HIS first coming was prophesied and it came to pass, so shall the second coming of Jesus the Christ be: it shall happen. His second coming was first spoken of more than two thousand years ago.

Jesus Christ Is Coming Again

Jesus is expected to come again and do some uncommon works as part of His return. There are too many prophesied details concerning His return which cannot be overlooked or misunderstood when He indeed returns. This return is referred to many times in one form or another throughout the New Testament. Here are a few of these references:

> And as it is appointed for men to die once, but after this the judgment, so Christ was offered once to bear the sins of many. To those who eagerly wait for Him He will appear a second time, apart from sin, for salvation. (Hebrews 9:27–28) For our citizenship is in heaven, from which we also eagerly wait for the Savior, the Lord Jesus Christ, who will transform our lowly body that it may be conformed to His glorious body, according to the working by which He is able even to subdue all things to Himself. (Philippians 3:20–21) See also 1 Thessalonians 4:15–18.

But the day of the Lord will come as a thief in the night, in which the heavens will pass away with a great noise, and the elements will melt with fervent heat; both the earth and the works that are in it will be burned up. (2 Peter 3:10)

Jesus Himself said that He was going away and would come again. He assured His disciples that

"in My Father's house are many mansions; if it were not so, I would have told you. I go to prepare a place for you. And if I go and prepare a place for you, I will come again and receive you to Myself; that where I am, there you may be also." (John 14:2–3)

Jesus is presently in Heaven, seated with the Father, waiting:

So then, after the Lord had spoken to them, He was received up into heaven, and sat down at the right hand of God. (Mark 16:19)
But he [Stephen], being full of the Holy Spirit, gazed into heaven and saw the glory of God, and Jesus standing at the right hand of God, and said, "Look! I see the heavens opened and the Son of Man standing at the right hand of God!" (Acts 7:55–56)
See also Acts 3:19–21.

Jesus's return is going to be quick, no lingering (Revelation 22:12).

"For as the lightning comes from the east and flashes to the west, so also will the coming of the Son of Man be." (Matthew 24:27)

When He returns, He is coming on the clouds:

Now when He had spoken these things, while they watched, He was taken up, and a cloud received Him out of their sight. And while they looked steadfastly toward heaven as He went up, behold, two men stood by them in white apparel, who also said, "Men of Galilee, why do you stand gazing up into heaven? This same Jesus, who was taken up from you into heaven, will so come in like manner as you saw Him go into heaven." (Acts 1:9–11)

All the tribes of the earth will see Jesus at His second coming:

"Then the sign of the Son of Man will appear in heaven, and then all the tribes [races, clans, kindreds] of the earth will mourn, and they will see the Son of Man coming on the clouds of heaven with power and great glory." (Matthew 24:30)

It is going to be a surprise, an unexpected coming:

"For as in the days before the flood, they were eating and drinking, marrying and giving in marriage, until the day that Noah entered the ark, and did not know until the flood came and took them all away, so also will the coming of the Son of Man be." (Matthew 24:38–39)

Just as we are living nowadays, that's how it was in the days before the great flood. People living as if there is no God—self-gratification, self-centeredness, sudden and unexpected end.

Before Jesus Christ Returns

Jesus has not come the second time, yet His return is still in the future. We are still waiting for Him. According to the book of Matthew, Jesus told His disciples there are some nine predictions that must happen first. Here is what He said:

> Now as He sat on the Mount of Olives, the disciples came to Him privately, saying, "Tell us, when will these things be? And what will be the sign of Your coming, and of the end of the age?" And Jesus answered and said to them: "Take heed that no one deceives you.

1. For many will come in My name, saying, 'I am the Christ,' and will deceive many.
2. And you will hear of wars and rumors of wars. See that you are not troubled; for all these things must come to pass, but the end is not yet.
3. For nation will rise against nation, and kingdom against kingdom.
4. And there will be famines, pestilences, and earthquakes in various places. All these are the beginning of sorrows.
5. Then they will deliver you up to tribulation and kill you, and you will be hated by all nations for My name's sake.
6. And then many will be offended, will betray one another, and will hate one another.
7. Then many false prophets will rise up and deceive many.
8. And because lawlessness will abound, the love of many will grow cold. But he who endures to the end shall be saved.
9. And this gospel of the kingdom will be preached in all the world as a witness to all the nations [gentiles, heathens, people, tribes and cultures], and then the end will come." (Matthew 24:3–14, emphasis and numbering added)

Keeping abreast of what is happening around the world today will give you a good perspective on where the world is on this timeline. Thanks to modern technology, you can receive audio and video footage of events from around the world as they are taking place. The mere fact that some of the nine telltale signs have already taken place and some are happening today gives some credibility to Revelation. Take numbers one to three above. Before John wrote this book of prophecy, there were persons calling themselves "Christ," so that was nothing new. Likewise, there have been wars and rumors of wars from time immemorial and even during John's era. There have always been earthquakes around the globe. In fact, there were major ones at the time of Jesus's death and His resurrection. But Jesus says that the fulfillment of these prophecies is not the end; in fact, it's just getting started. He is letting you know that the journey to the end-time is in progress, whether you believe it or not.

The first eight signs given by Jesus are in operation, and obviously so. As for the ninth sign, the gospel is being preached around the earth (through satellites, the Internet, cell phones, social media, missionaries, Bible distribution, books, personal testimonies, etc.) even in nations and among sects where it is strictly forbidden. The world is about ready for the end. When all the nations and various cultures of the earth have been presented with the gospel and have had the opportunity to accept Jesus Christ as Lord, know that Christ is soon to return. His publicized coming is supposed to give the believer hope and bring him comfort.

Before Christ Comes Again

Jesus Christ is coming soon. The Father is holding His Son back until

1. *the gospel of the Kingdom of Heaven has been preached in all the world.*

This is not about preaching on prosperity, security, peace, miracles, church membership, denominational doctrines, or anything carnal that makes this life more comfortable; these themes are what the counterfeit church preaches. The gospel of the Kingdom of Heaven is about Jesus Christ being "the only Savior of the world, the Redeemer of mankind, and the King of kings," and about grace and truth being found in Him alone. The gospel demands repentance from religion, traditions, and dead works to an acceptance of Jesus Christ as one's Lord in every sense.

2. *the restoration of all rights and privileges that were taken away from mankind or that mankind gave up through sin; the restoration of the function and operation of the church of Jesus Christ today to its former or original state or position as on the Day of Pentecost or until the Father chooses to restore all things.*

For example, in keeping with prophecy, Israel was established as a nation in one day, May 1948. In December 2017, US President Donald Trump formally recognized Jerusalem as the capital of Israel. Now the ancient temple has to be rebuilt in Jerusalem to complete the prophecy. The question is when? We do not know. Only the Father knows the time of Jesus's return (Matthew 24:36–37; 6:9–10; Acts 1:6–7) "that He may send Jesus Christ, who was preached to you before, whom heaven must receive until <u>the times of restoration of all things</u>, which God has spoken by the mouth of all His holy prophets since the world began" (Acts 3:20–21, emphasis added).

3. *there is a falling away of the saints.*

   People will turn away from Christ and the Christian faith, intentionally going back to paganism and sin and forsaking or denying the power and presence of Jehovah.

4. *Satan exposes himself.*

   Satan wants to be recognized as "the Supreme" God. Second Thessalonians 2:9 says that "The coming of the lawless one is according to the working of Satan, with all power, signs, and lying wonders." If this character (the man who is raised up by Satan) does not come quickly—like a flash of lightning—and perform his assigned role as redeemer, then he is definitely the antichrist (Matthew 24:24–27).

Let no one deceive you by any means; for that Day will not come unless <u>the falling away comes first</u>, and <u>the man of sin is revealed</u>, the son of perdition, who opposes and exalts himself above all that is called God or that is worshiped, so that he sits as God in the temple of God, showing himself that he is God. (2 Thessalonians 2:3–4, emphasis added)

In regard to Jesus's coming, a prophet from Africa who calls himself "Prime Minister" says that "this coming is imminent, in that it can occur at any moment since there are no predicated events which must precede its occurrence." In support of his claim, he said that the Rapture is to be distinguished from the Second Coming and should be dealt with separately, using John 14:1–3 and 1 Corinthians 15:51–57 as his references.

He further argued that there is another coming of the Lord, which he referred to as "The Day of the Lord," when Jesus comes down to the earth (ground) with all His saints. His reference for this claim is 1 Thessalonians 3:13. In his *WhatsApp* post of

April 3, 2020, in the Global Pastors Alliance chat group, Prime Minister wrote that Jesus's first coming will be in the air when the dead and the living saints will be transfigured and together caught up to meet the Lord. This first coming he referred to as "Coming for His saints," but it is what is generally called the Rapture (see chapter 7 for further discussion).

> For this we say to you by the word of the Lord, that we who are alive and remain until the coming of the Lord will by no means precede those who are asleep. For the Lord Himself will descend from heaven with a shout, with the voice of an archangel, and with the trumpet of God. And the dead in Christ will rise first. Then we who are alive and remain shall be caught up together with them in the clouds to meet the Lord in the air. And thus we shall always be with the Lord. (1 Thessalonians 4:15–17)

What's Next? Judgment!

The earth is now preparing for judgment and is reserved for a fire this time:

> But the heavens and the earth which are now preserved by the same word, are reserved for fire until the day of judgment and perdition of ungodly men. (2 Peter 3:7)

To understand prophecies with a time factor, consider this:

> But, beloved, do not forget this one thing, that with the Lord one day is as a thousand years, and a thousand years as one day. The Lord is not slack concerning His promise, as some count slackness, but is longsuffering toward us, not willing that any should perish but that all should come to repentance. (2 Peter 3:8–9)

Christ must come to pass judgment. Thrones are set for judgment (Psalms 122:5).

He who keeps his command will experience nothing harmful;
And a wise man's heart discerns both time and judgment,
Because <u>for every matter there is a time and judgment</u>,
Though the misery of man increases greatly.
(Ecclesiastes 8:5–6, emphasis added)
See also Malachi 3:5.
"Be afraid of the sword for yourselves; For wrath brings the punishment of the sword, That you may know there is a judgment."
(Job 19:29)
For we must all appear before the judgment seat of Christ, that each one may receive the things done in the body, according to what he has done, whether good or bad. (2 Corinthians 5:10)
"But I say to you that for every idle word men may speak, they will give account of it in the day of judgment." (Matthew 12:36)

Judgment Is Coming

"And behold, I am coming quickly, and My reward *(wages, pay for services)* is with Me, to give to every one according to his work. I am the Alpha and the Omega, the Beginning and the End, the First and the Last." (Revelation 22:12–13, emphasis added)

When you were a student and the teacher announced that there will be a test, a certain fear came over you and you began to make changes. You started to look over your classwork, to study the chapters assigned, to cut down on social activities, etc. The coming judgment is that same kind of announcement, but where is the fear? Where are the changes? Is there no belief that the Word of God will come to pass? Is this whole earth experience a big joke? Is there no purpose to life except to eat, drink, have fun, get fat, get rich, and then die?

The reward for ignoring, disrespecting, disobeying, not heeding, not believing God's Word is death, or to put it mildly, "separation from God" (John 3:17–18; Romans 6:23; 1 Corinthians 3:8; Hebrews 2:2–3). Eternal life can come only through Jesus Christ (John 3:15–16, 14:6). For you, will there be a "well done, thou good and faithful servant" or a "Thou wicked and slothful servant"? (Matthew 25:14–30, KJV). They are both rewards for your work.

There is a JUDGMENT coming, and Jesus Christ is the JUDGE. Here are more scriptural references to show the reality and seriousness of this matter: Exodus 12:12; Psalms 9:7–8; Ecclesiastes 11:9; Ezekiel 33:12; Matthew 10:15, 25:19, 31; John 5:22; and Romans 14:10–12.

Revelation 1:8 states, "I am the Alpha and the Omega." Isaiah 44:6 agrees. Who can circumvent Him! Only the Creator, the Almighty Himself, can make such bold declarations and execute them. Who can dare to challenge these words? These are the words of authority, sovereignty, and power. The claim alone—to be not only the "beginning" but also the "end" of anything—calls for originality, creativity, ultimate authority, unlimited resources, a fool-proof plan, production and life-sustaining abilities, etc. This claim makes God responsible for everything in between. If He started the beginning, then He must be outside of time because time began when He started it. The claim to be ever-present puts Him in a class all by Himself. No wonder the Creator is known as the eternal, omnipresent, omnipotent, and omniscient One. Even the sun—the most powerful natural force—obeys Him (Joshua 10:12–13).

What Is the Big Deal about Judgment?

Periodic assessments are necessary for all areas of life. The teacher will test students. The manager will conduct staff evaluations. The accountant will audit the company's books. The project officer will prepare progress reports. The contractor will call in the inspector after each stage. The realtor will appraise the property before selling or buying. The doctor will perform your annual physical. Even when you die the coroner will perform an autopsy on you. Likewise, in the last days, the Creator will judge the world.

Everyone and everything goes through some form of testing and evaluation exercise some time or another in life. You are no different. You are not here just to be here. Neither are you here only because of your father and mother copulating. You have a purpose, a mission, and you will have to give an account for your time spent here (2 Corinthians 5:10).

There is a time and a season for an assessment of everything in your life—whether you are ready for it or not (Ecclesiastes 8:6–7). There is a time when you must examine where you are and compare it to where you thought you should have been. And there is a season to undergo testing of all that has been entrusted to you. You or someone who is concerned about you, at some time or another, should want to know what is going on with your life. Furthermore, it is not wise to go through a long process and not have checkpoints along the way. It is even worse to finish the process and not know what the outcome is or to have an outcome that is not in your favor. You do not want to live thirty, forty, fifty, even sixty years as an adult and be unable to give a meaningful account of what you did in those years. Not doing regular assessments has brought surprise, frustration, regret, anger, stress, and even depression to many people. The medical profession constantly reminds us to have regular checks so that we can detect an illness or something unusual early because early detection could mean a greater chance of successful treatment. In other words, you could be in bondage and not know how and when you got there if you are not doing periodic evaluations. You could be heading for an eternity in torments and not realize it until you get there.

You Must Do Periodic Checks

Uncertain conditions will put and keep you in bondage, especially if the unexpected is also uncontrollable or not easily managed. If you are in bondage and you don't know how long you have been there, it is because you did not do periodic checks. Can you imagine spending twelve years in school and upon completion neither you nor anybody else knows what level you have attained? This would be akin to not going to the dentist or to the doctor in twelve years, not giving your automobile a checkup for twelve months. As unthinkable as these omissions might be, there are some people who do not want to be tested at any time.

When you are demanded to submit to a test, it is not that someone hates you or is trying to put you down. Neither is it that someone is trying to frustrate your life. Testing is a normal process that should be carried out in a timely manner. This testing should be the most truthful, thorough, and accurate assessment you can have for it will expose weakness and strengths, identify areas for change, tell specifically what should be accelerated or decelerated, and detect the problem areas so that corrective action can be taken among other long-term benefits.

You should submit yourself to evaluations throughout your lifetime; otherwise, you could be making a mess and not know it. Assessments help you to know where you are so that you can make the adjustments to get to where you should be. Time is precious, so don't waste it. Be true to yourself. No matter who you are, there is always room for improvement in your life. Allow the Creator of All Things to show you the best way forward. It may be different from what you have in mind, but it will benefit your life. Remember, the heavenly Father loves you, and He wants you to prosper. Trust Him to guide you by obeying His Word.

You have heard all this talk about Jesus Christ being the Savior of the world, the Redeemer of mankind, the Healer of the broken, the Soon-Coming King, the Truth, the Lamb of God, the Messiah, the only Son of God, yet you have done nothing to make Him a reality in your life? You, and you alone, are completely responsible for this decision. If you have not yet confessed Jesus Christ as Lord of your life, now is the best time to do so. There are prayers you can confess to activate the Kingdom of God in your life. Once you are in the Kingdom of God, you must work out your own salvation daily, with fear and trembling (1 Peter 1:3–10).

> Therefore, my beloved, as you have always obeyed, not as in my presence only, but now much more in my absence, work out your own salvation with fear and trembling; for it is God who works in you both to will and to do for His good pleasure. (Philippians 2:12–13)

The Son of Man will judge the nations and individuals. He will separate His saints from the followers of Satan and Baphomet (Revelation 22:12). Stay far away from those who associate with goats.

> "When the Son of man comes in his glory, and all the holy angels with him, then He will sit on the throne of His glory. All the nations *(people of all races and tribes)* will be gathered

before Him, and He will separate them one from another, as a shepherd divides his sheep from the goats. And He will set the sheep on His right hand, but the goats on the left." (Matthew 25:31–33, emphasis added)

Every Eye Will See Him

Remember that the prophecy concerning Jesus's return to the earth was written in AD 95. At first glance, one would think Jesus's second coming was so near that the soldiers who pierced His side would have been alive when He returned. At the time of John's writing, Jesus had been ascended to the Father for more than sixty years. In other words, the soldiers would have had to live as long to see Jesus's return as Simeon lived to see His first coming (Luke 2:25–26). But this was not the case. Matthew 24:30 says that "all the tribes of the earth will mourn, and they will see the Son of Man coming on the clouds." Therefore, not only the soldiers but every nation (race, clan, kindred) will see (gaze with wide-open eyes as at something remarkable) Him come.

Prophecies and mysteries are meant to be understood; however, the natural mind cannot conceive what God has in store for those who love Him. The puny mind is simply limited, and that's why the book of Revelation seems to contain so many mysteries. But the Spirit provides explanations. You may not understand everything, but you know how to obey God.

CHAPTER 3

Revelation 2 and 3—
Addressing the Churches
in Asia Minor

T HIS REVELATION WAS for the early church of
John's era and shortly thereafter. The phrase "things
which must shortly take place" is a reference to the judgment of
churches for that era. Consider Revelation 4:1 which indicates
that the revelation is for the distant future from the third
century and beyond even up to today.

In 1:19, Jesus commanded John to write three specific
things. He was to write *what was*, *what is*, and *what shall be*,
namely:

1. "write the things which you have seen." This speaks to
   the past. John was alive at the time of Jesus and he was
   aware of what had happened since Jesus's resurrection;
   these are John's experiences.

2. "write the things which are." This speaks to the present
   time in which John was receiving the instruction and
   to the recent changes.

3. "write the things which will take place after this." This
   definitely speaks to things that have not yet happened.
   Diverse things will happen in the future after this

encounter. John is about to be exposed to what is yet to come, where there is an expectation for significant changes.

Jesus is coming again, no question about it. He has to execute judgment on the earth.

> "Men of Galilee, why do you stand gazing up into heaven? This same Jesus, who was taken up from you into heaven, will so come in like manner as you saw Him go into heaven." (Acts 1:11)
> Behold, He is coming with clouds, and every eye will see Him, even they who pierced Him. And all the tribes [races, clans, kindred] of the earth will mourn because of Him. Even so, Amen. (Revelation 1:7)
> See also Revelation 22:12–13.

"I Was in the Spirit . . ."

Patmos was a deserted and barren island used as a prison and a forced labor camp by the Romans. John was exiled there in the fourteenth year of the reign of Domitian, where he lived in a cave for about a year and a half before returning to Ephesus. He was banished to Patmos because all the attempts by the Romans to take his life had failed.[1]

Being mistreated, hunted, wrongly imprisoned, lonely, depressed, rejected, hungry, and thirsty creates the perfect setting for a pity party, where John would sit and sulk his time away. Instead, John used the time to fast and pray and seek the Lord's presence. In his suffering and persecution, he had patient endurance. Thus, he was in the Spirit, not in the flesh. One cannot easily handle John's degree of physical and mental pressure in the natural. His suffering placed him in company with Joseph, David, Daniel, Jeremiah, Peter, Paul, and Jesus his

Master. Suffering as an evildoer is more tolerable than enduring hardship for the sake of the gospel.

> *You had better know how to pray and*
> *praise in the midst of tribulation.*

"On the Lord's Day"

This was not the Sabbath day but a Sunday. Christians had already shifted from fellowshipping only on the Sabbath to worshipping on the first day of the week (Acts 20:7). Sunday worship started on the first Pentecost after Jesus's resurrection. Jewish laws and customs were not nationally recognized at this time in this area of the Roman Empire. Even though some Jews lived in these cities, the world, for the most part, was under the influence of the Romans and was mostly settled by Greeks. Judaism was not the main religion in these cities because non-Jews dominated the world. Followers of Jesus Christ fellowshipping on a Sunday was a norm. Apparently, Sunday gathering was an issue for Jews back in Apostle Paul's day because he addressed it in his letter to the saints at Colossae (Colossians 2:16–17). The average Jew did not realize that Jesus and Paul did not preach Judaism but the Kingdom of Heaven. Any day was a good day to seek the Lord (Acts 2:46–47).

Letters to the Churches

John is writing to the seven churches in Asia Minor. These letters are not addressed to the world at large but to persons who have identified with Jesus Christ. However, just as Apostle Paul would write a letter to the church in Rome and all the other churches would benefit from that letter, so it was with John's letters.

There were churches all around the world (Rome throughout Macedonia and Mesopotamia, Memphis, and Jerusalem) at that time, yet Jesus addressed only some of the churches in Asia Minor. The churches at Philippi, Thessalonica, Antioch, and Colossae were not mentioned for reasons I know not. That the churches were mostly Gentile rather than Jewish gatherings is a clear indication that God's agenda for the salvation of souls had shifted from specifically the Israelites to the entire world. This thought corresponds with Jesus's instruction in Matthew 28:19 "to go into all the world." However, the matters John addresses to the churches are found in all local churches today in varying degrees and combinations. Therefore, if any of these churches help you to recognize a deficiency in the church where you fellowship, you now know how to deal with it positively and effectively.

In each of the churches addressed, John identifies the current condition, discusses how it got the way it is and states what needs to be done to fix it. Even though the churches were acknowledged for their many good deeds, their one or few bad deeds were enough to put them off course, requiring them to repent to get back in right standing with Christ. Christ is seeking a mature bride. Those who do repent and overcome will be given a reward (Ezekiel 18:21–24, 33:17–19).

One should also gather from these letters that whatever shortcoming your church is going through today is an age-old matter, and the Lord Jesus has already provided the remedies to fix it. It is comforting to know that you don't have to die in your sin or continue to fail.

What was called Asia Minor in the first century is called Turkey today. None of the city names used by John are around today. These places now have different names and different characters. Today the dominant religion in Turkey is Islam, not Christianity.

The principal objective of the letters is to unveil the purposes of the Lord concerning the different sections of His universal church. He is deeply concerned about the affairs of every sector of His church. The universal church has to be uniform; therefore, the Lord Jesus identifies the deficiencies of each one—confirming that none is perfect—to bring each one into the fullness of Christ in His efforts to prepare that spotless bride. The Lord's approach seems to be more corrective than condemnatory. There is no place for deviations and personal differences when it comes to kingdom doctrine—His church has only one Lord (Ephesians 4:3–6).

The Seven Golden Lampstands and Seven Stars

Here is a Polaroid of what the writer saw. As he turned to see from where or from whom the voice came, he saw "one like unto the Son of Man." John lived, traveled, and ministered with Jesus for three and a half years, yet he did not say emphatically that it was "the Son of Man." He said one similar in appearance to or character of the Son of Man. Apparently, the true image (the post-resurrection image) of his Master was still vague to him. Not Mary Magdalene or the two disciples on the road to Emmaus or any of His eleven disciples recognized Jesus right away after His resurrection. Yet today, folks would say with surety that they have seen Jesus. Did they see the same image John saw, or did Jesus make Himself known to them? Presenting Jesus as a tall, clean-shaven-faced blue-eyed Caucasian holding a lamb or a staff while it seems so sacred is a grave injustice to His image and likeness when people from those parts did not have those features (Exodus 20:4; Deuteronomy 4:15–16).

The statement by John is grounds to question the true likeness of the Son of Man. "What does Jesus look like today?" is a topic for another book. However, whatever John saw among the candlesticks was enough for him to identify the image with Jesus the Christ. There were several factors that helped John with his verification. First, the image had a holy and awesome presence about Him. Second, the image did not stop John from paying homage to Him, which an angel would have done. And third, the image confessed to His own deity and authority.

The mystery of the seven stars and candlesticks is no longer obscured. Jesus told John plainly what they are all about. The early church knew that Jesus was with them in their midst. That was a promise He had made to them (Matthew 28:20). Jesus in the midst of the candlesticks (churches) signifies that He has full authority and awareness and would not let their oil (anointing) run dry causing them, the source of light, to go out. The Son of Man had seven stars (angels/pastors) in His right hand, signifying that He is controlling, directing, preserving, and protecting them. Having them in His hand also signifies how precious they are to Him. The pastors who are no longer in His hand should not seek to enjoy these benefits (Exodus 15:6; Psalms 16:11).

> The mystery of the seven stars which you saw in My right hand, and the seven golden lampstands: The seven stars are the angels [pastors/leaders] of the seven churches, and the seven lampstands which you saw are the seven churches. (Revelation 1:20)

God dwelling with man is nothing new. John, seeing Jesus in the midst of the churches, is expected. It is a fulfillment of a promise made since the days of Moses (Exodus 25:8). The Son of Man is qualified to speak and judge because He is present and in control. Jesus is and will be in the midst of His church.

The Letters to the Pastors

These letters address the spiritual, moral, social, historic, and prophetic concerns of the various churches through eras and dispensations from Pentecost to the Second Coming. This means that the concerns are relevant for today. The letters commend, exhort, rebuke, and correct matters of significant interest to the Bridegroom concerning the preparation of His Bride. He does not want His Bride to look like or be confused with the harlot—she must be chaste. The concerns have all been addressed in the Scriptures already. Therefore, if He addressed them again in His letters, then He expects repentance because they matter to Him. The person who has been warned repeatedly can no longer claim ignorance. Ignorance of a law is no excuse, not even for the person who claims, "I didn't know." The good news here is that all who harken to the warnings will be overcomers and will receive a special promise.

Ephesus—the Loveless Church

The church at Ephesus is a well-disciplined people who can patiently endure. The fervency they had at first is now diminished, gone cold. Now they lack enthusiasm, zeal, and interest. They got so used to the regular that they became bored, merely following rituals. The things that first excited them about Christ and His Kingdom have faded drastically and their interest has shifted to other things. Maybe when the church was started, the people genuinely cared, shared, and loved each other, but as they prospered economically, the love shifted from people to things and possessions. Apostle Paul's biggest problem with this church in his day was the lack of Christian unity, but their pride and joy were their material possessions. Economic prosperity can cause people to put their business interests above their personal relationship with God (Matthew 6:33, 16:26).

The Ephesian church is commended for hating the "deeds" of the Nicolaitans while the church at Pergamos is blamed for having members who hold to their "doctrines" (2:15). The followers of Nicolas seemingly were a class of professing Christians who sought to introduce into the church false freedom or licentiousness, thus abusing Paul's doctrine of grace and were probably identical with those who held to the doctrine of Balaam.[2] Another view says that fornication (sexual immorality) and eating things sacrificed to idols were permitted by the Nicolaitans. Overcomers in this church will eat from the tree of life; they will live forever (2 Peter 2:15; Galatians 6:9; 2 Corinthians 4:16–18).

Smyrna—the Persecuted Church

Persecution and testing will come your way for a season. Stand firm! Some churches will experience more persecution than others, but every church will be persecuted at some time or another (Matthew 5:10–12). Muslims will persecute Jews and Christians. One Christian denomination will persecute the other. The state will persecute the church. Sinners will persecute people of whatever religion. Christians will persecute people of other religions and so on. The Spanish Inquisition (a scheme to cleanse the church) was the deadliest and most horrific movement in the fifteenth and sixteenth centuries. Hundreds of thousands of people were executed because the leaders of the Roman Catholic Church (RCC) took it upon themselves to purify the Church of heretics.[3]

If you are going through harassment right now, know that you are not the first to be persecuted, and you will not be the last. The good news here is that overcomers will not be maltreated and made to suffer again.

> Yes, and all who desire to live godly in Christ Jesus will suffer persecution. (2 Timothy 3:12)
> See also Mark 10:29–30.

It is one thing to live for Jesus, and it is a different matter to die for Him. There was mass persecution after Christ's death—and this was just the beginning. The effects of persecution are not all bad. When the church in Jerusalem was attacked, the disciples fled to faraway places, taking the gospel with them wherever they went. The good news here is that if you die in Christ, you are alive forevermore (1 Corinthians 15:22). Overcomers will not be hurt by the second death (Revelation 20:14).

By the way, there was an established synagogue of Satan in this city and in Philadelphia at that time. There have to be moral and other easily distinguishable differences between the two kingdoms; therefore, Jesus has to draw a line.

Pergamos—the Morally Compromising Church

This church did not succumb to the pressures around them even though they were where Satan lives; they had such strong faith. Just as Jesus lived in Nazareth, Satan's throne was in Pergamos. But this church showed that it is possible to stand despite what's happening around you. Fellowshipping among them were people (the Nicolaitans, the LGBTQ+) who have perverted lifestyles. This was a problem because these people could negatively impact the church (1 Corinthians 5:9–11, 10:20–22; 2 Corinthians 6:14–15; Galatians 5:19–21; Ephesians 5:11–12). One bad apple can indeed spoil the whole basket.

The church cannot look like the world; otherwise, baby Christians and non-Christians would not know the difference between the church and the world. There must be a clear distinction between the church and the world. When an individual receives Christ into his life, he should, at the same time, lose interest in the things of this world. The world and the church represent different kingdoms and have different value systems with different lifestyles. If you intend to bring the things of the world into the church, then you should stay in the world as there is no place in the church for you. The church should never become like the world because the church was set up to take people out of the world's system. When a person comes to Christ, he must repent (change the way he thinks); otherwise, the Word of God will destroy him.

Under the headline "Anglican Archbishop Tells Same-Sex Marriage Supporters to Leave the Anglican Church," the Archbishop stated that individuals should leave the church rather than "betray God's word." This statement was made by Dr. Glenn Davies while speaking to the 51st Synod of the Diocese of Sydney in his final address to the Anglican Church's parliament. He described same-sex marriage proponents as having "entered treacherous waters" and called on them to leave.

> My own view is that if people wish to change the doctrine of our church, they should start a new church or join a church more aligned to their views—but do not ruin the Anglican Church by abandoning the plain teaching of Scripture. Please leave us. [4]

He also said, "I fear the stability of the Anglican Church of Australia." His strong position leads one to think that he fears that God will fight against the Australian Church with the sword of His mouth. The Archbishop's sentiments are right in line with the letter to the church in Pergamos.

When churches today in Canada, the United States of America, and Europe conform to the prevalent immoral lifestyles of the world, churches for Christ must take a stand for their community. Those who overcome will be given hidden manna to eat, a white stone, and a new name as their reward.

Thyatira—the Corrupt Church

Commendation is given to the "good deeds, love, faith, service, perseverance, and improvement" of the church at Thyatira. The members are known for their works: very busy with numerous programs, outstanding projects, and civic activities. However, the Lord Jesus rebukes them for tolerating the "spirit of Jezebel," a woman whose teachings had misled others into sexual immorality. Those who follow her will suffer intensely; their children will be struck dead. Jezebel will be cast onto a "sickbed" and the sexually immoral (those who commit adultery—apostasy—by leaving their religion to go with her) will be sent into great tribulation. There is a price for sleeping with Jezebel (1 Kings 16:31–33).

There are several denominations and churches—going back centuries and continuing to the present day—whose doctrines are not in line with the early church. Some of these congregations were started by women. One such renowned group is Christian Science, which was founded in 1879 by Mary Baker Eddy. Her movement was classified as "spiritualism," but she rejected this label. She was known for mixing the Bible with science.[5]

Another group, the United Society of Believers in Christ's Second Appearing, was more commonly known as the Shakers. Mothers Jane Wardley, Ann Lee, and Lucy Wright were its founders. Having Quaker roots, the Shakers flourished from the mid-1700s. They spoke in tongues while dancing and singing in a trancelike state. The Era of Manifestations was a period from

1837 to the mid-1850s when Shakers came under a spiritual revival marked by visions and ecstatic experiences among the followers. They expressed their visions in song, dance, and drawings.[6]

Mother Ann Lee had a series of revelations, after which she regarded herself as the female aspect of God's dual nature and the second incarnation of Christ. She developed an elaborate theology and established celibacy as the cardinal principle of the community.[7]

Another movement started by a woman is the Seventh-day Adventist Church. Its founding is credited to Methodist Ellen G. Harmon-White, who, in the late 1840s, used her prophetic gift to give direction to a sect of people who were part of the Second Great Awakening. They were disappointed because of an unfulfilled prophecy concerning the coming of Christ in October 1844. Ellen White's efforts grew essentially because she preserved the balance between "spirit" and "order" to keep the movement alive.[8]

Jehovah's Witnesses believe that Jesus began ruling in 1914, an interpretation of Revelation 11:15. They believe that a relatively small number of people—144,000—will be resurrected to life in heaven to rule with Jesus in the kingdom.[9] This doctrine is found nowhere in the Holy Bible.

Today you can find teachers and doctrines that will support any of your desires. There are "seeker-friendly" churches that will accommodate whatever you want. You can find the "Top 10 Best Gay Churches in Atlanta, Georgia" through a web search. One of the churches on the list is called "Spirit and Truth Sanctuary."[10] Amazing! Will someone please publicly announce that the LGBTQ+ community and the Christian faith will never ever join as one. There is no ground for compromise between the two. Either the so-called Christians will outrightly reject God or the sexual perverts will repent and receive Jesus Christ as Lord and Savior (Romans 1:24–32).

Whether it was for money, power, fame, vainglory, land or to safeguard themselves, kings were known for taking their wives from potential enemy nations. Solomon also did this. He made a league with pagan nations and ended up worshipping their gods, even building temples for them (1 Kings 11:1–8). The church cannot entertain sexual perverts (Revelation 21:8).

Mixing with foreign nations usually has a negative side which can become a national issue. The Bahamas used to have the United States of America as its major trading partner for many reasons, but today she is trading—or sleeping—with China and still expecting the United States to treat her the same way as before. China was welcomed in for economic reasons, but she brought her god with her. Now statues of Buddha can be seen around the island of New Providence, and this does not seem to bother the residents, who are predominantly Christian. This is a subtle entry for the massive overthrow. The Chinese have used this strategy throughout Africa and in other Caribbean nations. The Bahamas is no different. It is only a matter of time before she, too, will be overthrown if Chinese expansionism is left unchecked.

The Spirit of Jezebel in the Church Today

The name Jezebel means unexalted. The woman Jezebel was notorious for corrupting her husband and the nation and for blatantly defying the God of Israel. She led Israel away from Jehovah to worship Baal and Astarte. She was the power behind the throne of her husband and two sons and controlled and orchestrated situations according to her will. She swore to kill Jehovah's prophet Elijah because he killed her prophets. She was so dreaded that the senior prophet ran and hid himself from her.

Jezebel was also known for wearing makeup or adorning herself (2 Kings 9:30). However, she was more notorious for being cruel, crafty, revengeful, influential, and domineering. Her doctrine will cause you to know the depths of (go deep with) Satan.

It is said that the Jezebel spirit is the spirit that hates prophets. While this is true, the spirit is not confined to hating prophets. Someone having a Jezebel spirit will use his or her authority irresponsibly. This spirit is known to do whatever it takes to get a task completed—lie, kill, steal, destroy, deceive, slander, fabricate, bribe, use emotions and the ignorance of others to manipulate persons to accept his/her stories, whatever. If a man of God or a woman of God gets in the way, this spirit will attack him or her also, as this spirit has no regard for love, order, authority, others, or God. It is a selfish spirit that gets what it wants at the expense of everything else and is not afraid of consequences. This spirit is still alive in the church today (2 Timothy 3:1–6, 4:1–5). Overcomers will be given power over the nations and receive the morning star.

Sardis—the Dead Church

Camouflage! Sardis looks like a true church but is dead. She experiences no healings, no salvation, no deliverance, no growth, no gospel being preached, nothing that shows life. She pretends to have life but there is none in her. This church is full of religion and rituals. The members put on a great show with their pomp and pageantry, but their works leave much to be desired, not impressive at all. They think they are saying something, but they are saying nothing. Actually, this church is living off faded glory, decayed religion. The only people fooled are the ones who are with her and the ones who don't want to make a serious commitment to Christ. She is obviously not fooling the devil.

The admonition here is to pay closer attention to what you are doing. REPENT! Change the way you have been doing church. "Strengthen the things which remain" means that all is not lost because there are some things which can still be revived. Examine carefully what you have left. If you put Christ back in the proper perspective, there is still hope. The remnant can spark new life (Ezekiel 6:8–9; Luke 21:34–36).

"A bruised reed he will not break,
and a smoldering wick he will not snuff out,
till he has brought justice through to victory."
(Matthew 12:20, NIV)
See also Isaiah 42:1–4.

There are a few people in this congregation who have not defiled themselves. Those who are watchful and repent will be counted as overcomers and will join this small group in receiving their white garments and have their names remain in the Book of Life. This reward can be glorious. Meanwhile, the understanding here is that it's possible for names to be removed from this Book (Ezekiel 18:24).

Philadelphia—the Faithful Church

This is the only church that seems to have received a good report card. Today it is still a city of considerable size. What was known as Philadelphia back then is now known as Alasehir or Allah-shehr ("the city of God"). It is in the district of Manisa Province in the Aegean region of Turkey. The city itself is built on a terrace 650 feet above sea level. It has several mosques and Christian churches. Philadelphia fell to the Arabs during the Muslim conquest of the seventh century led by the Islamic prophet Muhammad. Even though there were numerous invasions and conquests against the city over the centuries, it is still heavily influenced by the Muslims.[11]

It came into the possession of the Turks in AD 1392 and has several times been nearly destroyed by earthquakes. According to Edgar J Banks, Alasehir is still a Christian town; one-fourth of its modern population is Greek, and a Greek bishop still makes his home there.[12]

Philadelphia was recognized as the faithful church. Isaiah gave a prophecy about Eliakim the son of Hilkiah (22:20–23). Because of his faithfulness, God would choose him and put responsibilities in his hand. "The key of the house of David I will lay on his shoulder . . . he will become a glorious throne to his father's house." According to Prophet Nathan (2 Samuel 7:16–17), David's house and kingdom are established forever before him, and his throne is established forever. Jesus identifies Himself to the church at Philadelphia as "He who has the key of David." He, Jesus, has the authority and responsibility to open and close doors (Genesis 7:15–16).

What God opens, no man can shut, and what God shuts, no man can open. Even though this church is small, it kept Jesus's word. Therefore, the Lord Jesus will make those of the synagogue of Satan worship before their feet (bow down before them) and acknowledge Him. This church was commended for its faithfulness and was given "an open door" and a crown. An "open door" means access to God and the gateway to a great opportunity. It also refers to the opportunity for spreading the Gospel of Jesus Christ. They will witness the Satan worshippers and the liars worship Jesus. God promised He will keep this faithful church from the hour (day, hour, instant, season, a short time) of trial which will come upon the whole earth. Because they have persevered, they do not need further testing (3:10). He admonished them to hold fast to their crown and not get distracted now. Jesus said He will make those who overcome "a pillar in the temple of My God" (3:12).

Laodiceans—the Lukewarm Church

It was one of the most important and flourishing cities of Asia Minor with a strong Jewish following. It was also the wealthiest Phrygian city, known for banking, medicine, and black wool textile and was especially prosperous in this period. Zeus was the city's patron deity, but the Laodiceans also had temples for Apollo, Asclepius (the healing deity), Hades, Hera, Athena, Serapis, Dionysus, and other deities. At a very early period, it became one of the chief seats of Christianity (Colossians 2:1, 4:15). Today it is a deserted place that the Turks call Eski-hissar or "old castle."[13]

The charge here is that the church of the Laodiceans is neither cold nor hot. Rather, she is in the middle of the road, or on the fence. This is not a good place to be. The beverage is too hot for a cold drink and too cold for a hot drink. The church would not make a decision for one side or the other. When a war is going on you cannot not take a side. You must show your allegiance somewhere, or nobody will trust you. But it seems, this church wants the best of both worlds; instead, she will get none. It is like saying, "I am a Christian, but I don't want to be known as a 'Jesus freak'" (Romans 1:16). Therefore, the Lord Jesus will cut off the Laodiceans for He has no use for her. She is a bad taste in His mouth. Her riches have blinded her. Rich people tend not to need God or anything else (Matthew 19:21–24; 1 Timothy 6:17–19). Whatever they were rich in physically and naturally, they were poor in spirituality.

But those who desire to be rich fall into temptation and a snare, and into many foolish and harmful lusts which drown men in destruction and perdition. For the love of money is a root of all kinds of evil, for which some have strayed from the faith in their greediness, and pierced themselves through with many sorrows. (1 Timothy 6:9–10)

Nakedness is supposed to bring you shame, not glory (Genesis 3:7). But the Greeks lived by a different moral standard from the Jews and Muslims even in dress codes. Going naked or with little clothing was common practice in some cultures and is even so today. Jesus promised the Laodicean church white garments (purity) to cover their nakedness. As an overcomer, you get to share the throne with Jesus and His Father.

Every church gets the same message of Revelation 2:7, "He who has an ear, let him hear what the Spirit says to the churches."

It is important to note that Holy Spirit is in agreement with Jesus and that Jesus is in agreement with the Father.

This is He who came by water and blood—Jesus Christ; not only by water, but by water and blood. And it is the Spirit who bears witness, because the Spirit is truth. For there are three that bear witness in heaven: the Father, the Word, and the Holy Spirit; and these three are one. And there are three that bear witness on earth: the Spirit, the water, and the blood; and these three agree as one. (1 John 5:6–8)

CHAPTER 4

Revelation 4—a View into Heaven

THESE REVELATIONS ARE about what is to come later in the near and latter centuries. John gets a look into Heaven and sees the throne room of Jehovah. He describes the scene in layman terms using the knowledge common to the first century. When he arrives in Heaven, John meets a worship service in progress. He is an observer, a spectator. The scene evokes Psalms 100, written by King David 1,250 years earlier.

John has to go to Heaven for further revelation. How is he going to get into Heaven, where God's throne is? Isn't Heaven light-years away from the earth? The answer is that John got to Heaven the same way you would travel on vacation to Exuma, an island in The Bahamas, without your body ever leaving your bed. Heaven is a physical place. But flesh and blood cannot enter Heaven (1 Corinthians 15:50), yet John was there, still alive in his body. Second, man is spirit (Genesis 1:26); he only lives in an earth suit or body (Genesis 2:7). Therefore, John was teleported—as in, "Beam me up, Scotty!"—or translated like Pandora in the movie *Avatar*. Apostle Paul wrote of a similar incident he had heard about:

> It is doubtless not profitable for me to boast. I will come to visions and revelations of the Lord: I know a man in Christ who fourteen years ago —whether in the body I do not know, or whether out of the body I do not know, God

knows— such a one was caught up to the third heaven. And I know such a man—whether in the body or out of the body I do not know, God knows—how he was caught up into Paradise and heard inexpressible words, which it is not lawful for a man to utter. (2 Corinthians 12:1–4)

When John gets to Heaven there is a door or portal already open to receive him. He was not the first human to see into Heaven, so this is nothing new. Prophets Ezekiel and Isaiah and Deacon Stephen also saw what that glorious place looks like, and they, too, wrote about it. You will find their accounts in Ezekiel 1:1, 8:2; Isaiah 6:1–3; Acts 7:55–56.

There is a sound that precedes every move of God. This sound John heard could have been a voice, an instrument, organized music, thunder, unknown natural noise, sounds not initiated by man but by angels, etc. Whatever it was, it was an attention-getter. The voice is described as a musical instrument speaking to him. The trumpet—called a shophar or qeren back then—could have been a ram's horn, which made melodious sounds.[1] It was used by priests to announce an approaching festival (Numbers 10:1–7), and used in the military to sound an alarm and to give signals.[2]

John is now told, "I will show (reveal to) the next order of events, what is to come later" (4:1b). There is a major time-lapse right here, between the now and the admonitions to the churches. However, the "Spirit" that spoke to him concerning the churches is the same "Spirit" he is now inspired by and who can be identified as Holy Spirit.

What follows next is a very descriptive verbal picture of what and who John saw. But first, let's talk about the heavens for more clarity going forward. According to 2 Corinthians 12:2, there are at least three levels of heaven. The first heaven is the troposphere, where clouds hang and the birds and planes fly. The second heaven is the thermosphere, where the planets

REVELATION 4—A VIEW INTO HEAVEN

and the sun are. And the third Heaven is the exosphere, outer space, or outside of this galaxy, where God dwells.[3] The first thing John sees is a throne set in Heaven. The Lord's throne is in Heaven (Psalms 103:19; Isaiah 66:1).

> The Lord is in His holy temple, the Lord's throne is in heaven; His eyes behold, His eyelids test the sons of men. (Psalms 11:4)

A throne is defined as "a stately seat; by implication, power or (concretely) a potentate."[4] It is a royal chair or seat of dignity, authority, and power; and the exalted position of a king, ruler, or judge.[5] The understanding here is that it is not a common seat or just another chair for anyone to sit on. God's throne is one of mercy, grace, righteousness, justice, judgment, truth, and glory (Psalms 9:7–8).

Jehovah Is Ultimately Supreme

The sovereignty of Jehovah—and His right and power to sit on His throne—was not acquired by winning a war. It was not granted to Him by his ancestors/father, neither was it won by popular votes nor through a democratic process. Rather, it is because of His office as the Creator, independent, infinite, absolute, and universal. No one else has claimed or can claim this position. This means that every other throne is subject to His. God's Kingdom rules over all others. His throne is established above everything and everyone.

> For by Him all things were created that are in heaven and that are on earth, visible and invisible, whether thrones or dominions or principalities or powers. All things were created through Him and for Him. (Colossians 1:16)

Being with the Creator

Since God is the Creator of all things (Genesis 1:1; Psalms 8:3; John 1:3), there is nothing that is or was that is outside of Him or that He cannot perform again or that He cannot provide when you need/desire it. You are probably more obsessed with His creation than you are with Him. That is man's greatest problem: we love (worship) things rather than the Creator of all things. If you have God or are with Him, you have everything—including what does not presently exist. You don't have to stockpile, save for a rainy day, or hold onto just in case. Where God is, everything about Him is there also. Whenever you need something, simply get into His presence and wait for Him (Psalms 16:11). That is why prayer (communication with God) is vitally important. Having a personal relationship with Him is everything. That is also why "worship" comes before "petition" (Psalms 23:1–3; Matthew 6:9–11).

The One on the Throne

John begins to paint a prismatic picture of the One sitting on the throne. He does not see a figure, its size, shape, or any quantifying attribute. Instead, He sees colors. This may explain why God gave Moses the following instruction:

> "You shall not make for yourself a carved image—any likeness of anything that is in heaven above, or that is in the earth beneath, or that is in the water under the earth [to represent Me]." (Exodus 20:4, emphasis added)

The One on the throne is reddish-brown in color (jasper and sardius).[6] These stones are the first and the last on Aaron's breastplate (Exodus 28:17–20). Maybe because of the light coming from "The One," John could not get more definitions and features, just as one cannot look directly at the sun without its light causing irreversible damage to the eye. John saw this light before in Jesus while He was on Earth (Matthew 17:1–2; John 8:12; James 1:17).

Seeing God

Being around Bible scholars, one will hear repeatedly that "man is made in God's image and likeness." How does one know this to be true when nobody has ever seen God and knows His image or likeness? Furthermore, according to Judges 13:22, no one has seen God and lived, yet countless people claim to have seen God. Jacob claimed that he wrestled with Him all night long (Genesis 32:30). While in the mountain, Moses and the Israelite elders saw God (Exodus 24:10–11). The prophet Isaiah said that his eyes have seen the LORD of hosts (Isaiah 6:5). Job and King David made similar claims.

Exodus 33:20 brings some clarity to this matter. God told Moses that "you cannot see My face; for no man shall see Me and live." The key word here is "face." But the Hebrew word for face, which is *paniym* ("paw-neem")[7] is a plural word and can be used in a great variety of literal and figurative applications. Despite all this, other Bible writers have given their take on God's image and likeness. Another prophet gave his view on the appearance of God in Ezekiel 1:26–28. There is yet another in Psalms 104:1–2. Paul, writing to Timothy, described God as

[He] who alone has immortality, dwelling in unapproachable light, whom no man has seen or can see, to whom be honor and everlasting power. Amen. (1 Timothy 6:16, emphasis added)

The central theme in describing God's appearance is light. This goes back to Genesis 1:3. A misleading assumption here by non-Christians is that God (Elohiym) is one person. God's triune nature (the Father, the Son, and the Holy Spirit) must be made known before we go further in this presentation. To help with this, consider the explanation Jesus gave to His disciple Philip when he asked to be shown the Father. Understanding this passage will give you a better grip on understanding how others could claim they saw God when most likely they saw Jesus, "the only begotten Son of God," before He became Man.

> Jesus said to him, "Have I been with you so long, and yet you have not known Me, Philip? He who has seen Me has seen the Father; so how can you say, 'Show us the Father'? Do you not believe that I am in the Father, and the Father in Me? The words that I speak to you I do not speak on My own authority; but the Father who dwells in Me does the works. Believe Me that I am in the Father and the Father in Me, or else believe Me for the sake of the works themselves." (John 14:9–11)

The Rainbow

In carnal matters, the rainbow is a symbol of the female messenger of the pagan deity Iris, thus the Greek name.[8] In nature, a rainbow has no beginning and no end. You can see it, but you cannot tell where it starts or where it ends. Furthermore, light has to be present for a rainbow to be seen. You can see it, but you cannot touch it (behold but not handle). Its beauty, splendor, and majesty cannot be touched but only pleasurably enjoyed—a true display of the iridescence of Jehovah's natural beauty (Ezekiel 1:28).

The world has cheapened and distorted the symbol of the rainbow by making it an icon of sexual immorality, starting in the late 1970s.[9] The LGBTQ+ squad has used it to convince people that some kind of gaiety or serenity is derived from their lifestyle. This is a very good example of blasphemy as the rainbow, which the Bible regards as sacred because it represents God's presence and covenant, is used to promote and identify the basest form of sexual carnality. This can be very confusing to a new believer who discovers that this symbol is used to represent two distinctly opposite entities. It should not be surprising, though, that the kingdom of darkness would use the rainbow because deception and lies are two of the pillars of that kingdom. Also, Satan, the lord of darkness, is also known as "the angel of light."

There is a protocol for approaching a throne: never casually, always with reverence. Around the throne were twenty-four thrones, and on the thrones, John saw twenty-four elders sitting, clothed in white robes, with crowns of gold on their heads.

Around the Throne

On his first look, the twenty-four elders were sitting on their thrones and had their crowns on their heads. The twenty-four elders formed the second circle around the throne. Who were these elders? They were not angels because no angel was ever crowned. Therefore, these elders had to be persons who had earned their reward for the faithful work done on earth (Matthew 19:28). Whether these crowns were literal or symbolic, they represented the visual achievement of the persons who wore them. They also represented the right to the position attained and the authority that came with that position. An athlete wears the gold medal because he attained that award—"Well done, good and faithful servant." How these crowns (headpieces) stack on each other is another question.

Biblesoft's concordance defines a crown as "Gk, *stephanos* (stef'-an-os); (to twine or wreathe); a chaplet (as a badge of royalty); a prize in the public games or a symbol of honor generally; but more conspicuous and elaborate than the simple fillet; a diadem; a garland."[10]

A crown could have been made of any material—tree leaves, metal, cloth, wood, etc.,—and therefore could be corruptible and able to fade (1 Corinthians 9:25). A crown is something worn on the head that distinguishes a royalty from a commoner. It is a symbol of authority. It is something you put on yourself or that others place on you to show you as more honorable, and it is regarded as a symbol of victory and reward. The elders having crowns meant that they had attained an honored position and were rewarded for the exemplary role they played while they were still in the flesh on earth. Their crowns were golden— imperishable—and sturdy enough to take abusive treatment (being cast down). One would be hard-pressed to find on earth a time when a king would intentionally and intensely throw his crown to the ground. This act would signify defeat or disgust on that king's part. But John noticed that in Heaven the crowns (symbols of honor, authority, and achievement) meant little while in the presence of the Most High God. This speaks of the high level and intensity of the worship session in progress. In His presence, one would do whatever is necessary to worship the Creator because there is nothing greater than Him. The elders were wearing tangible crowns and sitting on tangible thrones; they were in a physical place.

There are numerous types of crowns in the Kingdom of Heaven. A "crown of thorns" was placed on Jesus's head recognizing Him as a king on the earth. The person who has been approved for his work done here on earth will receive the "crown of life." Apostle Paul told Timothy that there is a "crown of righteousness" laid up for him. Apostle Peter talked about a "crown of glory" which does not fade away while King David talked about man being crowned with "glory and honor."

The Elders

According to the Greek word *presbuteros*,[11] an elder is "a senior, an Israelite Sanhedrist, a member of the celestial council, or Christian presbyter." There were twenty-four elders. John did not see their faces, neither did he identify any of them. Twelve of them could very well have been the apostles of Jesus Christ in fulfillment of His promise (Matthew 19:28)—and John might have seen himself.

The other twelve could be major prophets and/or patriarchs of the Old Testament or one patriarch from each of the twelve Israelite tribes. Two of them could very well be Enoch and Elijah (Genesis 5:24; 2 Kings 2:11). Another possibility could be that these elders are a representation of the twenty-four courses of priests from the Old Testament temple set up by King David (1 Chronicles 24:3–19). Do not forget that priests are kings also:

> But you are a chosen generation, a royal priesthood, a holy nation, His own special people, that you may proclaim the praises of Him who called you out of darkness into His marvelous light. (1 Peter 2:9)
> See also Revelation 1:6.

Clothed in White

White robes are one of the rewards for the Sardis (dead) church mentioned in chapter 3. The color white symbolizes purity.

Lightning, Thunderings, and Voices

"And from the throne proceeded lightnings, thunderings, and voices" (v. 5a). A scene like this appeared before when Moses gave the Ten Commandments to the Israelites (Exodus 20:18–22). Such events represent the awesome power of God's presence. A new sound usually precedes a new move of God to signify that something different is about to happen. There will be more episodes of lightning, thunder, and voices along with earthquakes as time progresses. As they increase, so will the devastation upon the earth.

The sound of thunder appears to be "God is talking" (Revelation 8:5; 11:19; 16:18). As children, when we heard claps of thunder and saw flashes of lightning, we would say that "the devil and his wife were fighting for potcake" and make fun of it all. Our parents, on the other hand, would rebuke us and command us to be quiet and have reverence because "God is talking." Lightning and thunder were not seen as mere natural inclement weather conditions but as God's way of getting someone's attention.

> Now all the people witnessed the thunderings, the lightning flashes, the sound of the trumpet, and the mountain smoking; and when the people saw *it,* they trembled and stood afar off. Then they said to Moses, "You speak with us, and we will hear; but let not God speak with us, lest we die." And Moses said to the people, "Do not fear; for God has come to test you, and that His fear may be before you, so that you may not sin." So the people stood afar off, but Moses drew near the thick darkness where God was. Then the Lord said to Moses, "Thus you shall say to the children of Israel: 'You have seen that I have talked with you from heaven. (Exodus 20:18–22)

The Seven Lamps of Fire

The seven lamps of fire are the seven spiritual manifestations of Jehovah (see also Revelation 1:4). These manifestations are neither angels nor seven different spirits but rather the Holy Spirit with His seven-fold character. There is only one Lamb. These Spirits can be the gifts or graces given to the church (Revelation 5:6).

> There shall come forth a Rod from the stem of Jesse, and a Branch shall grow out of his roots. The <u>Spirit of the Lord</u> shall rest upon Him, the Spirit of <u>wisdom</u> and <u>understanding</u>, the Spirit of <u>counsel</u> and <u>might</u>, the Spirit of <u>knowledge</u> and of <u>the fear of the Lord.</u> (Isaiah 11:1–2, emphasis added)

The Four Living Creatures

Between the twenty-four elders and the throne are the "four living creatures" forming the innermost circle. The King James Version of the Bible uses the word "beasts," meaning "live things." They are "full of eyes," capable of seeing everything from every angle. They did not have to turn because they have eyes all around. Unlike man whose two eyes are only upfront or like the bird whose two eyes are on either side of the head but upfront or like the lobster whose two eyes can see all around but not underneath, the four living creatures have a 360-degree vision in 3-D. The eye is the lamp of the body, and it also speaks of wisdom, as it is the organ of perception (Psalms 119:18; Hebrews 4:13).

The living creatures represent Jehovah's creation giving Him praise for keeping His covenant after the Flood. The lion represents the wild beasts, the calf represents the domestic animals (cattle), the face of man represents mankind, and the flying eagle represents the bird family. In the natural, these creatures are the highest of their kind. The lion is known as "the king of the jungle," the calf the "choicest of meats for food," man "the apogee of God's creation," and the eagle "the lord of the sky." All these were saved in the Ark during the Flood. The Creator put man in charge because man came out of Him (Genesis 1:26). All of God's creation is important to Him and all worship Him in their own way. You don't have to acknowledge God; the rest of His creation will – even the stones (Genesis 9:10–11; Luke 19:40).

Prophet Ezekiel also spoke about strange-looking creatures in the presence of God. He, too, said that the living creatures were "full of eyes." According to McLean, "In the realm of the Spirit: the past, the present and the future is the now. They have eyes before and behind."[12] He is suggesting that the living creatures can see everything and have a full galactic vision from their present position because they operate outside of time.

Ezekiel gives a description of the living creatures he saw. It is similar to John's.

> Each one had four faces: the first face was the face of a cherub, the second face the face of a man, the third the face of a lion, and the fourth the face of an eagle. . . . This is the living creature I saw under the God of Israel by the River Chebar, and I knew they were cherubim. Each one had four faces and each one four wings, and the likeness of the hands of a man was under their wings. (Ezekiel 10:14, 20–21)

In addition to being full of eyes all around and having wings, the four creatures worked together (Ezekiel 1:13–15). The expression "living creature" is used to describe the beings because they were alive but neither completely animal nor completely man; they were hybrid creatures, like some of the exotic beasts portrayed in the *Star Wars* or *Avatar* movies.

Holy! Holy! Holy!

"Holy, holy, holy, Lord God Almighty, Who was and is and is to come!" (v. 8). This is clearly a worship session in progress. God's holiness or sacredness is paramount to those who are conversant with His greatness and are grateful to Him. In a regular worship service today, it is typical to hear worshippers singing out "Holy is the Lord God Almighty!" They, too, are honoring the magnificence of the Creator. Nothing and no one else in the universe can rightly accept this level of acclamation and be justified. Satan cannot accept this attribute—he would have to change his nature.

The Greek word for "holy" as used in this passage is *hagios*, which means "an awful thing; sacred (physically, pure, morally blameless or religious, ceremonially, consecrated); not defiled; saint; innocent; perfect; something to cherish."[13] The word is sometimes used as an adjective and as a noun. "Holiness of character in the distinct ethical sense is ascribed to God. From the holiness of God is derived that ceremonial holiness of things which is characteristic of the Old Testament religion. Whatever is connected with the worship of the holy Yahweh is itself holy. Nothing is holy in itself, but anything becomes holy by its consecration to Him. A place where He manifests His presence is holy ground."[14]

Visions into God's Temple

King Uzziah died in 758 BC.[15] That is the same year the prophet Isaiah had a vision of God in His temple in Heaven. He saw basically the same things Ezekiel and John saw, the living creatures, which he labeled *seraphim*.

In the year that King Uzziah died, I saw the Lord sitting on a throne, high and lifted up, and the train of His robe filled the temple. Above it stood seraphim; each one had six wings: with two he covered his face, with two he covered his feet, and with two he flew. And one cried to another and said: "Holy, holy, holy is the Lord of hosts; the whole earth is full of His glory!" (Isaiah 6:1–3)

According to *Nelson's Bible Dictionary*, *seraphim* are "mysterious angelic creatures" who ministered around God's throne.[16] *Seraph* is the singular of seraphim. It is amazing that from the time of Isaiah's vision to John's visit— some 850 years—these creatures are still crying out "Holy! Holy! Holy!" around the throne room, ascribing majesty, splendor, and glory to the One on the throne. Today, some 1,925+ years after John's revelation, mankind is still worshipping the Creator here on earth.

It is important to note here that in this era of John's visitation, there were still days and nights. During the worship session in Heaven, the elders joined in when prompted by the living creatures and fell down before the throne. Elders also fell down during the dedication of King Solomon's temple (2 Chronicles 5:11–14), but that was because they were overpowered by the glory of the Lord. The implication here in John's revelation is that the elders intentionally prostrated themselves before the throne because they all simultaneously and intensely thrust their crowns towards the throne of the Holy One.

Intensity and Sincerity in Worship

Notice here that everyone and everything present in the throne room is worshipping the One on the throne. Lying prostrate is an act of adoration and subjection. By casting their crowns, the elders humbled themselves in holy reverence, surrendering or giving back to the Holy One what He had given them. They owe everything they have to Him because it was He who had crowned them, awarding them for their work. In life, when one comes to this realization, nothing is too good or too valuable that God cannot have it. Whatever grace, glory, prestige, or honored position the elders are enjoying, these are all from the Holy One.

An encounter with God's holiness, awesomeness, and power will lead one to worship Him and to do so spontaneously. But experience teaches that what you don't adore you despise. The evil person does not want to be in God's presence (Psalms 65:4).

The casting of the crowns can also mean the admission that the Holy One's crown is greater and more glorious than the elders'. It is their pleasure (soul's desire) to worship the Holy One. No one is commanding or enticing them to worship. To stay on one accord, they take their cue from the living creatures (Daniel 3). Music and instruments were always a part of worship, as it helps everybody involved to stay together. If only we could worship the Lord today like the elders of John's vision, with our wealth, health, and strength (John 4:23–24).

The exaltation—"You are worthy, O Lord, to receive glory and honor and power; for You created all things, and by Your will they exist and were created."—is fitting for the Creator during worship here on earth. Even nowadays this is one of the many doxologies proclaimed in churches. It has been highly recognized as a congregational worship song. There are more doxologies throughout the book of Revelation.

CHAPTER 5

Revelation 5—the Worthiness of Jesus the Christ

"**A**ND I SAW in the right hand of Him who sat on the throne a scroll written inside and on the back, sealed with seven seals" (v. 1). The "right hand" represents power and authority. It is used for laying on of hands, greetings, and also for extending fellowship.[1]

According to *IVP Bible Background Commentary*, legal and official documents and certificates were sealed. They were sealed to give proof of authenticity and authority, maintain secrecy (marked closed until a certain time), and could not be opened without being noticed. In that era, a Roman's will was sealed with seven seals.[2] If this scroll is a will, then only on the death of the person could this scroll be opened. The scroll is labeled on the outside. This is mentioned because scrolls are not usually labeled, neither do they bear writing on both sides. John does not say who it is addressed to; therefore, it could have been meant to be opened at a particular time. The seven seals tell how mysterious (deep, strange, not easily understood or accepted) the contents were, signifying that the scroll should not be opened casually but after much deliberation. Maybe seven individuals (the seven Spirits) sealed the scroll, each with his personal seal, making it a team effort.

Finding the seal unbroken means that the contents of the document have been kept secured, confidential, and unaltered. When something is sealed, only an authorized person—not any

John Doe—can break the seal and open it. Whoever opens it must take full responsibility for what is revealed or exposed by the breaking of the seal.

> "You yourselves write a decree concerning the Jews, as you please, in the king's name, and seal it with the king's signet ring; for whatever is written in the king's name and sealed with the king's signet ring no one can revoke." (Esther 8:8) See also Matthew 27:65–66.

The Number Seven

The Babylonians use the number seven to mean "totality or completeness" and "perfection." It was sometimes used to mean "all."[3] The Hebrews adopted this symbolism from the Babylonians and expanded it to include "fullness." For example:

-   to forgive seven times means to forgive fully;
-   seven days complete a week;
-   seven days for a feast;
-   the seventh day is rest day, as eight starts a new week, the first day;
-   multiples of seven are just as significant (7x2, 7x7, and 7x10).

"Then I saw a strong angel proclaiming with a loud voice, 'Who is worthy to open the scroll and to loose its seals?'" (v. 2). The angel being referred to as strong could be a high-ranking angel as they have different strengths in keeping with their different functions. However, no one present was worthy enough to open the scroll, not even a stronger angel. There was no one worthy to even look at it. Everyone who was present knew their level of authority, and they stayed within their pay grade. Even though someone present might have had the physical ability to open the scroll, he had no authority to do so. Everyone knew their limitations. No one exalted himself higher than he ought, not the angels, not the elders, not the living creatures (Isaiah 57:15).

> [John the Baptist said,] "I indeed baptize you with water unto repentance, but He who is coming after me is mightier than I, whose sandals I am not worthy to carry. He will baptize you with the Holy Spirit and fire." (Matthew 3:11)
> See also Matthew 5:3.

Nowadays, one person only having access code for a high-level system is common. Because of the sensitivity of the operation and the potential impact, it can have on others and everything this power and authority have to remain entrusted to a responsible person if only for security reasons.

The Lion of Judah Is Here

It appears those in Heaven knew who was to take the scroll. One of the elders spoke up with words of comfort and cheer informing John that this high-level matter is taken care of (v. 5). This is an example of how nothing takes God by surprise. The elder also told him that the "Lion of the tribe of Judah," who is the "Root of [King] David," is ready to do the honors. Here is a prophecy by Prophet Isaiah concerning this matter from the beginning. David precedes Isaiah by three hundred years,[4] yet Isaiah is addressing David's forefather:

> "And in that day there shall be a Root of Jesse [King David's father],
> Who shall stand as a banner to the people;
> For the Gentiles [foreign nations, heathens, non-Jews] shall seek Him,

And His resting place [repose, abode] shall be glorious."
It shall come to pass in that day
That the Lord shall set His hand again the second time
To recover the remnant of His people who are left,
From Assyria and Egypt,
From Pathros and Cush [now Ethiopia],
From Elam and Shinar [Sinar],
From Hamath and the islands of the sea.
(Isaiah 11:10–11, emphasis added)

Notice that Isaiah said ROOT, not a shoot or fruit; therefore, the person of whom he spoke existed before Jesse. This root has a flag (standard or banner) that is recognized by people and nations all around the world.

The lion is a symbol of strength and authority. It is the most powerful of all carnivorous animals. Known for its courage, strength, and bravery, it is one of the living creatures around the throne (Proverbs 30:29–30). Jesus is hailed as the Lion of the tribe of Judah. Jesus overcame all the tests and temptations sent His way and is now victorious (Matthew 4:1–11). Among other feats, He freed the dead saints from Hades (Matthew 27:50–53). Now you can understand why "blessings, glory, honor, power, strength, riches and wisdom" (v. 12) are given to Him in worship. Who else is worthy to receive such an exaltation? "The fear of the Lord" is also attributed to Him. Jesus has never refused worship (Matthew 14:33, 20:29–32, 21:15–16; Luke 4:41). He has been found worthy to open the scroll.

Organizations usually charge only one person with the responsibility of a high-level matter. It is said that only the President of the United States can press the switch to release nuclear warheads. The IT department of an institution entrusts its system access codes or password to only one person. Only Jesus has the access codes to activate the end-time program (to break the seals). Jesus made it clear to His Disciples that He is the one and only way to the Father, the God of all creation (John 14:6).

The Lamb Who Was Slain

The Lamb in the midst of the throne, the One who had been slain, is present (v. 6). The Lion has now been transformed to the Lamb. Symbolically, a lamb is a type of meekness and innocence. Hence, it was the animal most frequently used in sacrifices. As Abraham set out for the place of worship, his son asked him, "Where is the lamb for a burnt offering?"

> And Abraham said, "My son, God will provide for Himself the lamb for a burnt offering." So the two of them went together. (Genesis 22:8)

Moses was about to lead the children of Israel out of Egypt, and he instructed them to slaughter a lamb for the family (Exodus 12:3–6, 11). A lamb was the daily sacrifice at the tabernacle (Exodus 29:38–42). Jesus of Nazareth became the real sacrificial Lamb of God for mankind. He was not a substitute but the actual Lamb.

> Again, the next day, John [The Baptist] stood with two of his disciples. And looking at Jesus as He walked, he said, "Behold the Lamb of God!" (John 1:29–30, 35–36, emphasis added)

Why didn't John address Jesus as "the Prophet" or "the Great Teacher"? Jesus was definitely a rabbi, a healer, etc. But a prophet or a teacher cannot redeem your soul. Mankind needs redemption most of all. This Jesus of Nazareth is the same Lamb that was slain for the redemption of mankind because He met all the Old Testament requirements for sin removal (Isaiah 53:4–7; 1 Peter 1:18–21).

Seven Horns

A lamb, which is a young sheep, does not have horns; it's too immature. In the event it does have horns, it has only two not seven. So this lamb in the midst of the throne is not a regular creature. Animals that have horns are fierce and use their horns when fighting (Daniel 8:5–7). The horn described here is not the instrument you blow, neither is it the most sacred part (edge) of the altar; it's a hard, bone-like pointed body part which grows out of the head. It is recognized as a symbol of royal dignity and power (Zechariah 1:18–21). It also represents strength (Deuteronomy 33:17). The seven horns speak of the complete honor, power, and strength with which the Lamb is endowed.

Seven Eyes

The eye is the natural organ that allows humans and animals to see in the physical realm. Symbolically, the eye refers to generosity, lust, pride, envy, and the stirring up of desires.[5] Having no eyes means darkness, ignorance, dependence, groping/fumbling rather than being organized. Taking out someone's eyes is meant to weaken and humble the individual. And because the eyes deal with sight, they are also a symbol of "all-knowing." The seven eyes mean that nothing misses His vision as they are the seven Spirits of God sent out into all the earth (v. 6).

Another Worship Session

The twenty-four elders are musically inclined; they play the harps while angels blow the horns. They are intercessors also. The golden bowls contain the worship/prayers of the saints. Their worship is like sweet incense, savory to the Father's nostrils. Here they go with a new song. They make up these songs as they go along (Psalms 33:2–3, 96:1–2; Isaiah 42:10).

> And they sang a new song, saying: "You are worthy to take the scroll, and to open its seals; for You were slain, and have redeemed us to God by Your blood out of every tribe and tongue and people and nation, and have made us kings and priests to our God; and we shall reign on the earth." (Revelation 5:9–10)

The Voice of Many Angels

"Then I looked, and I heard the voice of many angels around the throne, the living creatures, and the elders; and the number of them was ten thousand times ten thousand, and thousands of thousands, saying with a loud voice" (vv. 11–12a). Here, John is trying to quantify the number of angels he saw in and around the throne room. This number is too big to even call or put into a regular calculator. He said the number of them was ten thousand times ten thousand and thousands of thousands. That is 10,000 x 10,000, which is 100 million, plus 1,000 x 1,000, which is one million, for a total of one thousand trillion (the number one with fourteen zeroes behind it) heavenly bodies at least. And they spoke in a loud voice. The number would be thunderous in itself. Another doxology breaks out, with worship to the One who took the scroll. The angels and everyone present shout (v. 12):

"Worthy is the Lamb who was slain To receive power and riches and wisdom, And strength and honor and glory and blessing!"

The heavenly beings proclaimed seven significant and well-deserved attributes or meritorious qualities about the Lamb (not the Lion). This speaks volumes of His completeness and perfection and demonstrates why He is so highly adored.

Every Knee Shall Bow

Every creature (everything created and made) was speaking or making some sort of sound. They were delivering yet another doxology namely, "Blessing and honor and glory and power be to Him who sits on the throne [the Father], and to the Lamb [the Son], forever and ever!" (v. 13). This scene coincides with the prophecy of Prophet Isaiah, whom Apostle Paul quoted:

For it is written: "As I live, says the Lord, Every knee shall bow to Me, And every tongue shall confess to God." (Romans 14:11)
See also Isaiah 45:23; Philippians 2:9–11.

There are many questions arising from this scene, but an important one is this, were the people and creatures reading from the same script as they were all uttering the same praise at the same time? No, they were not reading from the same source because the people were from different nations and animals don't read! What language were they speaking—tongues, Hebrew, or their own native dialect? Were they on one accord? That should have been a loud noise. Maybe they were speaking in tongues because they were in the Spirit and there is the gift of interpretation of tongues. This universal display of honor to the Creator led to another worship session initiated by the four living creatures.

CHAPTER 6

Revelation 6—Opening the First Six Seals

THE DIVINE JUDGMENT is about to begin. You have seen or heard of divine judgments executed by God over millennia on Israel and other nations. Some examples are the Great Flood; Sodom, Gomorrah, and other cities; inhabitants of the land of Canaan (the Promised Land for Israel); and Achan and his family. These examples can be classified as "the wrath of God" against those who were in rebellion against Him. However, most of these were localized judgments. The final judgment will be global, encompassing every nation.

In Matthew 24:4–14, Jesus warns that destruction by judgments will come again. Go to chapter 2 of this book to refresh this scripture reference. Examine Zechariah 6:1–8. The fairness in God's judgment is expressed in Ezekiel 33:12–16.

The First Seal Opened

After drying his eyes from the weeping due to no one being found worthy to open the scroll and after having observed the intense worship session, John is settled enough to watch the opening of the seals. He said, "I saw when the Lamb opened one of the seals" (v. 1). The word "saw" here means "to know by seeing." Then he said, "I heard . . . a voice." The word "heard" here means "audible to the ears or audio-sensory." John, being able to see and hear, is now invited to move from where he was to "come (closer) and see" what is on the opened scroll. He looks and beholds with his eyes not writing but a series of pictures—maybe a motion picture—which he describes in detail.[1] One cannot precisely conclude "a crown being given" or a person going "out to conquer" from one still picture. Furthermore, John did not say that he *read* this but that he *saw* this (maybe like on a monitor screen). These pictures (or presentations) were in full color.

The "white horse" is a representation of the "pure, sanctified, and bold" believer of the early church who continued the advancement of the gospel of Jesus Christ around the world. Back in John's day, a horse was a symbol of war, strength, and conquest.[2] The "horseman with a bow" may remind us of the Parthians, who were very skilled at riding and shooting with accuracy at the same time. These third- to second-century BC horse archers, who traveled light and were well trained, were known for the "Parthian Shot," a highly effective military tactic.[3] This first seal speaks of the believer(s) of the early church engaged in high-level military warfare or hunting (evangelism) with good success—winning souls. You must be dressed for warfare (Ephesians 6:12–13). Like the apostle Paul, these believers were probably given a "crown of righteousness, of glory or of life" for their dedication and effectiveness (Psalms 8:4–5; James 1:12; 1 Peter 5:4; Revelation 2:10–11).

The Second Seal Opened

As in the opening of the first seal, it does not sound as if someone is reading from the scroll into John's hearing (v. 3). He is again invited to "come (closer) and see" what the Lamb is viewing on the scroll. He sees another horse going out, but this one is "fiery red." This rider has a different assignment because the horse is a different color. The red denotes "blood, fire, and destruction" with the same intensity and success that the color white symbolizes. His assignment matches his color—to take peace from the earth and cause bloodshed while bringing destruction wherever he goes.

The "sword," being sharp and destructive, is a symbol of "divine chastisement" (1 Chronicles 21:27; Judges 7:20). Gideon was known for bearing "the sword of the Lord" in battles. While John did not reveal who gave the rider the sword, it was given to him as his authority and power to accomplish his assignment. This bloody period follows the great accomplishment by the rider on the white horse. It seems that since the essence of the white horse has faded, mankind has reverted to his former status of sin and bondage with the church adopting pagan and worldly practices. This seal alludes to the persecution which came upon the church starting with Nero into the Dark Ages and is continuing even today. This seal marks the beginning and spread of Catholicism.[4]

Be reminded, though, that from time immemorial, there have been wars and murders where people would turn on each other. People who know each other—gangs, clubs, even family members—would turn on each other. Even Jehovah has used one nation to turn on another as an expression of His punishment (1 Samuel 15:2–3). Early in Jesus's ministry, He announced that He did not come to bring peace on earth because He knew that establishing His kingdom required warfare. There would be conflicts on earth, as He did not expect the enemy to lie down and play dead or to simply give up territory.

> "Do not think that I came to bring peace on earth. I did not come to bring peace but a sword [a sword represents judgment]. For I have come to 'set a man against his father, a daughter against her mother, and a daughter-in-law against

her mother-in-law'; and 'a man's enemies will be those of his own household.'" (Matthew 10:34–36, emphasis added)

In the phase of the second seal being opened, do not expect more peace on the streets (Matthew 24:10–12). Violence and bloodshed will be common occurrences, especially in places where wickedness is prevalent. Mankind will violently slaughter one another.

"And you will hear of wars and rumors of wars. See that you are not troubled; for all these things must come to pass, but the end is not yet. For nation will rise against nation, and kingdom against kingdom. And there will be famines, pestilences, and earthquakes in various places." (Matthew 24:6–7)

The Third Seal Opened

John is invited again to "come (closer) and see" what is about to happen (v. 5). At this time, a "black horse," with the rider holding "a pair of scales," is the main character. The black represents "calamity, famine, evil (nothing good), and death." The pair of scales or balances, which is generally used to represent justice and fairness in business and commerce, is carried by an unjust merchant (or economic system), which promotes inflation. In this context, the scales point to rationing. A voice from the midst of the living creatures is now narrating what John is seeing. "A quart of wheat for a denarius and three quarts of barley for a denarius" (v. 6). During that era, the value of the denarius would be about twenty cents, which was the ordinary wage of a soldier and a day laborer (Matthew 20:8–9).[5] It would have bought provisions for a few days.

I can vividly recall as a boy paying only sixpence (ten cents) for a twelve-ounce bottle of soft drink from a vending machine.

Today, fifty-plus years later, that same twelve-ounce soft drink costs one dollar (ten times more). There is going to come a time when the money you will earn daily will only be enough to buy food for that day. Inflation—or taxation—will be at such a high rate that it will put the cost of food out of reach of the common person, resulting in either famine or a high rate of theft and robbery. Many of the poor and weak will die. The high rate of inflation could also come from scarcity as the economic law of supply and demand takes effect and leads to rationing. In foresight, I can see the hand of the World Trade Organization (WTO) involved with this globally if only to protect the upper class.

> "For whoever has, to him more will be given, and he will have abundance; but whoever does not have, even what he has will be taken away from him." (Matthew 13:12)
> See also Matthew 6:19–21.

Oil, especially olive oil, was used for many household purposes, such as in anointing the body in acts of consecration, as an offering, in lamps to give light, as medicine, and for gladness, making it one of the most valuable products in the nation of Israel. It was abundant among the Hebrews.[6] Wine, a product of grapes, was popular also. It was used for daily sacrifices, consumed with meals, used to make raisin cakes, drunk on special celebrations like Passover, and used at the Lord's last supper with His disciples.[7] It was known for its intoxicating effect on the human brain and its potential to bring merriment to the drinker (Ephesians 5:18). For the Jews, olive yards and vineyards were necessities, the way farms are today, and that was probably the reason for the instruction not to hurt or destroy them.

Oil and wine are symbols of the Holy Spirit (Luke 4:18; Acts 10:38; Ephesians 5:18; Luke 10:34). They also represent the graces—love and joy—given to man from God. Hence, a voice from the midst of the four living creatures in Heaven instructs John, "Do not harm the oil and the wine" (v. 6b). In other words, do not take away the provisions for anointing and healing during this period of distress. Leave the Lord's presence among them as a reminder of His promise.[8]

The Fourth Seal Opened

John is invited a fourth time to "come (closer) and see" what is about to happen (v. 7). He looks and his eyes behold a pale horse, whose rider's name is Death, and Hell followed him. The pale (dull-greenish) horse represents death. I personally would associate green with life, but the pale green indicates that life is weaning. Death is given the power to kill the flesh of man while his accomplice, Hell (Hades, the place for departed souls),[9] is ready to assign the dead to his place until that day. The story Jesus told in Luke 16:19–31 about the "Rich Man and Lazarus" gives a very good picture of what happens after Death does his job. Verses 22 and 23 show that the body will undergo either peace or torment when one dies.

In this fourth seal, unlike the previous ones, the rider is now given the power to kill; he is now doing the killing. Death and Hades are given the power to kill a fourth of the earth using various methods. The four major causes of death will be wars (or violence), starvation, strange deaths, and animal attacks. The world's population in April 2019 was almost 8 billion.[10] If this seal was opened then, nearly 2 billion people would have died during that phase alone. The Old Testament nations were familiar with these massive judgments (Jeremiah 14:11–12).

Is This the Tribulation?

The four living creatures have each made their presentation of the seals being opened. Now there is a shift—no more horses with riders. It seems John was shown the future devastations which are to come on the earth. Are these first four seals part of the Tribulation? When did the Tribulation start if it has started? Is the Tribulation still going on? Were saints killed during this period? Is this the time Jesus spoke about in Matthew 24:4–14?

The Fifth Seal Opened

Under the altar were the souls of the saints who were martyred and are awaiting release (v. 9). Is this the same place which is referred to as Abraham's bosom? Where is this altar? This altar is on earth and is probably the one on which these persons (believers) were persecuted or offered. Some of these souls may have been sacrificed long ago. If this altar is in Heaven, the souls would have been free to move about like the rest of the beings up there, worshipping God. Are present-day believers casualties in the judgments above? Most likely they are because there are still more saints to be persecuted (v. 11). During the Protestant Reformation and the various Inquisitions of the fifteenth and subsequent centuries, many more souls experienced the same fate as those under the altar. Today, it is common knowledge that in Muslim and Hindu countries, it is a "good deed" to slaughter infidels (Christians) in the name of Allah or Brahman.

How long must they wait for relief and the conviction of their slayers? The Lord is not willing that anyone should perish, but that everyone come to repentance. By His delay, He is simply giving sinners (all nations) a chance to repent. How merciful and gracious!

The Lord is not slack concerning His promise, as some count slackness, but is longsuffering toward us, not willing that any should perish but that all should come to repentance. (2 Peter 3:9)
See also Romans 9:22–24.

Some time ago I heard an explanation of the place called Hades. I cannot recall to whom I should give credit, but it went like this. Hades is like the Remand Centre at the Bahamas Department of Correctional Services (state prison) in Fox Hill. Because the person has not been convicted, he cannot be placed into the main prison population with convicted criminals; instead, he must be confined to a secure place until his trial. Unfortunately, this secure place is within the prison walls, where hardship is experienced and freedoms are taken away. Such is the case for these martyred souls.

Each one was given a white robe and told to rest a little while longer until the number of their fellow servants and their brethren who would be killed as they were, was complete. They were rewarded according to the church at Sardis (Psalms 13:1–2).

John's seeing and hearing "dead souls crying out" is further evidence that there is life after death in the flesh. Unlike animals which have no spirit, man lives on, but in a different realm. Death is simply a medium to move man from one state to another.

The Sixth Seal Opened

According to John, he saw the earth and other heavenly bodies were thrown into disarray (v. 12). A major earthquake shatters the Richter scale; the sun's light is turned off for the first time ever. the moon appears bloodred; a shower of asteroids crashes into the earth, resulting in tsunamis; and the first level of heaven splits apart, along with a terrestrial shift of mountains and islands—these events are enough to bring any mighty person to his knees because of fear. They sound like the cause of the cosmic devastations that were on the earth before its recreation. Genesis 1:2 says that "the earth was without form, and void, and darkness was on the face of the deep."

The earth has experienced quakes before. The great earthquake of November 1, 1755, is still recognized for its devastation of Lisbon and the surrounding nations.[11] There have been a few already this century but none achieving the magnitude of the quake seen by John. This earthquake caused tremors and tsunamis all around the globe at the same time. The sun turned black, meaning there was no more light and no heat. The sun's rays give life and energy to everything on the planet. If the sun disappears for a long period, things begin to die or at least begin to lose their effectiveness. The moon turned bloodred, a reflection of what's out there (maybe fire from the stars in flight). The stars fell to earth like asteroids, hitting the ground, leaving craters, and destroying what was on the ground. This shower of stars will take out satellites, airplanes, and whatever else man has put up there, along with cities and nations on the ground. With the satellites down, global communication will be drastically affected. The sky receded, rent apart violently, now separated and divided as though one can now see into the other heavens. Every mountain and island is removed from their places, total chaos. Hollywood movies are a joke! Now the lords of the earth want to hide from the face (or presence) of Him who sits on the throne. This should remind us of Adam and Eve in the garden when they disobeyed God. There is a day of reckoning. Have you made preparation yet?

John sees all this unfolding in motion from the scroll. Is this devastation literal or symbolic? I think literal because there is going to be a new earth later on. Notice that the seventh seal is not yet open. All seven seals must be open for the full content of the document to be revealed. With the opening of each of the first six seals, we saw a new release of terror on the earth. All this signifies the beginning of the end. Each terror will last for only a season. How long? I cannot say (Romans 2:3–11, Revelation 6:17).

The Tribulation

There is a great tribulation period (Matthew 24:21–22) before the Rapture. Those days will be shortened for the elect's sake, meaning that believers are still on earth. Here Jesus references the prophet Daniel when he prophesies about the "abomination of desolation" (Daniel 11:31; 12:11). Daniel says there is coming a time when there will be so much detestable perverseness, filth, and idolatrous activities that it will stupefy people and bring destruction upon them. The people will continue in this way until they become numb, accepting it all as normal, just like in Sodom and in the days of Noah.

This great tribulation period is ripe. With the universal prevalence of idolatry, adultery, homosexuality, drunkenness, backsliding and covenant breaking, murder, hatred, greed, false information, sorcery, and satanic worship in the earth, mankind has moved himself very far from his Creator. Mankind has declared his independence from God as he sees God as no longer relevant for life and happiness. Here is the "falling away" (2 Thessalonians 2:3). Thirty years ago, this anti-God attitude was not so obvious and widespread. Today, we are in it.

Periods of Tribulation

There are more periods of tribulation. Trouble, affliction, extreme pressure, anguish, and persecution will be throughout the end-time. Some afflictions will be released because of God's wrath on the wicked, and some by Satan and his imps on whomever.

During the fifth seal, when the martyred saints asked, "How long . . . until You judge and avenge our blood?", they were told that there are more fellow servants and their brethren to be killed as they were (vv. 9–11).

During the sixth seal and after a tribulation period when the wrath of the Lamb is unleashed upon the earth, the 144,000, who are all children of Israel, will be sealed (vv. 15–17). However, nothing on the earth is harmed until after they are sealed (Revelation 7:1–3). After this sealing process, a rapture of "a great multitude" takes place. These are the ones who came out of the great tribulation and washed their robes and made them white (Revelation 7:9–14). Saints will still be on the earth during some stages of the tribulation process. The 144,000 are not taken out yet. Christ will come and take out (rapture) His saints and ignore the unbelievers (those left behind).

Some saints may be thinking that God has said that He will not allow the righteous to suffer from the wicked (Genesis 18:23, 32; Revelation 3:10); therefore, tribulation (affliction, anguish, persecution) should not come upon the righteous. Instead, the righteous should be taken out before the trouble or pressure starts in this wicked world. These saints are thinking that the church is not supposed to go through tribulation (Matthew 24:9). However, Jesus says, "Let both grow together until the harvest [reaping]" (Matthew 13:28–30). Yes! God will allow hardship and burdens to come upon the righteous because they know how to overcome. God allowed hardship to come upon Job, Joseph, Jeremiah, John the Baptist, and Jesus. Some overcame while some died in the process. The Father determines who does what. Your role is to remain faithful unto death even though you may not die (Psalms 116:1–8; Matthew 10:28; Revelation 12:11). However, if you die in Christ, you are secure (Philippians 1:20–21). Are you more righteous or essential than the apostle Paul, Martin Luther, or Myles Munroe? The Kingdom of God is not for the weak-hearted, fearful, and cowardly but for warriors and overcomers.

The Post-Tribulation Events

The Synoptic Gospels featured this post-tribulation event. Therefore, John could have heard His Master talk about it or read what other authors had to say about Jesus's return. This was not a small, concealed matter because the disciples asked Jesus about it before He left (Acts 1:6). Let's examine Mark's account:

> "But in those days, after that tribulation, the sun will be darkened, and the moon will not give its light; the stars of heaven will fall, and the powers in the heavens will be shaken. Then they will see the Son of Man coming in the clouds with great power and glory. And then He will send His angels, and gather together His elect from the four winds, from the farthest part of earth to the farthest part of heaven." (Mark 13:24–27, emphasis added)

Many of the major and minor prophets recorded some account of the heavenly bodies being affected in some way, rendering signs and wonders in the earth before the end comes. Here is Isaiah's account:

> Behold, the day of the LORD comes,
> Cruel, with both wrath and fierce anger,

To lay the land desolate;
And He will destroy its sinners from it.
For the stars of heaven and their constellations
Will not give their light;
The sun will be darkened in its going forth,
And the moon will not cause its light to shine.
"I will punish the world for its evil,
And the wicked for their iniquity;
I will halt the arrogance of the proud,
And will lay low the haughtiness of the terrible.
I will make a mortal more rare than fine gold,
A man more than the golden wedge of Ophir.
Therefore I will shake the heavens,
And the earth will move out of her place,
In the wrath of the LORD of hosts
And in the day of His fierce anger.
(Isaiah 13:9–13)

According to Uriah Smith,[12] who has excellent research and documentation on the subject, most of these events have taken place already namely:

The Great Earthquake. The gospels do not mention this, but John does. A great earthquake took place on November 1, 1755, popularly known as the earthquake of Lisbon. It covered a tract of at least four million square miles and killed about ninety thousand people in Lisbon alone. Entire cities were swallowed up as the quake moved at a rate of twenty miles per minute, even crossing the North Atlantic Ocean.

The Darkening of the Sun. This took place on May 19, 1780. Known as "The Dark Day," it started at ten in the morning and continued until the middle of the next night over all the New England States and the surrounding areas, at different degrees and duration in places. However, only North America recorded this.

The Moon Became as Blood. This took place the night following the day of the Darkening of the Sun. To prove that the darkening of the sun was not an eclipse, the moon did appear, but the appearance was like that of blood.

The Stars of Heaven Fell. This was the great meteoric shower of November 13, 1833. The falling stars of the north stayed in the north, etc., but none fell to the earth. The celestial show covered the whole of North America from the Atlantic Ocean to the Pacific Ocean from nine o'clock to twelve o'clock and continued until rendered invisible by the light of day. It was described as "a splendor of celestial exhibition . . . the most brilliant skyrockets and fireworks of art."

The Heavens Departed as a Scroll. This can also be referred to as "the shaking of the powers of the heavens." Smith states, "We wait for the heavens to depart as a scroll when it is rolled together." In other words, according to Smith, this has not yet happened. But he does say that "these are times of unparalleled solemnity and importance, for we do not know how near we may be to the fulfillment of these things."

Smith also thinks that the world is now ready for the opening of the seventh seal. How much longer do we have to wait?

The Second Coming: Literal or Symbolic? Ministers over the centuries have truly believed there is a literal second coming of Christ to the earth. Some have gone as far as to set an exact date of His arrival even though Jesus said that "no one knows" (Matthew 24:36). We were told to "watch and pray" (Mark 13:33) not predict a date.

> "But of that day and hour no one knows, not even the angels of heaven, but My Father only. But as the days of Noah were, so also will the coming of the Son of Man be . . .Therefore you also be ready, for the Son of Man is coming at an hour you do not expect." (Matthew 24:36–37, 44)
> See also Luke 17:34–36.

Here are a few of the more than one hundred presumptuous ministers and organizations who, nonetheless, have tried to predict the date of Jesus's return.[6]

Predictor	Predicted Date of Second Coming	Explanation
Pope Sylvester II	January 1, 1000	The Millennium Apocalypse would take place at the end of the first millennium. The world would end on that date.
Michael Stifel	October 19, 1533	Stifel, a mathematician, calculated that judgment day would begin at 8:00 AM. on October 19, 1533.
John Wesley	1836	The founder of Methodism forecast the millennium beginning in 1836. Revelation 12:14 refers to the years 1058–1836 as the period when Christ should come.
Jehovah's Witnesses	1914	The year 1914 marked the beginning of Christ's invisible presence (Matthew 24:3) as the King of God's Kingdom and the beginning of the last days of the human-ruled system of society.
Herbert W. Armstrong	1935, 1943, 1972, and 1975	Pastor-General and self-proclaimed apostle of the Worldwide Church of God predicted in *The Plain Truth* magazine on two occasions that Christ will come after 3 ½ years of tribulation. Then he predicted Christ would come before he died. Armstrong died on January 16, 1986.

Timothy Dwight	2000	President of Yale University, he foresaw Christ's Millennium starting by 2000.
Mark Blitz	September 28, 2015	Blitz believed Jesus's return would correspond with the September 28, 2015, lunar eclipse. This is known as the Blood Moon Prophecy.
Jeane Dixon	2020	This self-proclaimed psychic and astrologer claimed that Armageddon would take place in 2020 when Jesus would return to defeat the unholy trinity.

CHAPTER 7

Revelation 7—
Sealing the Saints

WE ARE STILL at the sixth seal on the scroll, which is still in the hands of the Lamb. Reading the statement about "four angels standing at the four corners of the earth" (v. 1) and knowing that the earth is round can throw you off a bit. However, when the clause "holding the four winds" is added, it makes the first statement clearer. The four corners are where the four winds originate, the major points on a compass namely, north, south, east, and west. The winds are different, but they are all under the Lord's authority. The north wind usually brings rain and blessings (Proverbs 25:23). The south wind usually brings peace and tranquility, good weather (Luke 12:55). The east wind usually brings widespread disaster (Genesis 41:27; Ezekiel 19:12). The west wind usually removes disaster and brings order (Exodus 10:19).

Let me hasten to add here that some, not all of these situations may be symbolic rather than literal. For example, winds and beasts may be interpreted literally, as well as winds can be symbols of wars and beasts of nations (Daniel 7:2–4). The 200+-miles-per-hour winds of hurricane Dorian were literal, but they had the devastating effect of war on the northern islands of the Bahamas in 2019.[1] Similarly, the four living creatures around God's throne can be actual creatures or beings, just like the twenty-four elders.

Everything stops until the servants of God who are still on the earth have been sealed, that is, stamped or marked with a signet or private mark for security or preservation. This seal is placed specifically on their foreheads. These servants of God are bondservants, people who have voluntarily submitted or subserviently rendered themselves to God without question. They have denied their freedom and now belong entirely to God. In this group are men, all from the tribes of the children of Israel (whose name was Jacob).

It is Jewish practice to start with the firstborn and end with the lastborn when listing offspring. Notice that the list (v. 5) does not start with Reuben but with Judah and that the rest of the sons of Israel are not listed in chronological order. Another strange notation is that the tribe of Dan is missing and is replaced by Manasseh. Manasseh was Joseph's firstborn. Twelve thousand men (a remnant) were sealed from each of the tribes listed. This brought the total sealed from Israel's clan to 144,000. Even though some tribes were significantly larger in number than others, the same number of persons was selected from each tribe.

However, the session does not stop there. John describes a mass of bondservants as "a great multitude which no one could number, of all nations, tribes, peoples, and tongues, standing before the throne and before the Lamb." This statement should remove the fear of not being sealed if you are not in the lineage of Jacob or cannot prove that you are Jewish. If you did not make the twelve thousand from your tribe, you are still covered in this "great multitude." In fact, the end-time judgment is not for Jews only but the entire world. Furthermore, the 144,000 and the great multitude are living human beings because the sealing is being done on earth (vv. 1–3).

A possible explanation for the tribe of Dan not being listed is that, according to chapter 18 of the book of Judges, Dan deliberately chose to neglect their heritage in Canaan and go farther north with strange gods, and they never repented. Ephraim, Joseph's other son, is represented by Joseph.

The Sealing Process and Matters about the Seal

An angel having "the seal" to mark or stamp foreheads is significant here because had the task of sealing been left to a man, he probably would favor his family and friends first. The sealing was done to clearly identify those selected by putting a mark of privacy or genuineness on them. How long did this sealing process take? Days? Months? Years? Angels are involved, so they could have done it supernaturally with one spoken word. Note that while the great multitude will be standing before the throne and the Lamb, the scripture does not say that they will be sealed as well.

While trademarks, copyrights, and patents have been around for centuries, the significance of the matter has only recently gotten international attention. It is promoted nowadays as "Intellectual Property" as governments seek to protect the rights and intangible creations of their citizens.[2] The Kingdom of Heaven is no different when it comes to the protection of its citizens. Nations going to war would uniform (clearly mark) their soldiers so that they are distinguished from the enemy or easily identified and therefore less susceptible to being caught in "friendly fire." The outward identification, whether it is color, a badge, a sound, or a symbol would be worn by all personnel involved, as it helps with security. A benefit of sealing one's people is that they would know whose cover they are under.

Putting this seal on the forehead of its citizens—making it known where to look for the identification—makes the recognition and validation process quicker. However, the question of counterfeiting is still in the air. Pretenders, hypocrites, talented copycats have been around from time immemorial. Satan is known to be an imposter masquerading as an angel of light (2 Corinthians 11:13–15). A big question is, can this seal (logo, trademark, or symbol) be counterfeited by the enemy? If so, then it will be. It is smart of John not to have given the exact image, nature, or design of the seal, but we do know where to look for it.

The call not to "harm the earth, the sea, or the trees till we have sealed the servants of our God on their foreheads" (v. 3) draws attention to something negative happening to occupants on the planet if they are not sealed. Just as Moses instructed the children of Israel to apply blood to their doorposts on the night of the Passover, a similar protection is now necessary for the saints so that they may survive what is about to come. Whether this seal is a RFID microchip,[3] some alphanumeric combination, a simple prominent indelible mark, or the blood of the Lamb (Revelation 12:11) is not clear (Ezekiel 9:3–6). The scenario seems to be a reverse of the various Inquisitions from the fifteenth to the seventeenth centuries in Europe.[4]

Exactly who are these 144,000? Revelation 14 sheds more light on them. This is where the idea of celibacy (abstention by vow from marriage and sexual activity) and the monastic lifestyle originated with regards to Christendom. A monk is a man who has withdrawn from the world for religious motives and is usually living under a vow of chastity, poverty, obedience, and self-denial.[5] Martin Luther, Thomas More, and John Wycliffe, for example, started out as monks within the Roman Catholic Church.[6] Here is a closer look at the persons who were sealed—all men:

> Then I looked, and behold, a Lamb standing on Mount Zion, and with Him one hundred and forty-four thousand, having His Father's name written on their foreheads. . . These are the ones who were not defiled with women, for

they are virgins. These are the ones who follow the Lamb wherever He goes. These were redeemed from among men [*anthropon*, human beings] being firstfruits to God and to the Lamb. And in their mouth was found no deceit, for they are without fault before the throne of God. (Revelation 14:1, 4–5, emphasis added)

The Rapture: Literal or Symbolic?

Sometime after God's sealing on earth was done—how long it took, I cannot tell—the scene shifts from earth to the throne room in Heaven. A great multitude from all nations, tribes, peoples, and tongues was present around the throne. Dressed in white robes (representing purity or spotlessness) and carrying palm branches (in preparation for worship and to celebrate victory), this group cries out with a loud voice singing salutations to the Lamb. Are the 144,000 in this multitude or are they still on earth? They are sealed (from harm and danger), so they are protected on earth. How did this multitude get from earth into the throne room which is in Heaven?

When the great multitude, who have just been taken out of the tribulation, screamed out "God, You and the Lamb are Savior and Deliverer!" (v. 10), they sparked another mass worship session, with everybody (angels, elders, and beasts) participating. The regular beings in Heaven answered the call of the great multitude with another of the seven attributes of God (v. 12). This doxology was slightly different from others but still of the same nature of giving full recognition to the Creator. First, they agreed with the multitude's call by saying "Amen!" Then they exalted the God of Heaven with "Blessing, glory, wisdom, thanksgiving, honor, power and might," and topped it off with another "Amen!"

I believe the Rapture will be literal, a live event which will be the vehicle to move the believers to God's throne room. A "great multitude" consisting of actual humans "of all nations, tribes, peoples, and tongues" will be present. More significantly, these humans from different nations, clans, tribes, and languages have kept their distinct cultural heritage over the generations. Despite present pressures to form a one-world order economically and socially, the nations have remained individualistic in their religious-cultural pursuits. The Bahamas contingent in Heaven will be recognized by its goatskin drums and cowbells (Junkanoo music), separate from other African cultures. Yes! Jehovah will remain the God of the Bahamas, and we do not have to Americanize our method of worship.

Many will make it out of the Great Tribulation. Those who came through the Great Tribulation will be given robes which will be washed in the Lamb's blood. How can you wash in red blood and get white robes? Prophet Isaiah and King David have the answer:

"Come now, and let us reason together,"
Says the LORD,
"Though your sins are like scarlet,
They shall be as white as snow;
Though they are red like crimson,
They shall be as wool.
If you are willing and obedient,
You shall eat the good of the land."
(Isaiah 1:18–19)
See also Psalms 51:2, 7.

The blood of the Lamb has that kind of cleansing power. When you put away evil and darkness from your life and begin to seek righteousness, things begin to light up around you. When you are serious about repentance, regeneration begins to take place which can cause you to become a new creation, transforming you from darkness to light. (Glory!)

The Rapture

I believe from Revelation 7:9 that the Rapture took place when the great multitude was brought into the throne room from earth. Rapture simply means "the act of carrying off." It is not a spiritual word but one that names an action. No, the word rapture is not in the Bible, but the act will take place, and that's how people who are still alive will get into Heaven from earth. Will it be similar to the "Beam me up, Scotty!" events in *Star Trek*? No, not exactly!

Here is an attempt to explain how the process will work to get humans into Heaven for a short period. Bear in mind that humans, unlike angels, were never designed to live in Heaven. Our purpose and design are strictly for Planet Earth. You might have already figured out that angels and living creatures have spiritual bodies which will last them their lifetime; therefore, they live in the heavens. The dead human bodies have been placed in a hole somewhere to rot, but their souls, which are celestial and cannot die, live on. Celestial bodies can travel to and from the heavens. You probably have heard by now that flesh and blood cannot be an heir to the Kingdom of Heaven. This means that some kind of transformation must take place for people who are still alive to be carried to Heaven. Let's pick up from Apostle Paul's first letter to the church at Corinth.

Now this I say, brethren, that flesh and blood cannot inherit the kingdom of God; nor does corruption [decay] inherit incorruption [unending existence]. Behold, I tell you a mystery: We shall not all sleep [die], but we shall all be changed [made different]—in a moment, in the twinkling of an eye, <u>at the last trumpet</u>. For the trumpet will sound, and the dead will be raised incorruptible, and we shall be changed. For this corruptible must put on incorruption, and this mortal must put on immortality. So when this corruptible has put on incorruption, and this mortal has put on immortality, then shall be brought to pass the saying that is written: "Death is swallowed up in victory." (1 Corinthians 15:50–54, emphasis added)

The apostle is simply saying that your mortal, corruptible earth suit (physical body) will be changed so quickly that you may not know when it happens. He is also saying that in the same way, our earthly bodies which die and decay are different from the bodies we shall have when we come back to life again for they will never die. The bodies we have now embarrass us for they become exhausted, sick, and die, but they will be full of glory when we come back to life again. Yes, they are weak, dying bodies now, but when we live again, they will be full of strength. They are just human bodies at death, but when they come back to life, they will be superhuman bodies. For just as there are natural human bodies, there are also supernatural spiritual bodies." (1 Corinthians 15:42–44, TLB).

There Are Different Times for the Rapture

The carrying off of persons from earth was promised on numerous occasions by Jesus to His disciples. Theologians, for the sake of discussion, have divided this event into segments, namely, "Pre-Tribulation Rapture," "Mid-Tribulation Rapture," and "Post-Tribulation Rapture."

Pre-Tribulation Rapture takes place before the tribulation. This is what lazy saints are counting on. They have their salvation package with "fire insurance" and are ready to leave the planet.

Mid-Tribulation Rapture takes place three and a half years into the tribulation. The saints need assistance as Satan and his goons make it more difficult for saints to live on the earth.

> "For then there will be great tribulation, such as has not been since the beginning of the world until this time, no, nor ever shall be. And unless those days were shortened, no flesh would be saved; but for the elect's sake those days will be shortened." (Matthew 24:21–22)
> See also Revelation 7:9–10.

Post-Tribulation Rapture takes place at the end of the tribulation. There will be wonders in the heavens, then the sign of the Son of Man will appear in Heaven coming on the clouds (Matthew 24:29–31; Mark 13:24–27; 1 Corinthians 15:52). However, there is still more of God's wrath to come on the earth.

Private Raptures take place with small groups or an individual:

o Two witnesses are raptured after being resurrected three and a half years after they were killed (Revelation 11:11–12).

o The woman's Child, the one clothed with the sun, "was caught up to God and His throne" (Revelation 12:5).

Pre-Wrath Rapture takes place before God releases His wrath on the earth (Revelation 14:14–16). Note that up to Revelation 14:6–7 there are still saints on the earth.

The return or second coming of the Son of Man is so significant that it is to be preached as part of the gospel of the Kingdom. Remember His promise:

> "Let not your heart be troubled; you believe in God, believe also in Me. In My Father's house are many mansions; if it

were not so, I would have told you. I go to prepare a place for you. And if I go and prepare a place for you, I will come again and receive you to Myself; that where I am, there you may be also." (John 14:1–3)

God and Man Together Again

The Lamb now becomes the Shepherd and leads the sheep (saints) to "living fountains of waters" (v. 17). God always wanted to be among His people, hence His name Immanuel, which means "God with us." He and Adam used to walk together in the cool of the day while Adam was still in the garden. And now that God and man will be together again, there will be no more hunger and thirst and no more scorching sun—or need for air-conditioning—and the Father will give them comfort.

In Heaven it is easy to dwell in safety because no sin and no tempter are there. You don't have to be careful of the schemes of the enemy or the wickedness of the ungodly. The weary shall have rest. Remember this prophecy made by David, "You will show me the path of life; in Your presence is fullness of joy; at Your right hand are pleasures forevermore." If only you could believe this while you are still on earth! But don't you pray "Thy kingdom come, Thy will be done in earth, as it is in heaven"? (Matthew 6:10, KJV). What gross unbelief!

CHAPTER 8

Revelation 8—the Shuddering Seventh Seal

T HE OPENING OF this seal will be the opposite of the previous ones. Instead of the accompanying horses, earthquakes, thunders, devastations, etc., this one starts with silence, as in a lull before the storm. There is an intermission in preparation for the grand finale. The time taken here seems to wrap up the previous events to close those matters and clear one's head in preparation for the next more substantial move. Hence, there is silence in Heaven for half an hour (one-twenty-fourth of a day). This is John's "half an hour" for God does not wear a watch. The silence is a break in the worship session led by the living creatures, which was triggered by the great multitude who acknowledged Jehovah and the Lamb.

The seven angels from Revelation chapters 2 and 3 are now present in the throne room. They are given each a trumpet (sometimes referred to as a horn or cornet or shophar). It is an instrument that makes sounds by reverberating and was made from an animal's horn or from metals. For celebrations, the trumpet was an instrument of merriment and worship (Daniel 3:5). Here are occasions where priests used the trumpet: Leviticus 25:9–10; 1 Chronicles 15:24; Psalms 81:3. In the Old Testament days, the priests blowing the trumpets meant impending danger. Only the priests blew the trumpets when announcing the approach of festivals and in giving signals of war. Trumpets were blown at special festivals and to herald the arrival of special seasons.[1] Regular people blew trumpets for celebrations (2 Chronicles 23:13). Military personnel blew trumpets for different reasons (see the story of Gideon in Judges 7). For the opening of the seventh seal, angels are playing the role of Old Testament priests, signifying that imminent destruction is near.

An Angel Offers—Not Answers—Prayers

Another angel with a golden censer was given "much incense" that he should assist with the prayers of the saints (v. 3). While this unnamed angel could be just another angel as John suggests, his presence is cause for great concern within the New Testament church today. There are some prominent Christian denominations that practice praying to angels (by name) and to dead saints with the intention of getting assistance with their prayers. The concern here is that angels are "ministering spirits" sent to <u>assist</u> with the work of salvation (Hebrews 1:14). They are fellow servants who carry out the instructions of the Father in the earth (Revelation 19:10). This angel's job was to "offer [incense] with all the prayers of the saints" (v. 3) and <u>not to answer</u> the prayers of the saints. According to Jesus Christ, His disciples were to pray to <u>the heavenly Father using His name,</u> not to angels, patriarchs, or even Mary, His mother.

> "And whatever you ask in My name, that I will do, that the Father may be glorified in the Son. If you ask anything in My name, I will do it. (John 14:13–14)
> "And in that day you will ask Me nothing. Most assuredly, I say to you, whatever you ask the Father in My name He will give you. Until now you have asked nothing in My name. Ask, and you will receive, that your joy may be full." (John 16:23–24)

The incense was added to cause the prayers (worship) of the saints to be savory and pleasant to the Father. In the same way that an anointed praise and worship session in the church today would make room for the glory of the Lord to dwell in the place, incense when added to the sacrifice would have a similar effect. This can explain why the angel was given plenty of incense to offer along with the prayers of the saints. Furthermore, not just anyone can offer incense before the Lord (Numbers 16:39–40) as priests died for doing so unworthily. There was a particular protocol for altars, sacrifices, and incense before the Lord, as these were all holy (Exodus 30:1, 7–9).

God responding to the prayers (worship) of His people is a common thing. The apostles Paul and Silas had a personal encounter with the presence of God during which the earth responded to their prayer and worship (Acts 16:25–26). King Jehoshaphat and his army had a similar experience during a battle when they decided to worship first (2 Chronicles 20:21–22). God answered by fire when King Solomon prayed and worshipped during the dedication of the temple (2 Chronicles 7:1–2).

It is clear from verse 4 of our chapter that God has been collecting the prayers of the saints over the years, centuries, and ages. He heard them, received them, and was waiting for an opportune time to answer them. In other words, when you were praying and you apparently got no answer, it seemed God did not hear you. However, God has reminded us in His Word that He hears the prayers of the righteous (James 5:16; 1 Peter 3:12; 1 John 5:14). Furthermore, it was He who commanded us to pray in the first instance (2 Chronicles 7:14; Psalms 55:17; Matthew 6:6). Praying to the heavenly Father was a norm for Jesus.

There is nothing novel about fire coming from heaven (v. 5) to bring destruction on earth as cities and nations have had this episode before.

Then the Lord rained brimstone and fire on Sodom and Gomorrah, from the Lord out of the heavens. So He overthrew those cities, all the plain, all the inhabitants of the cities, and what grew on the ground. (Genesis 19:24–25)

However, the angel throwing the fire is a bit more graphic. The golden censer (a container made of gold used for carrying live coals of fire into which incense is placed) is the instrument used for offering sweet fragrances during worship. In Heaven holy fire is taken from a holy altar—which is before a holy God from a holy place—and put into a holy censer. When this fire is thrown to the profane earth, what else can be expected but atmospheric and planetary disturbances? The throwing of the censer filled with fire to the earth could be the answer to the prayers of the saints from Revelation 6:9–10. Now could be that time to avenge the blood of the saints. Prophet Joel prophesied about this day in Joel 2:1–2, 10–11.

Sounding the Trumpets

The seventh seal releases more destruction and different kinds of destruction than the first six seals combined; judgment is being poured out. The seventh seal, comprising the sounding of the seven trumpets, goes all the way through to the Fall of Babylon. Joshua, after crossing River Jordan, had seven priests blow the seven trumpets for seven days to release a "woe" upon Jericho, utterly destroying the city (Joshua 6:2–4).

The first trumpet sounding (v. 7) released an attack on the vegetation and one-third of the trees and all the green grass was burned up. This attack would definitely negatively affect the food supply for humans and cattle, causing a national panic. If these trees are for medicinal purposes, then sickness will become an epidemic. The hail and fire would leave the ground barren for quite some time while blood would flow from wars or plagues. Symbolically, the nation will be exposed to unstoppable or unforeseen catastrophes which will catch the people unawares. California, USA, in 2019[2] and Australia[3] in 2019–2020 are modern examples of this woe. Since only one-third of the area would be affected, the other two-thirds would rally and support the less fortunate, hopefully.

The second trumpet sounding (v. 8) caused a volcanic mountain to erupt and released an attack on the sea. One-third of the sea became blood and one-third of the living creatures in it died, along with one-third of the ships being destroyed. This calamity would cause a disruption in maritime affairs because of delayed transportation of goods across oceans. Not to mention, the seafood supply would be negatively impacted also. Economically, industrialized nations that rely heavily on exports would be shut down and civil unrest would follow.

The third trumpet sounding (v. 10) released an attack on the inland waters (rivers, lakes, and springs). A falling star by the name of Wormwood, which means "bitterness and calamity,"[4] fell into the waters polluting a third of it, and many died from the bitter water. Prophets Moses, Amos, and Jeremiah along with King Solomon all spoke about wormwood since the Old Testament days (see Deuteronomy 29:18; Proverbs 5:4; Jeremiah 9:15). They wrote about it being poisonous and accursed. While some would want to treat this falling star as a prince or noble royalty falling from celestial grace to the lowly estate of the ground, they do so mainly as an expression of the symbolism. It can, to some extent, be likened to (interpreted as) the falling away of the saints (2 Thessalonians 2:3). The polluting or poisoning of the drinking waters with false doctrines, errors, man-made traditions, and spiritual corruption can easily kill a third of the church.

The next chapter will discuss a bit more about stars and their connection to humans. But stars falling through the sky is a normal occurrence. Comets, asteroids, or falling stars can be seen at night with the naked eyes because of their long, bright tail. Astronomers have been known to track these celestial objects as they travel through the galaxy. Because they can be tracked and identified, religious cults have been using them to determine the spiritual times. Christian sects such as the Seventh-day Adventists and Branch Davidians have been tracking the heavens to calculate the second coming of Christ for quite some time.[5]

The fourth trumpet (v. 12) sounded and the sun, moon, and the stars were darkened a second time, causing a third of the day and the night not to shine. These are all physical occurrences in the earth, initiated by the works of the angels blowing the trumpets. Just as darkness covered the earth for three hours when Jesus was on the cross and as hailstones fell on the Amorites, similar cosmic events can occur at the will and pleasure of the heavenly Father (Joshua 10:11). While some would credit hurricanes, tornados, earthquakes, thunderstorms, flash floods, etc., to Mother Nature or "acts of God," it is with certainty the Creator who allows these to happen (Job 38). Astronomy and astrology were always meant from the beginning to be a factor in man's intelligence and instruments to help him dominate the earth (Matthew 16:2–3).

> Then God said, "Let there be lights in the firmament of the heavens to divide the day from the night; and let them be for signs and seasons, and for days and years; and let them be for lights in the firmament of the heavens to give light on the earth"; and it was so. (Genesis 1:14–15, emphasis added)

Historians such as Barnes have likened the woes of the first four trumpets to the successive severe blows on the Roman

Empire by Alaric, Genseric, Attila, and Odoacer until the empire fell, to rise no more. "When the sun, moon, and stars were struck and were darkened" was a symbol of the reign of the Barbarians who had overthrown the Romans.[6] However, these are events of the fourth and fifth centuries, far too early to be considered as "the last days."

You Don't Have to Suffer Any Longer

John says, "And I looked, and I heard an angel flying through the midst of heaven, saying with a loud voice, 'Woe, woe, woe to the inhabitants of the earth because of the remaining blasts of the trumpet of the three angels who are about to sound!'" (v. 13). Plainly stated, there are more woes to come. You would think that after having experienced the anguish and undergone the unnecessary suffering during the previous trumpets and survived, by now one would have a change of heart toward God and repent without being prompted to do so. Despite the warning, there is a hardening of the heart of the wicked. Don't they know that every knee will bow (Philippians 2:10)? By the way, grace and mercy are gone.

> For you know that afterward, when he wanted to inherit the blessing, he was rejected, for he found no place for repentance, though he sought it diligently with tears, (Hebrews 12:17)
> See also Romans 1:21–25; 2 Peter 2:13–16; Revelation 22:11.

The question now arises of "predestination," which cannot be fully addressed at this time. Was not Abel favored above Cain? Was not Esau ill-favored from birth? Was not Pharaoh raised up to play an evil role so that God's power can be declared on the earth? Romans 9:14–18 tells how God reserves the right to do as He wills. The potter has power over the clay. There are some people who are destined to serve Satan and remain faithful to him until the end. And there are some whom the god of this age has blinded their eyes that they may not believe (2 Corinthians 4:3–4). And there are some people who will start out serving Satan but will eventually repent and submit to Jesus Christ as Lord and Savior.

CHAPTER 9

Revelation 9—the Bottomless Pit

T HE FIFTH ANGEL sounds his trumpet and another star falls, but not as Wormwood did in Revelation 8:10. What or who is this star? It is clear from the passage that a physical key cannot be given to a spiritual heavenly object. The clause "to him was given" (v. 1) indicates that there is a personage involved in the transaction, someone of notable stature. Today in the entertainment world, a person of distinction is referred to as a star, noting his or her brilliance and prominence. The concept of stars being identified with people is not new. The Greek word *astér* (as-tare') is correctly translated to mean "a star" (as strewn across the sky) literally or figuratively.[1] While some stars have a name and an identity and are associated with beings, I don't know if this is true of all stars. Here are a few examples of stars connected with a personality:

> Now after Jesus was born in Bethlehem of Judea in the days of Herod the king, behold, wise men from the East came to Jerusalem, saying, "Where is He who has been born King of the Jews? For we have seen His star in the East and have come to worship Him." (Matthew 2:1–2, emphasis added) See also Amos 5:25–26; Revelation 22:16.

The Key to the Pit

This star was given the key to the bottomless pit. John does not say who gave him the key; but coming from Heaven, the giver has to be one of God's agents. This character could not have been a planet, of sorts, but a being who has mental capacity and can handle physical objects. This is why astrology is so strong and the constellations are significant in the world's system. Having the key to the bottomless pit gives him access to the entire place with the power and authority to regulate it. He opens the pit and does not go in.

The pit with no bottom (abyss)[2] is the abode for demons (Revelation 20:1–2). It is the abode of evil spirits, more or less the prison for spirits who rebelled. This is a different place from "the place of fire and brimstone," the place of final punishment (Revelation 19:20). Where is this place geographically on the planet? I don't know, but it has to be somewhere below the earth's surface (Genesis 1:2). This is not Sheol or Hades, places of the dead.[3] This place is the Hebrew equivalent of Tehom. The Greek word used here is *abussos* (ab'-us-sos), meaning depthless, abyss, deep. The same word is found in Luke and Romans:

> Jesus asked him, saying, "What is your name?" And he said, "Legion," because many demons had entered him. And they begged Him that He would not command them to go out into the abyss. (Luke 8:30–31)
> See also Romans 10:6–7.

The pit was closed and locked all along. It was like a furnace, a place of torments. The key, figuratively, refers to power or authority or office;[4] the authority to act in the name of the one who gave the key. Nowadays, cities give deserving individuals "a key to the city." It's not a physical key that fits into a physical lock but rather a symbol of authority and appreciation, welcoming the individual to that city at any time.

From out of the dark smoke of the pit came locusts (grasshoppers) upon the earth. I wouldn't say they slipped out camouflaged with the smoke. Instead, they were intentionally let loose so that they can do their assigned job. Locusts, which are known to totally devour the vegetation in swarms, are very destructive (Exodus 10:4–5; Joel 1:4). However, here, they are commanded not to harm the earth's vegetation but men instead. These strange-looking creatures with scorpion abilities were given limited power and authority to perform an assigned task, which was not to kill men but to torment them for a period.

The idea seems to be one of afflicting the physical body, that which they have been trusting in, and take away peace from their soul (2 Chronicles 32:8). Many people, especially those with the financial means to do so, spend significant time and money on their physical body, thinking that as long as their physical body holds out, they can remain on the earth. Recently, the demand for stem cell research, replacement of worn body parts, cosmetic surgery, medical breakthroughs, new drugs, over-the-counter cosmetics, physical fitness programs, special diets, organic foods, alternative medicine, etc., have increased tremendously, all in the name of trying to stay youthful (1 Timothy 4:8–10; 2 Corinthians 4:16–18). Now that their prized bodies are all messed up, their souls have no rest (Matthew 10:28; 1 Peter 3:3–5). Jesus has already announced a remedy for restlessness:

> "Come to Me, all you who labor and are heavy laden, and I will give you rest. Take My yoke upon you and learn from Me, for I am gentle and lowly in heart, and you will find rest for your souls. For My yoke is easy and My burden is light." (Matthew 11:28–30)

The Locust-Scorpion Creatures

The earth has never seen these creatures (vv. 7–11) before for the simple reason that they have been locked up. Their fake golden crowns on the faces of men with women's hair and teeth like a lion, wearing iron breastplates are signs indicating which kingdom they are from. These cannot be of the Kingdom of God. These creatures are a combination of locust, horse, scorpion, lion, and human. Their size is not mentioned. A regular locust in the Western world is about two and a half inches (six to seven centimeters) long. It is my opinion that the size of a regular locust is too small to bear all these details. They must have been larger than the regular or they represent an organization/nation. However, with a swarm of locusts, their size does not matter; they are destructive wherever they go. Historians (Smith[5] and Barnes[6]) say that these locust-scorpions are symbolic of Muslims with turbans as fake crowns, long hair like women and have human faces. Furthermore, the fact that they had a king over them and insect locusts do not have a leader gave rise to the argument in favor of symbolism. However, questions arise. Has the allotted time passed since the sounding of this trumpet and the next woe? The Muslims did massacre (instead of torment) the nations they fought against. Why? Secondly, the flight of Muhammad (Hegira) began in AD 622 or AD 629 and lasted for one hundred and fifty years, bringing the time to AD 772 or AD 779.[7] This is now the twenty-first century. Therefore, the locusts cannot be the Muslims. Space does not permit me to take the argument further.

A scorpion sting can cause severe pain with some common accompanying symptoms, especially tingling or burning at the sting site, numbness, difficulty swallowing, difficulty breathing, blurry vision, or seizures. The good news here is that a sting from a scorpion does not usually kill a man. The bad news is that the sting is so painful, one would rather die than suffer the torment. However, the Spirit of Death is on vacation at this time, and only the Spirit of Death is authorized to kill.

Here John gives a specific duration for all this to happen. "Five months" could literally mean five months or one hundred and fifty days (v. 10). Others consider the month as being prophetic months, each day being reckoned for a year; therefore this period could amount to 150 years (Ezekiel 4:5–6), counting thirty days to each month as was the general custom of the Asiatics.[8]

Abaddon or Apollyon

Their king "Abaddon" or "Apollyon," who was locked up with them in the pit, was given the authority to release this havoc on those who are still alive (v. 11). His name means destruction. He is identified as the "angel (demon) of the bottomless pit." Abaddon has been in the pit all along and the patriarchs are familiar with his existence (Job 26:6; Psalms 88:11). At this point, the saints (the 144,000) are still moving about in the earth untouched by all this drama. They are sealed, remember? They are living in the earth as believers should be living in the earth today—in this world but not of this world. This world is not home for the believer. Believers are sojourners and pilgrims passing through (1 Peter 2:11).

The Sixth Trumpet

When the sixth angel sounded, it was as if God Himself spoke as the voice came from the four horns of the golden altar (vv. 13–21). Instructions were given to the angel who blew the trumpet to release the four angels who are bound in the

Euphrates River. This is one of the four rivers mentioned in Genesis 2:10–14, but there nothing is said about it. We hear now that an army had been prepared at the river for some time and for this particular occasion.

Today, the river Euphrates, originating in the Armenian Highlands (eastern Turkey), flows through Syria and Iraq to join the Tigris in the Shatt al-Arab and empties into the Persian Gulf.[9] All the countries through which this river runs are heavily dominated by Muslims.

Are the four angels the angels who were placed at the Garden of Eden with a flaming sword to keep man away from the tree of life? If so, they were in place already. It seems the Creator has staff fixed in place or assigned for a particular task all over the universe. On the contrary, Adam Clarke says that "these four angels bound—hitherto restrained, in the Euphrates, are by some supposed to be the Arabs, the Saracens, the Tartars, or the Turks; by others, Vespasian's four generals, one in Arabia, one in Africa, one in Alexandria, and one in Palestine."[10]

Here is Smith's take on the four angels, "These are the four principal sultanies of which the Ottoman Empire was composed, located in the country watered by the Euphrates. These sultanies were situated at Aleppo, Iconium, Damascus and Bagdad. Previously they had been restrained; but God commanded, and they were loosed." Smith sets this stage at the close of the 150-year period, in late 1448.[11] The point being made here is that they both believed and agreed that this event has already taken place. If this is true, then we are beyond this stage in the fulfillment of end-time prophecies.

Whether it happened over 391 years ago or one year and thirty-one days ago or one hour ago or has not happened yet, a third of mankind was (will be) killed by the release of these angels. A note must be made that the people whom the Muslims would take pleasure in destroying back then were predominantly Christian. Mention must be made here of the size of the army, 200 million, not an easy number to quantify for an army of horsemen. Today India and China have the ability and manpower to put an army of this size together, but they both would not be using horses and are not near the Euphrates. When looking for a geographical location on earth where the final events and activities leading up to them might take place, the Middle East is a very good speculation.

Out of the mouths (openings) of cannons, rifles, and guns came fire, smoke, and brimstone (v. 18). This is how John tried to describe weapons that use gunpowder. Their power is in their frontal openings.

Here is Smith's summary and explanation of the four angels who had been prepared for the hour and day and month and year to kill basically unsealed persons and non-Muslims:

> On August 11, 1840, the period of three hundred ninety-one years and fifteen days, allotted to the continuance of the Ottoman power, ended; and where was the sultan's independence? — Gone! Who had the supremacy of the Ottoman empire in their hands? — The four great powers; and that empire has existed ever since only by the sufferance of these Christian powers. Thus was the prophecy fulfilled to the very letter.[12]

No Repentance

Is there a possibility that "no repentance" (v. 20) can be caused by one not being conscientiously aware of the matter at hand? Yes! But the gospel had been preached to every nation, so there is no excuse for anyone being unaware.

Those who did not die still did not have a change of heart. God is expecting us to repent of what we are doing wrong, especially when we hear of the calamity that hit others (Matthew 11:23–24). Some people learn by what they experience. Experience may be the best teacher, but it does not have to be your experience. It is amazing that Satan is allowing the people who are still alive on the earth and still loyal to him to be afflicted with torments, plagues, and death. Can't Satan do something to save his people? Why won't these people come to their senses and repent? Are they thinking the lies they have been told will eventually come to pass? Are they still thinking that Jehovah God and judgment are fictitious (Hebrews 9:27)? Are they thinking that Satan can actually challenge God and win? Did they consider that Satan is a created being, a steward and he has been fired?

From the outset of his mission to lead the children of Israel to the Promised Land— the land flowing with goodness—Moses preached righteousness. He took it further by presenting the Ten Commandments to the people, telling them that Jehovah God is righteous (different from other gods) and requires righteousness from them. The people had a customary way of life; therefore, Moses had to use the laws he presented to make a definite statement about how they should live. Everything the laws addressed were common practices of the people (Exodus 20). Thus, "Thou SHALT NOT," beginning with the worship of demons and idols. It is fine to worship something. Man will worship whatever he honors even though it might be worthless or unworthy. Murder, the shedding of innocent blood and the taking of human life for any reason except in Deuteronomy 19:4–5, is forbidden in the Kingdom. Sorcery of any form, including but not limited to witchcraft, black or white magic, Ouija boards, séances, obeah, voodoo, spell casting, meta-science, divination, occultism, spiritualism, Tarot, etc., are prohibited (Leviticus 20:6, 27). Sexual immorality— fornication, adultery, harlotry (including homosexuality, lesbianism, incest, and bestiality)—is also prohibited.

"For out of the heart proceed evil thoughts, murders, adulteries, fornications, thefts, false witness, blasphemies. These are the things which defile a man, but to eat with unwashed hands does not defile a man." (Matthew 15:19–20)

The Misunderstanding about Sexual Sins

Please allow a bit of divergence here because the matter of sexual sins has been misunderstood for so long that a lot of people have taken it for granted and have suffered needlessly for their ignorance. As an adult, you have full control over your own body, and you have the freedom to make choices concerning the use of your body. Since you may not be offending anyone by the way you use your body, you go right ahead and mix and mingle your body with any other body you choose, not considering that there are grave consequences attached to your actions.

Because most of these consequences are not immediate and are seemingly not detrimental to life, you, like most people (especially during their teenage years), casually use your body as you see fit for sexual pleasures. You then continue this practice throughout the rest of your life.

Sexual sin is any sexual act you participate in outside the confines of your marriage. A marriage is a love covenant between one man and one woman for as long as they both shall live. Love is the key factor here as intimacy and togetherness (oneness) are the results of the "love glue" which is activated in such a covenant relationship.

The love feature in a relationship is what comes alive and flourishes as the bond is nourished and maintained. Love grows and intensifies because it is a pure character trait that originates in and flows out of the Creator. Love is of God and God is love (Deuteronomy 7:9; Daniel 9:4; 1 John 4:7–8). That is why every human being (mankind) can love. Love comes out of

God and man came out of God. Therefore, man has a portion of God in him. This explains why not only Christians can love as God loves. Every human being has the potential to love the way God loves. So the desire for intimacy and oneness which is found in love and expressed in sexual activities is also sought after by persons who have not made a covenant. This is why sex outside of a marriage covenant is totally offensive to God—no commitment. No commitment, no responsibility, no sacrifice, yet you want the same privileges and pleasures as a person who made the commitment? That can't be right!

Furthermore, if the love of God is in you and you choose not to operate in a righteous manner (doing things in a way that is right, straight, proper, just, innocent, holy, equitable), then your standard would be perverted (turned away from the right course; turned to improper use, distorted, misguided) and what should have been pure love now becomes polluted and upsets the applecart of decent living. When love is not mixed with righteousness, perversion and confusion are the outcomes (1 John 3:10).

Who Is Authorized to Have Sex?

This means that if you are not married, you are not authorized to have sex. The violation is not confined to sexual organs (penis and vagina) but extended to any body part used for sexual pleasure. Here are some of my quick definitions of various forms of sexual activity:

- Undefiled Bed (Marriage)—having sex *within* a covenant. "Marriage is honorable among all, and the bed undefiled, but fornicators and adulterers God will judge" (Hebrews 13:4).

- Fornication—having sex *without* a covenant (Ezekiel 16:26; 1 Corinthians 6:18).
- Adultery—having sex *outside* the covenant (Leviticus 20:10).
- Masturbation—performing sex acts on oneself, self-gratification where there is no possibility of a covenant.
- Prostitution—offering sexual pleasures for profit and where there is no love (Proverbs 6:26, 7:6–23).
- Rape—having sex with a person without that person's consent (against his or her will) (2 Samuel 13:1–17).
- Immorality or Abomination—having sex with anyone of the same gender or with close relatives or with under-aged persons or using body parts not designed for sex purposes in sex activities or having sex with anything that is not human (Leviticus 18, 20:11–21; Revelation 22:15).

Sex between unmarried people (outside a covenant)—or "sweethearting" in the Bahamian vernacular—is not a light thing before the Creator. It is the covenant that makes husband and wife one flesh. "Holy Matrimony" is the name that describes the covenant two humans (one male and one female) make. Humans are not like the other animals, mating with whomever or whatever is available. Sexual partnering outside of marriage is strongly forbidden by God. He sees it as giving worship to another god or having more than one god. Breaking a marriage covenant (divorce) is not acceptable. Caution: You should not be switching sexual partners simply because you want to. Why not? Because a female carries a part of every male with whom she has sexual relations.[13]

Isn't having sex just a fact of life? Maybe because sex is so easy and simple to perform, the question appears to be rhetorical. But it is not true! This lie is so subtle and seemingly insignificant that it is not even considered a lie. The lie is that "this matter is so meaningless and personal that it is literally nobody's business, and it is really not bothering or hurting anyone else, except for a third party (if they find out)." Sex is more than a physical act as it involves the soul of each person involved. It is how soul ties are formed. Creating a soul tie and not having a covenant to validate it is a touchy matter. Soul ties are what breed ownership and jealousy. Unlike the other Commandments—murder where you kill another person or lying where you tell an untruth on another person or stealing where you deprive another person of their property, all of which are wrong—you commit a sexual sin against yourself with your neighbor. Even though sex is a personal and private matter, sexual sins are placed in the same category as killing, lying, and stealing. Sex is serious business with God, no matter how private you make it simply because it is connected to love. Where there are laws against murder, giving false information, and stealing, there should also be laws against all sexual immorality according to the Kingdom of Heaven:

> By swearing and lying, killing and stealing and committing adultery, they break all restraint, with bloodshed upon bloodshed. (Hosea 4:2)

CHAPTER 10

Revelation 10— the Little Book

BETWEEN THE TWO last trumpets sounding, there is another mighty angel without a name but with an awesome, unique description (v. 1). He is clothed with a cloud with a rainbow on his head. His face is like the sun and his feet like pillars of fire. The position he takes is also of significance—right foot on the sea and left foot on the land, making representation in both worlds. His position indicates his size, dominion, and sphere of authority. Another factor about him that John makes mention of is that he had a little book in his hand, opened as if to read or make a statement.

However, before he reads from the book, he roars like a lion. His roaring triggered seven thunders to utter their voices, speaking in an understandable language. These intelligible utterances by the thunders (seemingly something prophetic) prompted John to begin to write what he heard, but he was instructed to "seal up the things which the seven thunders uttered, and do not write them." Understanding thunder when it roars is not new to mankind. Thunders have a voice. Yes! They are saying something of significance which can be understood. It sounded like a roar to John in the natural, but remember that he was in the Spirit.

Just as the birds of the animal kingdom make a sound when communicating among themselves, a noise could be a language you are not familiar with. In the same way that tongues and groanings in the Spirit are unintelligible expressions, thunders may have a communication type of their own. If you have been dabbling in the spirit realm for some time, you would have found that sounds have meanings. According to the Greek word *fone* (fo-nay'), there is no difference between a voice, a noise, and a sound.[1] All noises have a meaning; they simply may not be intelligible to you. Consider the following passage:

> "Father, glorify Your name." Then a voice came from heaven, saying, "I have both glorified it and will glorify it again." Therefore the people who stood by and heard it said that it had thundered. Others said, "An angel has spoken to Him." (John 12:28–29)

No More Delay for the Next Sounding

There is a time and a season to reveal certain things. It seems God uses a need-to-know policy—if you don't need to know, He doesn't tell you. An angel now swears by the Creator that there should be no more delays before the sounding of the seventh trumpet (vv. 1–7). In the days when he is about to sound, the mystery of God would be finished (completed, accomplished, or fully discharged) as He declared to His servants the prophets. In other words, what God is about to do in the seventh trumpet has already been foretold by the prophets. Just as Moses foretold the ten plagues over Egypt, a prophet has been told of the plagues following the seventh trumpet.

> The secret things belong to the Lord our God, but those things which are revealed belong to us and to our children forever, that we may do all the words of this law. (Deuteronomy 29:29)

See also Amos 3:7.

There as some mysterious things that must come to an end before the sounding of the seventh trumpet. Let's examine them. The last time a book was commanded sealed that dealt with a prophecy of the end-time was the book of Daniel.[2] The prophecy is found in Daniel 12. In verse four of that chapter, Daniel is instructed to "shut up the words, and seal the book." Here one angel from the side asked the one standing above the river, "How long shall the fulfillment (it be to the end) of these wonders?" His sworn response was "that it shall be for a time, times, and half a time; and when the power of the holy people has been completely shattered, all these things shall be finished" (Daniel 12:7). Prophetically speaking, a "time" is a year (Daniel 4:16).[3] Thus, one year plus two years plus half a year equals three and a half years or forty-two months.

Here is the time factor the question was about: "And from the time that the daily sacrifice is taken away [Jesus' death in AD 33 took away the daily sacrifice], and the abomination of desolation is set up [the full persecution of the church], there shall be one thousand two hundred and ninety days [or forty-three prophetic months]. Blessed is he who waits, and comes to the one thousand three hundred and thirty-five days [or forty-four and a half prophetic months]" (Daniel 12:11–12). Prophetically speaking, a "day" is interpreted as a year, so we are actually looking at one thousand three hundred and thirty-five years. Considering this with other factors, Smith now puts 1798 as the year the end-time began.[4]

The mystery in question is that the church will be undergoing 1,335 years of persecution. The suffering of the righteous and the triumph of the ungodly over them will be allowed. The church will be beaten in sunder, broken in pieces, scattered, and dispersed (Daniel 12:7). The church has to be fully persecuted for righteousness's sake. She will suffer as Jesus did—a lamb led to the slaughter—then all these things shall be finished. That is why in Revelation 6:10–11, after asking "how much longer we have to suffer?", they were told, "Until both the number of their fellow servants and their brethren, who would be killed as they were, was completed."

> Many shall be purified, made white, and refined, but the wicked shall do wickedly; and none of the wicked shall understand, but the wise shall understand. (Daniel 12:10) Also see Daniel 8:23–26.

Wake Up, Church!

Since we are still in this same era, the church of Jesus Christ today can expect intensified persecution. Taking prayers out of schools and public meetings, giving restrictions on preaching the gospel of Jesus Christ and His Kingdom, not praying in the name of Jesus Christ publicly, removing the Ten Commandments from public places, allowing other religions to infiltrate the media, promoting pagan festivals, and decriminalizing ungodly activities are only the tip of the iceberg. Politicians, lobbyists, pressure groups, and other religions will invent ways to challenge and suppress the church of Jesus Christ. The wicked are not only out of the closet but also out to advance the kingdom of darkness. They are effectively using the seven mountains to negatively transform a nation's culture while "Christians" are busy playing church and not preaching the gospel of the Kingdom.

The Little Book

This little book is distinguished from the scrolls and other sources of information used to educate John about what is happening in the heavens (vv. 8–11). Let's recall the prophecy in Daniel 12. It was commanded sealed until the end-time for obvious reasons. Since the book is now in the hand of the angel and is open, this must be the end-time to which the prophecy referred. Roughly 700 years later, John obeys the instruction of getting the little book but is now told to "take and eat it" (v. 9b). John is instructed to get all the contents of the book in his system, chew them thoroughly, meditate on them, digest them, understand them, receive them, and be familiar with them before he publishes or shelves the book. The prophet Ezekiel had a similar experience of having to eat a scroll (Ezekiel 2:9–3, 3). The book was sweet in John's mouth because of the excitement and novelty of having firsthand information of what God is doing. The excitement increased as the promises were refreshed, but as he digested the contents of the book and the revelation of the scattering, suffering and painful persecutions which are about to come made his stomach bitter.

With the angel releasing the book to John without hesitation, you can assume here that it is not God's intention to withhold anything good from you (Psalms 84:11). On the contrary, the book was made available for this occasion. There is a time and a season for everything under the sun, something that should be beneficial can cause more harm than good if it is done prematurely. This is not so in John's case. Having eaten the book, John is now ready for another instruction from the angel, who says to him, "You must prophesy again about many peoples, nations, tongues, and kings" (v. 11). Your work is not done.

Don't Take Persecution Personally

Oh, the reality of the bitterness of persecution! That is probably why ministers do not preach the true gospel of the Kingdom but instead stick to the prosperity messages. People would prefer to hear "Bless me!" messages than to hear "Repent! The Kingdom of Heaven is here!" They want to know what they can get for free rather than what they have to give up. The Master has taught you that harassment is something you should be happy about:

> "Remember the word that I said to you, 'A servant is not greater than his master.' If they persecuted Me, they will also persecute you. If they kept My word, they will keep yours also. But all these things they will do to you for My name's sake, because they do not know Him who sent Me." (John 15:20–21)
> See also Matthew 5:10–12.

Persecution is a reality of Christian life. All you have to do is walk uprightly and you will draw the haters to you. Apostle Paul assured Timothy that "all who desire to live godly in Christ Jesus will suffer persecution" (2 Timothy 3:12). This is part of the Believer's package. Apostle Paul admonished the Romans not to take it lightly (Romans 8:35–39).

Bear in mind that all persecutions do not end in death, so do not be afraid to face them. Remember the fearlessness of David as a young man, when he boldly declared, "Yea, though I walk through the valley of the shadow of death, I will fear no evil; for You are with me; Your rod and Your staff, they comfort me" (Psalms 23:4). As a Disciple of Jesus Christ, you are to remain a faithful and wise steward. There are many rewards outlined in the early chapters when the letters were written to the churches to encourage the saints in their faithfulness and diligence to overcome the challenges of this world (Luke 12:42–43).

CHAPTER 11

Revelation 11—the Kingdoms of This World

THE STAGE IS still set on earth where the angel has his feet on the land and the sea. The scene appears to be near the city of Jerusalem. John is shown the temple in Heaven so that he may have a better perspective of it. If he has to replicate it, he has the measurements already. He has the standard, the pattern, and the size in case he has to make changes to it or restore it. This is not the first time God is giving measurements of things in Heaven. Noah had to measure the ark (Genesis 6:14–16). Moses had to measure the tabernacle and the Ark of the Covenant (Exodus 25:8–12). Ezekiel had to measure the city (Ezekiel 40:3–5). Are these things replicas of what are in Heaven where God lives? Why is God so exact with the measurements and patterns? Does He want Heaven on earth or a second home?

God is the Master Builder. He is meticulous and precise. He determines the size, pattern, type of material, and other specifications of what He wants to be built. He does this for His purpose and glory and not according to our pleasure or finite understanding. Just as He does with His church today, He sets all the standards, guidelines, methods of operation, rules, criteria, and levels of involvement. You have to bring yourself in line with Him or rebel and do your own thing. If you are thinking about pleasing God or doing things His way, He has a pattern set already. Like the faithful patriarchs, you simply conform to it.

> "And I also say to you that you are Peter, and on this rock I will build My church *[not yours, what presently exists is not serving the purpose],* and the gates of Hades shall not prevail against it *[the one I will build]."* (Matthew 16:18, emphasis added)

If you are trying to please God, you cannot give Him whatever (Genesis 4:3–5).

John has to measure (ascertain the size and specification using a fixed standard)[1] the temple (which represents the place where God meets with His people), the altar (which represents the place where people offer their sacrifice to Him), and those who worship there (the people who call upon Him as their God) (v. 1). The court outside the temple does not matter to God. The outer court is for anybody as this is the closest pagans want to get to the truth, so don't bother to measure it. The pagans who have nothing to do with God will trample there. They have this area for three and a half years (forty-two months).

The Two Witnesses

The two witnesses will emerge and prophesy for three and a half years (v. 3). Using thirty-day months, this equals 1,260 (days or) prophetic years. This is the same time and period when the pagans would trample the outer court of the temple. Some say that the two witnesses are Enoch and Elijah (men who never died in the natural), but there is no reference to this. Some say that they represent the Jews and the church, both representatives of the Kingdom of God on the earth today. Zechariah 4:11–14 explained who these witnesses are. In any event, they are faithful ministers (entities) who are bold enough to preach the gospel of Jesus Christ in such dreadful times and without fear of persecution. They are dressed in prayer clothes, interceding for the world. Sackcloth is clothes worn by mourners and as a sign of repentance (Genesis 37:34; 1 Kings 21:27; Esther 4:1). They will foretell events, declare God's purposes, and exercise the powers which go along with their heavenly assignment to counter and subdue the heathens. Two witnesses are enough to establish a thing (John 8:17).

The Third Woe Is Coming Quickly

There are no more delays. The situation gets worse with each "woe." Brace yourself for more devastation and dreadful judgment. The seventh angel sounds his trumpet after three and a half years of delay, a time for retrospection and rethinking (v. 15). This is the last trumpet of the last seal to be opened. This is the end of world governments and powers as we know them today. With this last trumpet sounding, Christ now has control of all the kingdoms, and the report has gone throughout Heaven.

> Then the seventh angel sounded: And there were loud voices in heaven, saying, "The kingdoms of this world *[orderly arrangement]* have become the kingdoms of our Lord and of His Christ, and He shall reign forever and ever!" (Revelation 11:15, emphasis added)

Will the voices heard in Heaven also be heard on earth? Will earth get this same message as Heaven at the same time?

You Are a Steward Only

The only authority mankind has on the earth is stewardship. He does not own anything. His instructions were to "be fruitful and multiply; fill the earth and subdue it; have dominion over the fish of the sea, over the birds of the air, and over every living thing that moves on the earth" (Genesis 1: 28). Consider these:

- God owns the earth (Psalms 24:1–2; Exodus 9:29). He has never given up ownership.
- God is not reigning in the earth at present. Man is supposed to be dominating (just like Jesus of Nazareth demonstrated), but he (Adam) gave this authority to Satan (Genesis 3; Romans 6:16). Man has to give God the right to interfere in earth matters or take dominion himself (Matthew 16:19). However, God will intervene when He sees fit.
- These are the very kingdoms the devil offered to Jesus as a reward for worship (Matthew 4:8–9). Jesus now has them, and He did not worship the devil to get them. Instead, He defeated the devil and took back what belongs to Him. This is your lesson: You don't have to worship the devil for anything on earth.
- The parable in Matthew 21:33–39 talks about the wicked vinedressers who want to kill the son so that everything could be theirs. They have no title, yet they want ownership. They will kill the heir to get it. This is the same attitude mankind has towards owning the earth—he wants to fight God and kill for it.

As in the days of Moses, when the plagues inflicted on Egypt weakened Pharaoh's hand, the kings of the earth are now weakened to the point where they have no resolve to fight back; instead, they can only hate God for being relentless in His efforts to reclaim what is His. Who can stand against the Lord God Almighty and prevail?

"Look to Me, and be saved,
All you ends of the earth!
For I am God, and there is no other.
I have sworn by Myself;
The word has gone out of My mouth in righteousness,
And shall not return,
That to Me every knee shall bow,
Every tongue shall take an oath."
(Isaiah 45:22–23)
See also Romans 14:11–13; Philippians 2:9–11.

This is the establishment of that eternal government of which Daniel and Isaiah prophesied millennia ago:

"I, Daniel, was grieved in my spirit within my body, and the visions of my head troubled me. I came near to one of those who stood by, and asked him the truth of all this. So he told me and made known to me the interpretation of these things: 'Those great beasts, which are four, are four kings which arise out of the earth. But the saints of the Most High shall receive the kingdom, and possess the kingdom forever, even forever and ever.'" (Daniel 7:15–18)
See also Isaiah 9:6–7.

The Seven Mountains/Kingdoms of Influence

Even though a government has the power to govern its citizens, there are pockets of influence within a nation which subtly steer that nation. These pockets or "mountains" of influence are a part of every society with some operating on a larger scale than others. Some are more vocal and visible than others. The seven mountains are controlled by select persons or organizations that dictate to the nation what happens.[2] These persons all work as one, supporting each other. This is happening right now in 2021. The media will support the antagonistic politicians in an attempt to destabilize governments while the education system and religion will promote whatever dishonors God. Here is a general description of the strategies of the seven kingdoms or mountains and their sphere of control under the satanic influence:

Media and Communication: control all media networks (Internet, social media, cell phone, TV, radio, cable, satellite, newspaper, books, magazines, tabloids). They will publish lies, fake news, etc., to deceive the public. They will be bias and careless when releasing information with the intention of disrupting the normal flow of life. A timely example of this dreadful deed is the reporting on the novel coronavirus, which was identified in November 2019. Labeled as COVID-19, this man-made virus was released in Wuhan, China, and has spread around the world. The coronavirus has received a tremendous amount of media attention compared to previous viruses which threatened the world in the last four decades. It was given pandemic status in late 2019 when it was still only in China. It was at the forefront of seemingly every newscast (local, national, and international) with reporters detailing, step-by-step, every event that concerned the virus. While COVID-19 received the most attention from the media, it was responsible for only 0.12 percent of deaths worldwide in the first quarter of 2020. It did not even make the "top ten killers" list. The regular (seasonal) flu, which is similar, was five times more deadly but received no attention. Here is a breakdown of deaths from other causes for the same period.

Deaths Worldwide
January 1 to March 25, 2020

Cause of Death	Number of Deaths	Cause as Percentage of All Deaths (%)
COVID-19	21,297	0.12
Seasonal Flu	113,034	0.66
Malaria	228,095	1.32
Suicide	249,904	1.45
Traffic Fatalities	313,903	1.82
HIV/AIDS	390,908	2.26
Alcohol	581,599	3.37
Smoking	1,162,481	6.73
Cancer	1,909,804	11.06
Hunger	2,382,324	13.80
Abortion	9,913,702	57.41
Total Deaths	**17,267,051**	**100.00**

As reported by ASK.com, a reputable US-based website[3]

It is obvious that the intent of the media was to promote lies and fearmongering and to cause panic among people in all nations. The withholding of helpful, pertinent information while releasing lies and distorted facts was the strategy the media employed to negatively influence the public, knowing that the public would look to the media to be informed. It is apparent to some in the United States that the media is working with Bill Gates, Dr. Anthony Fauci, George Soros, and others to advance their agenda to drastically depopulate the world as quickly as possible. This plan is totally contrary to God's agenda as stated in Genesis 1:28, which is for mankind to "be fruitful and multiply, fill the earth." Worse still, the world's economy was shut down for months because of the way the information concerning COVID-19 was pessimistically presented and the fear that was generated. It is rumored that the coronavirus scheme was designed to be an open door for the introduction of a vaccine that will not only deal with COVID-19 but also allow the implantation of a RFID (Radio Frequency Identification) chip, or some other device, which has GPS capabilities and one's personal data. It is also rumored that the vaccine will be designed to alter one's DNA.

When is the media going to focus on cancer, abortion and hunger? These are hundreds of times more deadly than the coronavirus. According to Google WHO reported that in 2019 1.4 million persons worldwide died from tuberculosis (also a communicable disease) and another 10 million fell ill. Where was the fearmongering or media concern?

Arts and Entertainment—encourage perverted and obscene shows; produce defiled music; produce movies and shows that coincide with their agenda; introduce, legalize, and promote mind-altering drugs under the label of entertainment; introduce new cultures which will destroy morality, bedrock institutions, and value systems.

Education—indoctrinate the young with unethical, immoral behavior and beliefs; introduce children to perverted material so that they are comfortable with it as they grow older; propagate strange philosophies and ideologies; teach in favor of moral relativism and against moral absolutes.

Family—redefine marriage, take away children from parents, regulate childbirth, destroy the male/father/husband image, encourage divorce and abortions, downplay the sanctity of sexual intercourse, promote gender neutrality.

Business and Finance—control the flow of money and the banking system, control the production and sale of goods, determine marketing and distribution restrictions, press for the global economic decline, destroy middle-class citizens, control the economies of small and developing nations.

Religion—suppress and persecute Christianity, alter the Bible, allow other religions to persecute Christians, make room for new gods, enforce stiff regulations on churches and the preaching of the gospel, encourage public satanic worship.

Government—aim for a one-world government, overthrow governments and nations, encourage civic unrest, overtax citizens, initiate strange foreign policies, track or spy on citizens, permit unfair judicial systems, use foreign agencies to determine governments, require and enforce allegiance to international regulating authorities.

Dr. Lance Wallnau's seven kingdoms concept shows that today the kingdoms are still under the world's influence. New ideas and matters which appeal to the comfort and pleasure of mankind have been the strongest factors drawing the masses away from the truth. People with influence (money, fame, power, anointing, and who have control of the media) will continue to lead unsuspecting folks <u>away</u> from the things of God. The masses will not be won by the sword or violent domination; the Inquisitions proved this. Age-old institutions and concepts like the family, morality, and righteousness will fall and be replaced by whatever gives physical gratification. Lifestyles will be centered around "the here and now" with very little emphasis on the future. However, if you can remember that there is a judgment day, or a day of reckoning, whether you are alive or dead, then you can overcome what this present age is presenting to you. Only with the spread of Christianity can these kingdoms be occupied by persons and organizations for the glory of God.

The Kingdom of God is entered here on earth when an individual comes to Christ and repents of his or her former life. Because Christ is purposed to live and reign forever, to be with Him or in Him, you have to be a part of His Kingdom. As you overcome the challenges around you, be prepared to rejoice when the announcement is made concerning the kingdoms of this world becoming those of our Christ.

The Elders in Another Worship Session

Kingdoms or nations shifting at the sounding of the seventh trumpet is a time for jubilation and a great celebration for the elders (vv. 15–19). They got up from their seats after having been seated for three and a half years; the culmination of all things is coming to an end. The elders got into worship mode again, on their faces, saying thanks to the Almighty God as they adored Him. They praised Him, You have taken back Your power, asserted Your rights and will to reign over Your creation. The people who were against you are now angry and Your wrath has come upon them. This is the time for judgment—for rewards and punishment, to bless the saints and condemn the wicked, and those who destroyed the earth will now be destroyed.

CHAPTER 12

Revelation 12—the Woman and the Dragon

THEOLOGIANS LIKE MATTHEW Henry say that the contents of these two chapters are not prophetic at all but rather a recapitulation and representation of things past.[1] Now is a very good time to talk about the methods of interpretation used for understanding this book. There are four basic schools of thought:[2]

Preterist—believes that all the prophecies of Revelation have already been fulfilled. This is the view of the renowned Apostle John Eckhart which has been causing great concern for Bishop Bill Hamon, two respected apostolic and prophetic fathers in the church today.[3] While this interpretation may be correct up to the time of the persecutions and the Dark Ages, it is not for the rest of the book as the manifestation of Daniel 12:2–4 is still pending. Examine these scriptures for further verification:

> Now, brethren, concerning the coming of our Lord Jesus Christ and our gathering together to Him, we ask you, not to be soon shaken in mind or troubled, either by spirit or by word or by letter, as if from us, as though the day of Christ had come. Let no one deceive you by any means; for that Day will not come unless the falling away comes first, and the man of sin is revealed, the son of perdition, who opposes and exalts himself above all that is called God or that is worshiped, so that he sits as God in the temple of God,

showing himself that he is God. (2 Thessalonians 2:1–4, emphasis added)

See also Matthew 24:3–31, 36–44.

"Assuredly, I say to you, this generation *[age, period, time]* will by no means pass away till all these things take place." (Matthew 24:34, emphasis added)

Futurist—holds that the book contains a forecast of universal history. The events mentioned are still unfolding today and there are still more to come.

Historicist—sees the events of the book as symbolic portrayals of church history from New Testament times to the end of the age. We have already seen the Dark Ages and some of the great persecutions and Inquisitions against the saints. These were not symbolic but actual.

Eclectic (or Idealist)—stresses the spiritual principles of the book and does not attempt to dogmatize details of the more mysterious visions. The idealist selects and uses whatever is considered best in all the methods presented, taking the best of all worlds and not committing to any one method. This method is more inviting because there are mysteries still waiting to be revealed. However, because man is limited by time and seasons and the scope of his finite knowledge is limited to the era in which he and his forefathers live, only the Holy Spirit can give a divine understanding of what is written in the book of Revelation.

There are many who were adamant that their revelation was genuine and one hundred percent accurate, only for this self-confidence to bring them shame and disgrace as time unfolded. There is no need for pride to get the better part of you. Simply follow James's advice, "If any of you lacks wisdom, let him ask of God, who gives to all liberally and without reproach, and it will be given to him" (James 1:5). God invited Isaiah to ask Him of things to come:

Thus says the Lord,
The Holy One of Israel, and his Maker:
"Ask Me of things to come concerning My sons;
And concerning the work of My hands, you command Me.
I have made the earth,
And created man on it.
I—My hands—stretched out the heavens,
And all their host I have commanded."
(Isaiah 45:11–12)

A Woman in Heaven

A great sign (wonder) in Heaven is a woman (vv. 1–6). The way she is dressed is also a factor. This is only the second reference to women thus far in the book. Everything else was in reference to men. When the Bible makes reference to gender, it is on purpose. For example, 1 Timothy 3:1–2 states that "if a <u>man</u> desires the position of a bishop, he desires a good work. A bishop then must be blameless, <u>the husband of one wife</u>, temperate, sober-minded, of good behavior, hospitable, able to teach." Therefore, since a woman (female) cannot be a husband and there are no qualifications stated for her, a woman cannot validly be a bishop in the Kingdom of God. In the natural, the Bible does not neutralize genders.

While in the natural here on earth the distinction between a man and a woman is strictly adhered to. A woman can never be a man, and neither can a man be a woman – no matter what manmade law says otherwise. No surgery, no medication, no hypnosis, no re-educating, no hormones, no roleplaying, no satanic intervention, no new technology or scientific breakthrough, nothing can change God's design and purpose. Participating in transgender activities are all exercises in futility and are promoted by Satan in rebellion to the Creator. A man is innately physiologically, spiritually and soulishly different from a woman. Remember that Eve came out of

Adam – the woman was taken out of the man. God has assigned and designed them to play different roles.

There is a belief that females will not play a major role in end-time events. Judaism, Islam, and East Asian religions are adamant about this while for some Europeans and Westerners, it does not matter. Consider that all the references to angels so far are males, the twenty-four elders are males and the 144,000 are all males. There is no biblical record of a female angel. The only place thus far to accommodate women and children in Heaven is in the "great multitude" mentioned in Revelation 7:9 if that is any consolation. But this should not bother you because in the spirit your gender, age, social status, race, country of origin, and family ties will not matter. Bear in mind that when God created man, Eve was still in Adam. Also, when asked about marriages (the roles of males and females) in Heaven, Jesus responded:

> "You are mistaken, not knowing the Scriptures nor the power of God. For in the resurrection they neither marry nor are given in marriage, but are <u>like angels of God in heaven.</u>" (Matthew 22:29–30, emphasis added)
> For you are all sons *[kinship, children]* of God through faith in Christ Jesus. For as many of you as were baptized into Christ have put on Christ. There is neither Jew nor Greek, there is neither slave nor free, <u>there is neither male nor female;</u> for you are all one in Christ Jesus *[in the spirit].* (Galatians 3:26–28, emphasis added)

How to Interpret the Symbols

<u>Horse</u>—"the meaning of this symbol must be drawn from the natural use to which the symbol is applied, or the characteristics which it is known to have; and it may be added, that there might have been something for which that was best known in the time of the writer who uses it, which would not be so prominent at

another period of the world, or in another country, and that it is necessary to have that before the mind in order to obtain a correct understanding of the symbol. The use of the horse, for instance, may have varied at different times to some degree; at one time the prevailing use of the horse may have been for battle; at another for rapid marches—as of cavalry; at another for draught; at another for races; at another for conveying messages by the establishment of posts or the appointment of couriers. To an ancient Roman the horse might suggest prominently one idea; to a modern Arab another; to a teamster in Holland another. The things which would be most naturally suggested by the horse as a symbol, as distinguished, for instance, from an eagle, a lion, a serpent, etc., would be a war, as this was probably one of the first uses to which the horse was applied. So, in the magnificent description of the horse in Job 39:19–25, no notice is taken of any of his qualities but those which pertain to war. Therefore, see the horse as connected with war."[4]

Woman—the reference here to a woman is symbolic. Most theologians say that this woman represents the true church of Jesus Christ and is not even a real physical woman. She is the Bride of Christ, the Church (Ephesians 5:25–27, 32; Revelation 21:9–10).

> "Let us be glad and rejoice and give Him glory, for the marriage of the Lamb has come, and His wife has made herself ready." And to her it was granted to be arrayed in fine linen, clean and bright, for the fine linen is the righteous acts of the saints. (Revelation 19:7–8)

This wonder woman in Heaven is clothed with the sun. The sun represents the "light of the gospel" with its rays beaming from every angle touching everywhere, reaching farther than this galaxy. The sun also refers to future glory (Malachi. 4:2).

Moon—the moon is a lesser light reflecting the sun. Moreover, the moon is of this planet and is confined to this planet. It is under the woman's feet because she is with Christ and everything is under His feet. This woman is "the Church of Jesus Christ." The passage also speaks of the dominion she has over the heavens and earth as she reigns with Him.

> For as in Adam all die, even so in Christ all shall be made alive. But each one in his own order: Christ the firstfruits, afterward those who are Christ's at His coming. <u>Then comes the end</u>, when He delivers the kingdom to God the Father, when He puts an end to all rule and all authority and power. For <u>He must reign till He has put all enemies under His feet</u>. The last enemy that will be destroyed is death. (1 Corinthians 15:22–26, emphasis added)
> See also Psalms 18:9–15.

Some also say that while the sun represents the Son of God reigning over the heavens and covering His bride (the church), the moon represents the weak and faded Jewish laws (Judaism).[5] This interpretation reinforces the view that in the end. Disciples of Jesus will have more clout than the Jews in the Kingdom of Heaven because Jesus will be married to the church and not to the Jews.

<u>Stars</u>—the twelve stars on the woman's crown are either the twelve apostles of Christ or the tribes of Israel. In either case, they represent governmental authority. Stars are connected to people and have an individual identity. See the notes on Revelation 9:1 and consider Daniel 12:3.[6]

> So Jesus said to them *[His disciples]*, "Assuredly I say to you, that in the regeneration, when the Son of Man sits on the throne of His glory, you who have followed Me will also sit on twelve thrones, judging the twelve tribes of Israel." (Matthew 19:28, emphasis added)

She Has Labor Pains

As she is not a real physical woman, an understanding of symbols is all the more necessary at this time. She (the church) is pregnant with expectations of deliverance and is about to give birth (be delivered from persecution). Can you hear the screams of pain and anxiety, feel her discomfort and fears, hear her erratic breathing? Nothing else matters to her right now, just get this baby out. She needs a deliverer from the pressures of this world's harassment. She needs to get this gospel out and into all the world. How much longer, Lord?

This woman was impregnated by Christ's word and teaching to her. What did she bring forth? She brought forth a male Child, the Living Word of God, the pure gospel of the Kingdom not mixed with pagan doctrines, man-made rituals, ungodly traditions, or satanic influences. The teachings of Jesus Christ, and not the traditions of men or the Old Covenant, are to govern the church. What Jesus taught His disciples is what His church should be about today. Verses five and six explain this:

> She bore a male Child who was to rule all nations with a rod of iron. And her Child was caught up to God and His throne. Then the woman fled into the wilderness, where she has a place prepared by God, that they should feed her there one thousand two hundred and sixty days *[three and a half years or 1,260 years]*.
> (Revelation 12:5–6; 13, emphasis added)

The revelation Peter had concerning the identity of Jesus was the determining factor in what would happen next (Matthew 16:15–19). When Peter answered, "You are the Christ, the Son of the living God" and Jesus responded that "flesh and blood has not revealed this to you," this revelation changed the landscape of how religion was to operate going forward. Jesus told Peter that He is now going to "build My church, and the gates of Hades shall not prevail against it." Jesus was telling Peter that the institution he had made use of as church (the synagogue) was not doing the job as intended. Therefore, He must build (start something different from what you and the Jews now have) a new church so that it can accomplish the will of the Father. That is why Jesus presented a "New Covenant." There is a new order of business in town (Acts 6:14).

As righteous as priest Zacharias (John the Baptist's father) was, what he and the old order were doing was not getting the salvation and deliverance job done. That is why the Lord raised up John the Baptist, who introduced "the Kingdom" and led the way for Jesus to fully present His church. The church of Jesus Christ is a different work from the old synagogues and requires repentance of attitudes and beliefs by anyone who wants to benefit from it. At one stage, Jesus told His followers that

> "unless your righteousness exceeds the righteousness of the scribes and Pharisees *[the old order]*, you will by no means enter the kingdom of heaven *[the new church He is building]*." (Matthew 5:20, emphasis added)

Contrary to some denominational beliefs, this male child cannot be Jesus Christ because Jesus is the One who impregnates the woman. This woman cannot be Mary because Jesus has already come, died, and resurrected at this time. Also, this is a *prophecy* which was given in AD 95, when Jesus's death had been <u>history</u> since AD 33.

The Fiery Red Dragon

Another sign (wonder) appeared in Heaven—a fiery red dragon (v. 3). This, too, is symbolic. The dragon is not one of the living creatures or a good angel or an angel working under the Father's authority. This is an evil spirit in the heavens; that's why it is a wonder. Furthermore, it is making war against Michael and the heavenly hosts (v. 7). The dragon is a fabulous kind of serpent. It represents evil, a dreadful power-wielding entity that is destructive and merciless, inflicting terror at will. It is pictured as a great monster which can traverse the sky, the land, and sea, and has a strong defensive mechanism with which to protect itself. The color red and dragons are usually associated with China. However, this is not China the nation but an organization.

What Are These Seven Heads and Ten Horns?

I was told years ago that if a thing has more than one head, it is a monster. I fully agree with this saying. However, there is no real animal with seven heads and ten horns, so this strange-looking creature has to be symbolic. To gain a perspective of these symbols, let's jump ahead to chapter 17:9 of the book of Revelation, where John is given an explanation:

"Here is the mind which has wisdom: The seven heads are seven mountains on which the woman sits. There are also seven kings. Five have fallen, one is, and the other has not yet come. And when he comes, he must continue a short time. The beast that was, and is not, is himself also the eighth, and is of the seven, and is going to perdition.
"The ten horns which you saw are ten kings who have received no kingdom as yet, but they receive authority for one hour as kings with the beast. These are of one mind, and they will give their power and authority to the beast. These will make war with the Lamb, and the Lamb will overcome them, for He is Lord of lords and King of kings; and those who are with Him are called, chosen, and faithful.

And the ten horns which you saw on the beast, these will hate the harlot, make her desolate and naked, eat her flesh and burn her with fire. For God has put it into their hearts to fulfill His purpose, to be of one mind, and to give their kingdom to the beast, until the words of God are fulfilled." (Revelation 17:9–17)

Today there is an international intergovernmental economic organization consisting of the seven largest IMF-advanced economies in the world. This body is known as the G7 or Group of 7. It comprises finance ministers and central bank governors of seven industrialized countries with supposedly stable and advanced economies. In alphabetical order, these countries are Canada, France, Germany, Italy, Japan, the United Kingdom, and the United States of America. When the European Union is added, the group becomes the G8. The G7 was started in 1975 to discuss current world issues, but nowadays, the body exists to discuss primarily economic issues at a macro or global level. They make decisions which affect the entire world with their own authority. They represent about two-thirds of the world's total wealth. The body meets every year with emergency meetings whenever necessary. They monitor developments in the world economy and assess the economic policies of nations, a role now played by the International Monetary Fund (IMF) at a lower level. The G7 has the power to influence positively or negatively the economy of any nation.[7]

In 2009 a total of ten international organizations were represented at the G8 summit. These international organizations influence global politics in some way or the other as agents of the United Nations (UN): International Monetary Fund (IMF), World Bank (WB), World Trade Organization (WTO), World Health Organization (WHO), Food and Agriculture Organization (FAO), International Labor Organization (ILO), International Fund for Agricultural Development

(IFAD), United Nations Educational, Scientific and Cultural Organization (UNESCO), Organization of American States (OAS), and North Atlantic Treaty Organization (NATO).[8]

Large nations such as China, India, Brazil, Egypt, South Africa, and Saudi Arabia are invited to these summits from time to time. Even though China's economy is now ranked the second largest in the world by nominal GDP (US$14.3 trillion or 99 trillion Yuan in 2019), it is still not regarded as a developed nation by the G7.[9] Nevertheless, China has its hand in every nation around the world—including the United States—through financial, political, and economic matters. Time will reveal how much religious influence China will exert on nations that seek its financial help. Meanwhile, the Muslims are still subtly evangelizing Islam and agitating for Sharia law in every nation or city they are allowed.

Just as in the days of Nimrod more than 4,300 years ago, mankind today is still trying to set up a one-government system for the world, something known as "New World Order" (NWO).[10] They are coming together again, still trying to get into the heavens to challenge the Creator.

The dragon's tail—not his head, which signifies trickery and deception—will displace many saints (stars, high-profile Christian leaders) from their celestial (high-profile) position. They were to be seated in heavenly places with the Father and Christ (Isaiah 9:15–16). Adam, Eve, and Cain are early examples of this deception which is still rampant today (Matthew 24:24).

The Woman in the Wilderness

The woman's child, which represents the principles of the Kingdom, can stand on its own merit before God, man, and the kingdom of darkness. The woman (the church of Jesus Christ) fled to the wilderness because of heavy and relentless persecution. John the Baptist, Jesus Christ, Apostle Paul, and John the writer of this book all found themselves in a wilderness at one time or another. Being in a wilderness is not necessarily a bad place even though it may be desolate, lonesome, and dry. It can also be a place for quiet deliberations and transformation. Just as John received these revelations in a dry place, the woman is about to receive protection and sustenance for 1,260 days or 1,260 prophetic years. Because I cannot say when the church was first given this special protection, I cannot say when the 1,260 years will end. Just as angels ministered to Jesus and other patriarchs during their tough times, so are angels to minister to the church during her tough times. Jesus did promise His disciples that He would never leave them (Matthew 28:20; 16:18).

By attacking the advancement of the gospel, discrediting church leaders, restricting their finances, blocking the church from new revelations, and cutting-edge attempts to build the body of Christ, the dragon is out to destroy the woman. The enemy is trying hard to stop the spread of Kingdom principles throughout the world by keeping Christians practicing the same old synagogue-style rituals and traditions and seeking after perishable things rather than the Kingdom. For the church to be the church of Jesus Christ, it has to go beyond the four walls, leaving behind the Pharisaic rituals, Levitical laws, Mosaic traditions, and pagan mythologies. The church must put away the pagan gods, witchcraft, and the worshipping of demons. The church must make the transformation from Easter to Passover and from imaginary Santa Clause and fake trees to the living Christ. In some of our churches today, we are still singing songs from the 1700s and 1800s that are highly emotional but have no spiritual basis, while condemning singing and praying in tongues as demonic, archaic, and barbaric.

A War in Heaven

As was discussed in chapter 4, there are three levels of heaven: the troposphere where clouds hang and birds and planes fly; the thermosphere where the planets are, including this galaxy; the exosphere, outer space, or outside of this galaxy.[11] The Greek word used in verse 7 is *ouranos* (oo-ran-os') meaning "the abode of God" or where God lives.[12] This war took place in the third heaven but not anywhere near God's throne room because the exosphere is a vast place.

Satan Is Thrown out Again

Because there seems to be a break in the chronology of events, some interpreters see this war (vv. 7–12) in heaven as another recapitulation, that is, an actual event which took place long ago with reference to Isaiah 14:12–17. I would like to agree, but apparently this was not the only war or altercation between Satan and Michael. Jude 9 and Daniel 12 both speak of squabbles involving Michael. Ezekiel 28:14–19 also speaks about a celestial confrontation. Are all these different accounts of the same event? No! The war in Revelation 12 is the only one that makes reference to the dragon, and the only one stating that Satan and his angels were cast to the earth or ground (from the heavens) (Ephesians 2:2; 6:12). Satan still operates in the air. Daniel's end-time account speaks of deliverance and of the dead awakening, which has not happened yet. Satan will be thrown down again for the final time.

After Satan is cast out this time, a loud voice in heaven is making a declaration of how one, the accuser of the brethren is cast down to the earth, and two, there is renewed availability of

- salvation—deliverance, health, rescue, and safety;
- strength—miraculous power, ability, might;
- the Kingdom of our God—the reign or sovereign rule of the Lord Jesus; and
- the power of His Christ—the authority, jurisdiction, and liberty of the Messiah.

Satan is still accusing the brethren today and every day. He has not stopped accusing the saints; thus, he is not cast down yet. The saints will overcome the great dragon (the devil or Satan) by the blood of the Lamb (the redemptive works of the Messiah) and by the word of their testimony. Because the saints have been sealed by the blood of the Lamb and their lifestyle bore out their testimony, they are able to stand while undergoing great testing.

What Is Satan Doing in the Heavens Now?

It is generally held that God and Satan cannot be in the same place at the same time, just as light and darkness cannot dwell in the same place at the same time. While in the natural world this is certainly true in the spirit world it is different; otherwise, how could they contend with or confront each other? In 1 Kings 22:19–23, a lying spirit stood before the Lord. The introduction to the book of Job contains a record of a conversation between the Lord and Satan:

> Now there was a day when the sons of God came to present themselves before the Lord, and Satan also came among them. And the Lord said to Satan, "From where do you come?" So Satan answered the Lord and said, "From going to and fro on the earth, and from walking back and forth on it." (Job 1:6–7)

Satan presented himself before the Lord (in Heaven). Let it be established and known that the Lord is not afraid of Satan in any way, neither is He intimidated by Satan's presence. The Creator has no fear of His creation (Ezekiel 28:15–16). They had a conversation and decisions were made. Bear in mind that Satan (or Lucifer, his name before his fall) is regarded as a fallen cherub. He is a spirit being that can traverse the heavens just as Michael and Gabriel do, both of whom are cherubim. Before this war, Satan still has access to the heavens.

Where did this dragon come from? What is his assignment? Who gave him power and authority to operate? Who initiated this war? These are some of the questions still unanswered after John's revelation.

This war was prophesied in Genesis 3:14–15, some 6,000 years ago. Isaiah also prophesied this war (Isaiah 14:12–17).

Jesus tells His disciples about an altercation He witnessed involving Satan before He became "the Son of Man":

> Then the seventy returned with joy, saying, "Lord, even the demons are subject to us in Your name." And He said to them, "I saw Satan fall like lightning from heaven. Behold, I give you the authority to trample on serpents and scorpions, and over all the power of the enemy, and nothing shall by any means hurt you. Nevertheless do not rejoice in this, that the spirits are subject to you, but rather rejoice because your names are written in heaven." (Luke 10:17–20, emphasis added)

Historians (preterists) believe that this war, and the particulars of it, happened during the time of Constantine (a fourth-century Roman Emperor),[13] giving him the privilege to be called a saint. Even though many rulers had opposed God over the centuries, none of them had claimed "that he himself is God." Consider the passage from 2 Thessalonians 2:1–4, which is in opposition to preterists' beliefs. This last criterion has yet to be met—the man of sin is not revealed.

Heaven Rejoices while Earth Mourns

An accuser (a complainant at law, one who brings a charge against another), particularly Satan and his cohorts, will bring charges against the saints, trying to bring guilt and shame on them, with intentions of discouraging them in the faith. Just as Satan would accuse the brethren, non-believers will accuse and attack the church. The earth will mourn because saints, too, will be accusing and judging each other (Matthew 10:34–37; Romans 14:10–13). Saints should not be judging one another because they have an adversary already (Psalms 109:6; Isaiah 50:8; Zechariah 3:1–2; 1 Peter 5:8–9).

Jesus the Christ, the apostles, and Apostle Paul all had false accusers. Satan knows that he is doomed. He is doomed because of his deliberate rebellion and disobedience to the Creator. Because he will try to carry as many others with him to destruction—the lake of fire or the place of torments (Revelation 20:10)—he will continually point out or identify the sins of all those who have disobeyed the Father even of the saints who have been forgiven. His assignment is to bring great wrath on the earth. His intention is to wreak havoc on the earth irrespective of who is affected in the process, whether you have sworn allegiance to Satan or not. Everybody and everything affected is collateral damage as far as he is concerned, and there is no remorse for friendly fire. Therefore, he must be resisted and his works negated until he is removed from his influential celestial position.

Why doesn't Satan ask for forgiveness? If he were to do so, it would be an admission that the Father is greater than him and that he was wrong. Bear in mind that he is an adversary;

therefore, he cannot do anything but play his role. Also, his future doom has been prophesied and enmity is set between him and mankind. Having this knowledge about Satan's assignment and knowing that he will always be Satan, the saints must govern themselves accordingly. Satan has a short time; therefore, he must intensify his work. See one of Apostle Paul's admonitions on how the saints should respond at Ephesians 6:10–18.

The Accuser Is Still at Work

Satan is busy accusing the saints in Heaven and hindering, tempting, and destroying them on earth. Satan is also out to persecute the church and to dismantle its godly influence. Do not think it strange when you are attacked innocently with sickness, lack, confusion, broken relationships, sudden losses, death of loved ones, hatred from unexpected sources, and unexplainable setbacks. These are tools of Satan's kingdom and he will use them at his will. The mere fact that you are in this world makes you a candidate for these calamities to come your way, nothing personal. Our Master, Jesus of Nazareth, went through the same tests you have been or are about to go through. He overcame, so can you!

They (not just Jesus but our brethren who remained steadfast) overcame Satan by the blood of the Lamb and by the word of their testimony, and they did not love their lives to the death when it questioned their loyalty to Christ. They not only had reasons to live for Christ but also to die for Christ. Just as others who have gone before you overcame the devil, you have that same opportunity. Your faith in God and obedience to His Word will strengthen you to endure every hardship as a good soldier (1 Timothy 2:1–3). Your reward (crown) comes after the testing (James 1:12). Here is an excerpt from the "Hall of Fame of Faith" of your brethren:

Women received their dead raised to life again. Others were tortured, not accepting deliverance, that they might obtain a better resurrection. Still others had trial of mockings and scourgings, yes, and of chains and imprisonment. They were stoned, they were sawn in two, were tempted, were slain with the sword. They wandered about in sheepskins and goatskins, being destitute, afflicted, tormented—of whom the world was not worthy. They wandered in deserts and mountains, in dens and caves of the earth. (Hebrews 11:35–38)

These examples are for you. For God will make the way of escape that you may overcome whatever He allows you to come your way (1 Corinthians 10:11–13), just as He gave the woman "two wings of a great eagle" (Isaiah 40:28–31). Job is a prime example of what the patriarchs went through and how they overcame. Hold fast to your faith and strengthen whatever belief you have because persecution is about to increase.

The Greek word *dioko* (dee-o'-ko) means to "pursue (literally or figuratively); ensue, follow (after), given to, (suffer) persecute (-ion), press forward."[14] It also means to oppress with injury or punishment for adherence to principles or religious faith, to pursue with harassing or oppressive treatment. To comfort you, not all persecutions end in death. Apostle Paul and our Master have more encouraging words on this subject:

persecutions, afflictions, which happened to me at Antioch, at Iconium, at Lystra—what persecutions I endured. And out of them all the Lord delivered me. Yes, and all who desire to live godly in Christ Jesus will suffer persecution. (2 Timothy 3:11–12)
See also Mark 10:29–30; Matthew 5:10–12; John 15:20.

The Meek Shall Inherit the Earth

In Christendom, saints are not given the right to attack lost souls or pagans even though the saints are the first to be attacked and persecuted. Jehovah does not promote the killing of unbelievers as do some religions. Instead, He is long-suffering that none may perish, that all come to the knowledge of the truth. The Kingdom of Heaven is such that it encourages life and gives hope to all in an atmosphere of peace and love (John 3:16). Prophet Isaiah and our Lord expressed this clearly:

> He was oppressed and He was afflicted,
> Yet He opened not His mouth;
> He was led as a lamb to the slaughter,
> And as a sheep before its shearers is silent,
> So He opened not His mouth.
> He was taken from prison and from judgment . . .
> Because He had done no violence,
> Nor was any deceit in His mouth.
> (Isaiah 53:7–9)
> See also Matthew 10:16–20.

Saints are covered and protected from the enemy by the love of the heavenly Father, who will not allow His children to be abused unworthily.

> Who shall separate us from the love of Christ? Shall tribulation, or distress, or persecution, or famine, or nakedness, or peril, or sword? As it is written: "For Your sake we are killed all day long; we are accounted as sheep for the slaughter." Yet in all these things we are more than conquerors through Him who loved us. (Romans 8:35–37).
> See also Matthew 5:5.

The Serpent Spewed out of His Mouth

Satan also is able to do phenomenal feats, spewing out an enormous amount of "water" from his mouth, enough to drown the woman or wash her away. He does this by speaking lies and heavily organized destructive propaganda through the media (John 8:44; 1 Timothy 4:1–2; James 2:4–6). He releases waves of deception, false doctrines, counterfeits, pagan practices and cultures, strange gods, superstitions, sorcery, and anything that looks attractive to the carnal-minded person. By providing and promoting alternatives to Christianity, he uses people of foreign cultures to infiltrate the Christian communities. The church itself becomes a subtle tactic the enemy has been using in nations to destroy or weaken the religious fabric. Today, there is an organized movement in the United Kingdom and Canada that is not only allowing but making room for Muslims in key political positions in these nations that once were heavily Christian based.[15] The "flood alert" must be sounded.

Several years ago in the Bahamas, the then government introduced a festival called "Junkanoo Carnival" to the country. It was presented as another avenue to use the culture theme to bring fresh money into the country. In reality, it was a tactic to distract the Christians from their God and introduce them to a Greek god by the name of Bacchus, hence the bacchanal or carnival celebration. This was so clever that even the leading churches bought the scheme hook, line, and sinker. The Chinese are making similar inroads into the society and are setting up their statutes of Buddha in strategic places with no objections from the church. According to Revelation 17:15, the "water" represents "peoples, multitudes, nations, and tongues." These foreigners will weaken or destroy any local culture because of their multitude.

The woman is delivered from the hands of her enemy by supernatural means. One way is through a simple truth released or exposed that will substantively negate the lies and deception of the enemy. In September 2019, God supernaturally intervened and utterly removed the obeah and witchcraft altars that were set up in three areas occupied by Haitians on the island of Abaco in the Bahamas. God used one hurricane that lasted for thirty-six hours on one spot to cleanse the land of the obeah, the witchcraft, and the people who practiced the evil. This hurricane, by the name of Dorian, allowed the ground to open its mouth and swallow up the water of foreign culture's invasion, the insurgence of pagan worship, and the practice of witchcraft. Just as He dealt with the sorcerers, serpents, and the prophets of Baal, Jehovah will deal with those who rise up against you.

No weapon formed against the saints will prosper <u>unless the Lord allows it</u>. Just as the Lord protected (sealed) the children of Israel from the plagues that devastated the Egyptians, so will He cover His people from the wickedness of the enemy.

"Behold, I have created the blacksmith
Who blows the coals in the fire,
Who brings forth an instrument for his work;
And <u>I have created the spoiler to destroy</u>.
No weapon formed against you shall prosper,
And every tongue which rises against you in judgment
You shall condemn.
This is the heritage of the servants of the Lord,
And their righteousness is from Me,"
Says the Lord.
(Isaiah 54:16–17, emphasis added)

The woman (the church) had more than one (male) child (doctrines and principles). Since Satan could not conquer the woman, he went after her children (other institutions which stem from the church—schools, orphanages, hospices, care centers, etc.). Jehovah will deliver His people from the hand of the enemy. Jesus has assured Peter that the gates of hell shall not prevail against His church (Matthew 16:18).

CHAPTER 13

Revelation 13—the Beast and His Mark

The Beast from the Sea

EARLIER THERE WAS a red dragon with seven heads and ten horns appearing in heaven. Now let's go back to the earth realm where there is a beast rising up out of the sea with almost the same description (vv. 1–10). The sea represents the peoples, multitudes, nations, and tongues. The beast comes out of the Western world from among the people (the United Nations). In John's days, there was nothing to the west but the sea. The many different animals (nations) making up the one beast suggests an international organization. This first beast is neither Papal Rome nor the Pope.

This is a different beast from the dragon in chapter 12. The dragon also has seven heads and ten horns, but he has only seven crowns instead of ten like this beast from the sea, representing different power structures and purposes. Each beast is fierce-looking and is devised for causing great destruction of and terror upon people.

This is close to where we are now in prophecy.

"Thus he said: 'The fourth beast shall be
A fourth kingdom on earth,
Which shall be different from all other kingdoms,
And shall devour the whole earth,

Trample it and break it in pieces.
The ten horns are ten kings
Who shall arise from this kingdom.
And another shall rise after them;
He shall be different from the first ones,
And shall subdue three kings.
He shall speak pompous words against the Most High,
Shall persecute the saints of the Most High,
And shall intend to change times and law.
Then the saints shall be given into his hand
For a time and times and half a time.'"
(Daniel 7:23–25)

The time expressed here is three and a half years or forty-two months. Or is it three and a half millennia? The period between Daniel and Jesus Christ is more than 600 years.

The beast and the leopard are not persecuting or coming against other nations, not even against other sects of people, tribes, territories, races, or classes. It will not be the Chinese against the Muslims or the United States of America against Iran. It is not the communists against the capitalists or NATO or the UN against the terrorists. Instead, the beasts are against the church of Jesus Christ. The entire end-time battles are about worship and not about land, wealth, natural resources, or nuclear weapons. It is every nation against the church in that nation.

Who persecuted Jesus Christ? It was the Jews. Who persecuted Apostles Peter, James, John, and Paul? It was the synagogue, the religious leaders of the day. Who persecuted Thomas More, Martin Luther, and other martyrs? It was the counterfeit church, the Roman Catholic Church.

The end-time battles are about who gets the worship of the people. The Creator says, "I made them; so, they should worship Me" (Psalms 100:1–3). Satan says, "I will get them to disobey the

Creator and come after me." "Follow me!" is the message Jesus Christ preached. The kingdom of darkness tries to counterfeit the Kingdom of Heaven. The dragon gives his authority to the beast as the heavenly Father gave His authority to Jesus Christ His Son. The beast wants the same kind of worship that was given to Jesus Christ. The heavenly Father gave Jesus authority on the earth. Jesus preached and demonstrated the Kingdom of Heaven for three and a half years; now the beast is given authority for three and a half years.

People will worship whatever or whoever gives them what they want or makes them feel good. They will worship imaginary gods, lifeless idols and statues, an animal, a strange thing, something that seems to have extraordinary powers, or anything that seems to have influence, including another man (Exodus 34:14–16; Acts 10:25–26). People will give reverence to angels and demons. It is very important to know that an angel (or any of the heavenly hosts) would never receive worship from a man (Revelation 22:8–9)—but a demon would. Pay attention!

This book of Revelation was given so that you could live your life from "The End" perspective. If you do this, you will win, and if you do anything else, you have lost. Simple! Today, you have the pleasure and advantage of seeing (and knowing) the end before it happens. Here is an incentive for hearing and adhering to these things:

> Blessed is he who reads and those who hear the words of this prophecy, and keep those things which are written in it; for the time is near. (Revelation 1:3)

The Heavenly Father Makes His Plans and Purposes Known

That's how the heavenly Father works. He shows you the end from the beginning. He loves to prophesy, to make known His thoughts to man. He sets the rules upfront (Genesis 2:16–17). He is the God of light and knowledge and not of darkness and ignorance. He gives you this information so that you can have "hope and knowledge" instead of "fear and doubt." You know the expected end. You don't have to operate by guessing or wondering what will happen in the end. There may be some gaps, missing pieces, and surprises in the middle, but the end is certain. When you make Jesus Christ your Lord and Savior. Even if you don't know something, it does not matter because whatever happens, He has you covered.

When you are in the Kingdom of Heaven you have spectators and cheerleaders (the Holy Spirit, the Gospels, the Epistles, the recordings of the patriarchs, the legacy of departed saints, your leaders, intercessors, all the prophecies and promises since Adam, and the book of Revelation) in your corner encouraging you to succeed, to be an overcomer as they were. You also have Jesus the Son as your example. For best results, do what Jesus did. You have a major role to play in whether you overcome or not. You have to make it happen (Hebrews 12:1–2)!

Jesus was told of the joy prior to His leaving Heaven. He knew the end before He began. For it was prophesied (Isaiah 9:6–7).

Speaking Blasphemes

What is blasphemy? Blaspheme, the verb, is to vilify, specially to speak impiously (lacking reverence); defame, rail on, revile, speak evil.[1] When Jesus claimed to be the Son of God,

He was said to have blasphemed. He said something which was worthy of death. To speak evil or irreverently of God, to not give God credit due to Him, and to claim to be God or able to do what God does are all examples of blasphemy (Matthew 26:64–66; Acts 13:44–45).

Watch how you speak against the things of God. Blasphemy puts you in league with Satan. Because the beast spoke blasphemies, we know that he is against God.

All who dwell on earth at this stage will worship the beast, except those whose names have been written in the Book of Life. You have to know who you are worshipping and why. This is not the time to simply follow the crowd.

Greater persecution is coming against the church, and it will be because of religion. The supremacy of Jehovah is the main issue. Remember the doxologies in the previous chapters? They gave worship to Jehovah only. He who controls the earth is the Supreme Lord (Genesis 1:1; Psalms 24:1–2, 37:9–11). What is religion? James 1:26–27 gives a proper definition:

> If anyone among you thinks he is religious, and does not bridle his tongue but deceives his own heart, this one's religion is useless. Pure and undefiled religion before God and the Father is this: to visit orphans and widows in their trouble, and to keep oneself unspotted from the world.

The Greek word for religion is *threskeia* (thrace-ki'-ah), which means "ceremonial observance; worshipping." It is the quest for the values of the ideal life, involving the ideal, the practices, and the theology.[2] It can be further defined as a particular system in which the quest for the ideal life has been embodied and the practice of sacred rites or observances.[3] Obeying the Lord, not participating in religious activities are what defeat Satan.

According to Uriah Smith, the reasons for the persecution of the church were that "Christianity was prevailing against paganism, sweeping away its superstitions, overturning its idols, and dismantling its temples. The religious elements of that power were touched, and persecution was the result."[4] The Lord's command to "go into all the world and preach the gospel" was carried out, and it produced such significant results that Satan, who was losing too much ground, had to fight back (Matthew 28:18–20; Mark 16:14–20). Christ is not coming back until every nation has been touched by the gospel. Therefore, if you want Christ to come soon, you have to get busy now.

> "And this gospel of the kingdom will be preached in all the world as a witness to all the nations, and then the end will come." (Matthew 24:14)
> See also Revelation 14:6–7.

Some nations have already been preached to and have made a decision to turn away from Jehovah and go after Satan and his demons (Matthew 25:32–34).

When you preach and demonstrate the Gospel of Jesus Christ,

- people will come into the knowledge of the truth;
- people will be set free from bondage and satanic strongholds;
- people will be healed from sickness and diseases;
- people will be delivered from bad doctrines and demonic influences;
- people will get rid of idols and counterfeits;
- lives will be redeemed from destruction;
- people will begin to go after what is rightfully theirs with a passion;
- people will help to set others free; and

- people will ultimately set out to destroy the kingdom of darkness.

If you say that you are a Christian and you are not preaching the Gospel of Jesus Christ (the gospel of the Kingdom), then you are being persecuted for nothing. Since you will be persecuted anyhow, do something to earn your stripes.

What Goes Around Comes Around—Be Patient

The one who held the saints captive will be captured and imprisoned. Job and Jesus Christ are excellent examples today of patience and faith. They both appeared to be abandoned by the Father; both were allowed to be attacked by Satan; both held fast to their testimony of who God is and who they are in Him; and they both, like other saints, overcame the evil one (Revelation 12:11). There is a repeated promise from the Lord that "I will make your enemies your footstool" (Acts 2:34–35). The tide will turn. The saints have to believe this (Galatians 6:7; Matthew 26:52; Isaiah 33:1).

There will be numerous testing of your faith; therefore, you must purpose to stand. Adam fell victim to Satan. You don't have to. He was not obedient to the Father, as he did not endure the temptation. The trial of your faith works patience in you (James 1:3–4; 1 Peter 1:7). Because Jesus overcame, He was given the highest level of worship (Revelation 5:12–13). James, for many good reasons, tells you to be patient in your walk with the Lord (James 5:7–11).

Reflections on the Pope and the Roman Catholic Church

The pope is considered the head of the Roman Catholic Church. Popes, since the eighth century, have had political and spiritual powers. They operated and lived more like kings than priests. They controlled states and territories, not just parishioners. The Church provided the best education for quite some time. They commanded armies and made alliances or enemies as they saw politically fit. They judged in civil matters and they were as corrupt as secular politicians in every respect (simony, nepotism, bribery, sale of indulgences, etc.). Here are some of their more popular customs:

- Simony—the sin of buying or selling of ecclesiastical benefices (Acts 8:18–19).
- Indulgences—(n) remission of the temporal punishment still due to sin after it has been forgiven. When God forgives sins, He puts them in the sea of forgetfulness and remembers them no more with complete cleansing (Jeremiah 31:34). However, the RCC priest would supposedly take away your guilt for a price.
- Contrary interpretations and practices—the RCC made contrary interpretations of laws and initiated corrupt religious practices (the worship of statues, dead saints, and art: Exodus 20:4–5). Their belief is that priests (not the Holy Spirit) have the exclusive authority of the Bible and its interpretation (2 Peter. 1:20–21). Consequently, they promoted strange (ungodly) doctrines (purgatory, the Eucharist, a priest can forgive sins [Mark 2:7], etc.).
- Purgatory—a condition or place in which the souls of those dying in a remorseful state are purified from excusable sins or undergo the temporal punishment,

after which the guilt or mortal sin is remitted; a place of temporary holding before one goes to Heaven or hell (Luke 16:22–23, 23:42–43; 2 Corinthians 5:6–8).

-   The forgiveness of sins and transgressions—only God can do this. The blood of the Lamb is necessary for the forgiveness of sins, not money or indulgences (Isaiah 43:25–26; Matthew 26:27–28; Hebrews 9:22).[5]

A Beast from the Earth

He comes up out of the earth, a pagan entity (vv. 11–18). Pagan means counterfeit religion. A pagan is considered a person or community professing a religion other than Christianity. It is one who is neither a Christian nor a Jew and is also referred to as a heathen. Most likely, this is Papal Rome, the pope for Rome has always supported idolatry. He is soft and gentle, like a lamb, but his speech betrays him. Promoting false doctrines, changing established laws, and ordering the death of those who disobey him are some of the things that will distinguish him.

He is a great pretender under the disguise of religion. A lot of these charlatans are around today. But this one has "miraculous powers," enough to convince the masses of his supernatural abilities. These so-called miraculous powers are actually sorcery, magical tricks, and delusions. A good magician today does the same thing by deceiving you with his speed, skills, and knowledge of science. This is the same type of Chaldean spirit from the days of Abram's fathers (Genesis 11:27–29).

> But there was a certain man called Simon, who previously practiced sorcery in the city and astonished the people of Samaria, claiming that he was someone great, to whom they all gave heed, from the least to the greatest, saying, "This man is the great power of God." And they heeded him

because he had astonished them with his sorceries for a long time. (Acts 8:9–11)

See also Exodus 7:8–12.

Magicians are not new. They are tricksters who know their craft well enough to deceive and astonish others. Calling down fire from heaven and other similar tricks can be done by deception, witchcraft, chemistry, and uncommon knowledge. If the beast from the earth can genuinely do this, then he is on par with Jehovah because Jehovah is the God who answers by fire (see the story of Elijah on Mount Carmel in 1 Kings 18:20–24). Other than that, it is pure deception. People who go about looking for "signs and wonders" can easily be deceived. Lazy people—persons who want something for nothing—and fools are known to be gullible.

To control the people, the beast would use:

- **blasphemies**—tell lies about how great he is and who the other beast is while minimizing Jesus as the Christ.
- **deception**—wonders and phenomenal works. He will undo some of the evil he has initiated to make it look like he is undoing what God has done.
- **worship of the former beast, false gods**. There is always a problem with giving worship to the wrong object.
- **programs and projects** to keep the people busy and distracted from the truth.
- **fear**—evil rules by fear and control. Satan and his crew will kill, using the secular power, those who do not worship the beast and those who did not accept their lies and deception. Sect leader Jim Jones and his followers in Jonestown, Guyana, during the late 1970s are very good examples of evil-minded persons wanting to control others.[6]

He makes an image of the beast (an idol or statue) for the people to worship, then he gives the image life as if this beast is a god that requires worship. When the worshippers are under his influence or have his confidence, he will cause them "to receive a mark on their right hand or on their foreheads" (v. 16). He will require their commitment to do any kind of commerce or have an association with them. The stipulation requiring that no one may buy or sell except one who has the mark or the name of the beast or the number of his name is welcomed because it speaks of relationship. The people who have not yet made a commitment to God will gladly accept this offer because they have no other choice. It will help to show their allegiance and build a connection with the beast.

The Mark or the Name

The English word "mark" is translated from the Greek word *charagma*, which means "a scratch or etching; a stamp (as a badge of servitude); sculptured figure (statue)."[7] It can also refer to something that is graven. The implication here is the use of a sharp point to cause the mark. This mark may also be symbolic, a verbal or written commitment, or an expressed desire to affiliate. The "mark of the beast" presumably can be anything that identifies with the beast. It is meant to show allegiance or bring one under its control.

In 2017 there was a business known as 3 Square Market in a town called River Falls in Wisconsin, USA, that offered its employees the opportunity to receive a chip (mark) in their hand to do business within the company.[8] This mark was the size of a grain of rice and was injected under the skin into the flesh of volunteers. After implantation, the employee could do whatever business he or she wanted, for example, clock in and out of work and conduct business without cash. The program seemed so successful that hospitals, universities, and foreign governments sought after it. The mark can be an RFID microchip. Nowadays nanochips are available.

In September 2015, on an episode of the CNN show *Anderson Cooper 360*, reporter John Surubba revealed in an interview that members of a church in South Beach, Miami, Florida, USA, had begun tattooing the image of "666" on parts of their bodies. They were not forced to place it on their right hand or on their foreheads. They chose to do so because the pastor claimed to be a "christ," and the members voluntarily followed him. The pastor is Jose Luis De Jesus Miranda, of Puerto Rican descent.[9]

From the late nineteenth century, some thought the use of credit cards and charge coins was the implementation of this mark which would become mandatory to transact business. We now can see that this was not the case. The possibility of a mark (a chip or etching, whether internal or external) being applied to, in, or on a person's forehead or right hand is not a question anymore. The technology is now available internationally. The Patient Protection and Affordable Care Act, commonly known as Obamacare, in the United States, has already authorized the implanting of a chip to be used on participants in this government-sponsored venture.

No Mark

Not accepting the mark is easier said than done. Not having the mark means that you do not participate in any public activity—no shopping, no travel, no government transactions, no business dealings, no medical attention, no more family and friends, and the like (Revelation 13:16–17). The government will probably deem you a "health risk" or "a rebel." You will be an outcast in that society. You might have to live in the wilderness like a caveman or a hermit. Your confidence and trust have to be in God alone, knowing that He will take care of you (Philippians 4:19). You will have to live by your faith (Romans 1:17). Living by faith is something you should be doing now as a Believer (Hebrews 11:6). With the onslaught of severe testing and persecutions, you will begin to understand why Jesus repeatedly said that he who overcomes will be greatly rewarded (Revelation 3:21).

The Influence of the Second Beast

The second beast enforces the acceptance of the mark. Bear in mind that the saints are still on the earth and great persecution is still going on. The Lord knows that some of the saints will not survive the persecution, but there is still hope for them (John 6:39–40).

This beast has jurisdiction (authority, influence, and power) over the earth. He has influence over every class of people. This influence has to be religious or spiritual as it is not economic, not educational, not cultural, and not athletic. It has no age barrier, no family connections, no national identity, and no social status or civil ranking such as a prime minister, senator, member of parliament, judge, permanent secretary, commissioner, pastor, police, doctor, chairman, janitor, prison inmate, beggar, or invalid. However he does it, he makes the people receive his mark. Whether by lies, trickery, deception, or compulsion, there is basically no choice. You receive it or wish you had. Those who want the easy way out will fall for this.

The enemy is a late counterfeiter. There is nothing original in him (Ezekiel 9:4–6). The Creator has already sealed His people (Revelation 3:12, 7:2–4). There is a strong admonition to not receive the mark of the beast, no matter the pressure (Revelation 14:9–11).

You Can Overcome These Beasts

You have to learn how to trust in God. Go back to Abraham, Job, Joseph, David, the prophets, and the apostles, and study their lives and learn from them. They are a part of that great cloud of witnesses. It is possible for you to overcome the beast and his mark. It calls for obedience to God's Word and patience (Revelation 14:12). Start practicing your faith and obeying God now! (Hebrews 10:32–39).

You have to come to the point of Apostle Paul when he said, "For I consider that the sufferings of this present time are not worthy to be compared with the glory which shall be revealed in us" (Romans 8:18). To overcome the beast and his threats, you will need all the Word of God, spiritual principles, kingdom teachings, prophetic words, Bible promises, and Holy Spirit encounters which come your way. If your church doctrines and denominational beliefs, the advice from your newspaper or talk-show host, the pledge of your fraternity, the laws of your government, the privileges of your private club, etc., are different from God's Word, they cannot help you. You have to follow Jesus Christ as your Lord and Master (Matthew 10:24–33; Acts 5:29–32).

There is a reward for not receiving the mark of the beast. When you believe and obey God, your end is predetermined. You are never abandoned or left hopeless. Those who are faithful and overcome shall inherit the Kingdom.

> And I saw thrones, and they sat on them, and judgment was committed to them. Then I saw the souls of those who had been beheaded for their witness to Jesus and for the word of God, who had not worshiped the beast or his image, and had not received his mark on their foreheads or on their hands. And they lived and reigned with Christ for a thousand years. (Revelation 20:4)

Calculating the Number of the Beast

The normal intellect would not be able to decode this number. To do this correctly requires the wisdom of God. "Six" is the number for man. It is referred to as the unlucky number and is dreaded by Jews. It is just short of completion—the perfect number seven—and the highest that one can go, outside of God. Nebuchadnezzar, Pharaoh, Hitler, the popes, Alexander the Great, Apostles Peter and Paul, all were sixes; only Jesus Christ is a seven.

The name tells you the character of the thing. "Three" is a deity; therefore, the three 6s are three times man trying to be God. The number 666 "Six hundred sixty-six" is a triangular number, but most ancient readers would not know that. It has been thought a parody (imitation, mockery) on the divine number seven. This is possible, but scholars more often turn to another explanation. Counting a name or word was a common practice in Greek and Hebrew, which used letters as specific numbers. Then Jewish teachers played with the numerical values of words. This form of calculation was known as *gematria*.[10] Many ingenious proposals have been made for the meaning of 666. Irenaeus, a second-century Christian scholar, listed among the possibilities Lateinos, Rome, as the final kingdom. The most popular proposal among scholars today is not Nero Caesar. Although his name comes out to 1,005 in Greek (which would have been obvious), his name comes out to 666 if transliterated into Hebrew.

Other Possibilities as the Antichrist

According to *Christian Forums*, other possible candidates for a present-day antichrist are Barack Obama, Donald Trump, Jared Kushner, and Pope Francis. Add Bill Gates to flavor the pot. The best candidate so far is Emmanuel Jean-Michel Frédéric Macron, the current President of France since May 14, 2017. A *Forums* writer noted, "[Mr. Macron] has generated more end-time buzz than any other world leader that I know!" His sudden rise from obscurity to national prominence, and his charisma cause attention to remain on him. Here is the meaning of his name: Emmanuel—God with us. Jean—Gift from God. Michel—Who is like God? Frédéric—peaceful ruler (Prince of Peace is the title for Jesus Christ). Macron—a short, straight mark. His name adds up to 666. There are 36 total characters in his name: 32 letters, 1 dash, 3 spaces. If you give each character a value of its position and calculate the sum, you get 666: (1+2+3+ . . . +36 = 666). His birthday is the winter solstice. He was born on December 21, 1977, which is the shortest day of the year. The reason December 24 and December 25 were picked for Jesus's birthday is that those days were considered the winter solstice or the shortest day of the year. *Prophecy Update* is basically in agreement.[11]

CHAPTER 14

Revelation 14—the Lamb and the 144,000 Saints

JOHN IS STILL in the earth realm but observing the heavens (v. 1). The reference here to Mount Zion is the Holy City of Jerusalem. Jesus the Christ is the Lamb. The 144,000 men are in Heaven with the Lamb. This is the same group from chapter 7:3–4, but they have been through more tribulation. None of them died or was martyred like other saints because they were all sealed on their foreheads. Verse 3 says they were redeemed from the earth.

Heaven is a noisy and melodious place. There is loud noise like thunder and noise like many waters while harpists are playing their harps. Angels (or saints) are harping, making joyful melodies in the presence of the Lord. Yes, there are musical instruments and worshippers singing loudly in Heaven. God enjoys noise. These virgin men are ministering before the throne and rendering a selection which only they knew. Can you imagine a choir of 144,000 male voices simply worshipping God? (And Bahamians praise the Rahming Brothers so highly!)

This choir in Heaven is a special group of men. It does not say what five-fold office they hold, but they are known for their moral purity and for being overcomers. Their character is promoted more than anything else, including their ministerial or secular office. They have been delivered from the evil one and from the guilt of sin. This is a level one achieves only through spiritual maturity because it does not come overnight or haphazardly. Eunuchs and suicide bombers set themselves aside for Allah, why not for Jehovah? This is one of the main reasons monasteries and convents were established to provide a place where one can be in the world but not of it. These men were faultless (blameless, unblemished) like a lamb to be sacrificed. They were purchased, "redeemed from among men, being firstfruits to God and to the Lamb" (v. 4). The term "firstfruits" suggests that they are converted Israelites who accepted Jesus of Nazareth as the Christ from His first coming. Today, some Jews still do not acknowledge Jesus as such.

Not Defiled by Women

This statement (v. 4) should be taken literally with reference to sex and intimate relationships with a female person. However, because in the book of Revelation the "woman" represents "the church," some scholars would read their bad experiences into the statement. Some would read that these men were not defiled by churches. It is suggested that these men cut from the church before they could have been defiled by it. A local entity can defile you by its false doctrines, irreverence for the things of God, rebellious practices, denial of the supremacy of God, lack of display of the love of God, condemnation of fellow saints, etc. But this is not a proper interpretation of this passage. There are good churches and there are bad churches.

What Will Be Preached in the Last Days?

Worship the Creator only, not the counterfeit. You must be confused if you worship anything other than the best or the original. There is only one creator of a thing. Only one person can create a thing, so once it is created, all else are counterfeits, duplicates, or wannabes. There is only one Creator of the heavens and the earth. That indisputable position has already been claimed by Jehovah. Therefore, everything else is created, which means they are secondary. Your fear and worship should be for the one who has the ultimate power and authority, the Creator (Matthew 10:28–33).

In this present dispensation (of grace), the preaching is on the Kingdom of Heaven. John the Baptist, Jesus Christ, and His disciples all preached the same thing with emphasis on repentance. The word "repent" here means "to think differently or afterwards; reconsider; feel compunction."[1] It calls for changing the way you used to think on a matter. Apostle Paul preached Jesus Christ and Him crucified and resurrected. Do not declare or bring a different or substitute kingdom or gospel.

> In those days John the Baptist came preaching in the wilderness of Judea, and saying, "Repent, for the kingdom of heaven is at hand!" (Matthew 3:1–2)
> See also Matthew 4:17; Luke 4:17–19.

The Proclamations of the Three Angels

The First Angelic Proclamation—"Fear God, and give glory to Him" (vv. 6–7). Strangely, an angel is preaching to men. Angels usually only deliver the message, and then they are on their way. This angel could be symbolic, or this event could have taken place outside of this present age. The first angel invites people to turn from what they are doing and to worship the true and living God.

There are a few key elements in the message the first angel brought. These elements are crucial to effectively present the gospel today (evangelism). If you positively receive this message and follow through with the corresponding actions, then you are secured in the Lamb's Book of Life. If you are serious about evangelizing, then your message, like the angel's, must include:

- **fear God**—having reverential respect for God is paramount in any message that points to Jehovah. If He is not recognized for His creative and divine architectural works, supremacy, might, wisdom, holiness, love, mercy, etc., then there is no need to acknowledge Him (Psalms 111:10).
- **give glory to Him**—all the power and glory (honor, praise, worship) belong to Him. This must be voluntarily and sincerely bestowed (Matthew 6:13).
- **the hour of His judgment has come**—people need to be sensitized to what time frame they are working with and what awaits them. This helps to determine the urgency or triviality of the matter. People don't have all day or forever to make a decision about their life, especially when they are in trouble. Examining this statement from a different angle, preterists would interpret this as the Final Judgment not yet taken place. Here are two scriptural references that prove this: Matthew 11:21–24 and 2 Corinthians 5:10. In your preaching, you can stress that "judgment is coming," but do not say that the "hour" has come, because no man knows that hour.
- **worship Him who made heaven and earth**, the sea, and springs of water—adore (bow before) the Creator. If it is common protocol to pay obeisance to earthly kings, then the King of kings deserves greater (Psalms 95:5–7).

Saints have been given a "Mission Possible." Should you accept this mission, your job is to make it difficult for your neighbor to go to hell. Your neighbor is anyone you come into contact with. This is not the feel-good gospel but the everlasting good news which is meant to deliver the sinner from hell. If you love your neighbor, give him the truth. This proclamation the angel made could be the last opportunity for someone to make Jesus Christ his Lord and Savior before his physical (first) death or before Christ returns (Romans 10:14–15; 1 Corinthians 8:4–6).

The Second Angelic Proclamation—"Babylon is Fallen!" (v. 8). The best that you have, the epitome and glory of your works, has crumbled. The second angel announces that the Babylonian system (the best the world has to offer) has failed them. The physical city has been destroyed already as prophesied by three major prophets.[2] Babylon was the most organized, powerful, and sophisticated world system that ever existed, based on the wisdom of man. It represented the economic and political systems of the world. It was known as "the glory of kingdoms." Its kings were known as "king of kings" (Isaiah 13:19–20; Ezekiel 26:7–8; Daniel 2:36–48).

Babylon was not known for anything spiritually good. It was first mentioned in Genesis 11:1–9. "Babel" means "the Gate of God" and is known for the confusion of languages. It is the short form of Babylon. The city of Babylon dates back to 2300 BC and was headed by Nimrod.[3] It was started shortly after the flood and about 300 years before God called Terah (Abram's father). Nimrod was an administrator, organizer, architect, warrior, and visionary strategist[4] (Genesis 10:8–10).

The first Babylon started out as a rebellion or a substitute, an alternative for what Jehovah intended. The people wanted the things of God but not God. They wanted to find their own method of how to live forever (Genesis 11:2–4).

Genesis 11:1–9 tells the story of how the tower and the city started and were stopped, scattering the people. The Tower of Jupiter Belus was 650 feet high and a quarter of a mile square base. Archeological investigations have found a mound eleven miles north of the ruins of Babylon, the last city before it was destroyed, claiming this to be the famed Tower of Babel. Around 520 BC, the city of Babylon fell to the Persians led by Cyrus, then to the Macedonians (Alexander the Great), then to the Romans[5] (according to Daniel's interpretation of Nebuchadnezzar's dream in Daniel 2:31–40). It is believed that Ancient Egypt came out of Babylon (Babel).

The physical ancient city of Babylon is in today's Iraq. The area is controlled by Muslims who claim that Jehovah is their God, but they have no relationship with Jesus the Christ.[6] Muhammad is their prophet, who came on the scene about 570 years after Jesus of Nazareth left the earth.

Babylon fell because she had a negative influence on every nation.[7] She led the nations away from Jehovah and into worshipping false gods (Jude 7). This negative influence was seen before in the church at Thyatira (Revelation 2:19–22).

Archeological Discoveries of the First Babylon

On the west bank of the Euphrates, about fifty miles south of Baghdad, there is found a series of artificial mounds of vast extent. These are the ruins of this once famous, proud city. These ruins are principally the great mound called Babil by the Arabs, which was probably the noted Temple of Belus, a pyramid about 480 feet high, and the Kasr (that is "the palace"), which was the great palace of Nebuchadnezzar. It is almost a square, each side of which is about 700 feet long. The little town of Hillah, near the site of Babylon, is built almost wholly of bricks taken from this single mound.[8] A lofty mound, on the summit of which stands a modern tomb, is called Amran ibn-Ali. This is probably the most ancient portion of the remains of the city, and it represents the ruins of the famous hanging gardens or perhaps of some royal palace. The utter desolation of the "The glory of kingdoms" was foretold by the prophets (Isaiah 13:4–22; Jeremiah 25:12, 50:2, 3; Daniel 2:31–40).

The Roman Catholic Church today is truly universal as it is spreading false doctrines, giving worship to the wrong things and many other matters that were publicly addressed by Martin Luther in his *95 Theses* in 1517.[9]

The Third Angelic Proclamation—"the wine of the wrath of God" (vv. 9–11). The third angel warns the people of the impending danger of putting their trust in the Babylonian system and the beast as these would be destroyed. There are serious and eternal consequences for siding with Satan. This is obviously a great sin, as it carries a great punishment the same as Satan's. However, you can circumvent the punishment by your full submission and obedience to the Creator. You will eventually worship the beast if you don't promote the gospel of Jesus Christ. This can easily happen because who you fear most is who you will serve. If you are afraid to preach the gospel of Christ, then you are actually afraid of persecution. You will refuse to be openly identified with Christ (Matthew 10:32–33). You will be ashamed of or have reservations about the power of the gospel (Romans 1:16; 1 Thessalonians 1:5). This is so because you don't believe that God can deliver you from the enemy, and, therefore, you will reject the gospel for your comfort.

This is a clear warning to those who think Satan has the power to deliver them. These graphic details tell the end of the story. They are given so that those who experience them would know without a doubt what it is they are going through and why. There are no long-term benefits for taking the easy road with the beast. It is more beneficial to suffer persecution for Christ's sake for a short while than to live forever in torment. You can reign victoriously forever with Christ or live in temporary comfort for three and a half years. The choice is yours. Once you have made the decision to receive the mark of the beast, you cannot switch later. The mark is a seal and you will get the same reward as Satan and his staff.

Satan is a loser. Leave him alone! Don't be deceived!

It is proper for a judge to witness the execution of the judgment written (Psalms 149:5–9). Jesus Christ is the Lamb and the Judge. The fire and brimstone on Sodom and Gomorrah were temporary, a few hours, or maybe a full day. But this judgment prepared for Satan and his cohorts will last forever.

The Patience of the Saints

This is the season (v. 12) where the patience of the saints must be made alive. This is the season when the doers—not hearers only—are tested and rewarded for their faith and obedience to God. The three and a half years of persecution during the Tribulation are going to be so tough you will need special preparation—a fresh infilling of the Holy Spirit—to make it through. However, you can and should endure because of God's promises and the fabulous eternal benefits (Romans 8:18–19; 2 Thessalonians 1:3–7; Hebrews 12:2).

Those who abide in Christ will be the ones who manifest the faith and patience needed to overcome. The word "abide" means "to stay (in a given place, state, relation or expectancy); continue, dwell, endure, be present, remain, stand, tarry (for), thine own."[10] They will follow the Lamb wherever He goes and do whatever He says. They are faithful unto death. Jesus has already given us "the formula" on how to acquire the faith and patience necessary to overcome in those tough days. While on earth with His disciples, He told them:

"As the Father loved Me, I also have loved you; abide in My love. *[How do you abide in My love?]* If you keep My commandments, you will abide in My love, just as I have kept My Father's commandments and abide in His love." (John 15:9–10, emphasis added)

Jesus also taught His disciples, saying:

"But before all these things, they will lay their hands on you and persecute you, delivering you up to the synagogues and prisons. You will be brought before kings and rulers for My name's sake. But it will turn out for you as an occasion for testimony. Therefore settle it in your hearts not to meditate beforehand on what you will answer; for I will give you a mouth and wisdom which all your adversaries will not be able to contradict or resist. You will be betrayed even by parents and brothers, relatives and friends; and they will put some of you to death. And you will be hated by all for My name's sake. But not a hair of your head shall be lost. By your patience possess your souls." (Luke 21:12–19)

You cannot rely on your flesh and willpower alone to bring you through. How many times have you said that you would not do something, and you still did it? Your willpower alone is too weak. There are some spiritual characteristics necessary to help you overcome tough times; acquire them now. If you take Apostle Paul's knowledge which he shared with the Galatians concerning having the "fruit of the Spirit," you would be better prepared to handle the persecution when it comes.

But the fruit of the Spirit is love, joy, peace, longsuffering, kindness, goodness, faithfulness, gentleness, self-control. Against such there is no law. (Galatians 5:22–23)

Apostle Peter shared similar wisdom in 2 Peter 1:5–8.

Blessed . . . Who Die in the Lord

Being faithful to the end and dying in the Lord (v. 13) counts for much, so do not take your commitment to Christ casually. Don't take any commitment or vow—whether it be your salvation, marriage, friendship—as trivial (Numbers 30:2; Deuteronomy 3:21; Ecclesiastes 5:4–5) because your works follow you.

It is a joy (special glory) to die for and in Christ. People choose to die in battle for their nation, their gang, their political or religious belief, or some other worthy cause, but they will not receive the reward one will get for "dying in the Lord." There are eternal and glorious benefits for remaining faithful (Romans 6:8–10; Philippians 1:20–21). Among these benefits are being "blessed," happy, fortunate, and well-favored. Those who remain committed also will have "rest" from their labor, no more tribulation and persecution, and no torments in the hellfire. There is a "peace" for the righteous dead, which is not so for the wicked. "Rest In Peace" is only for the dead <u>in Christ</u>. There is no peace outside of Christ, the Prince of Peace (Isaiah 9:6–7). This blessing is recorded so that the believer may be assured of his ultimate victory over the enemy and the kingdom of darkness.

There Is a Rest for Those Who Believe

Hebrews 4:9–10 says, "There remains therefore a rest for the people of God. For he who has entered His rest has himself also ceased from his works as God did from His." This rest (Gk. *sabbatismos*, the repose of Christianity) is a type of heaven, where believers will finally have peace and tranquility. This is the type of rest promised to the children of Israel upon entering the Promised Land. But you know this did not happen in this form. You also are fully aware of all the wars, famine, confusion, stress, persecutions, etc., that are still being experienced today by believers. Furthermore, King David talked about a specific "rest day," which he himself did not experience. Therefore, this promised rest is still to come, and it cannot come now or be realized the way the world is today with all the evil that is around. This repose is for all Believers in the "new earth."

Unbelief will cause you not to enter this repose, even though God has made provisions for you to enter. Isaiah prophesied about this when he said:

> It shall come to pass in the day the LORD gives you rest from your sorrow, and from your fear and the hard bondage in which you were made to serve. (Isaiah 14:3)

Jesus, when He was rebuking the cities which rejected Him, warned them of the consequences of not repenting. He told them of the impending Judgment Day when they will have to give an account. At that time, He also offered them the true rest they are looking for; the rest that is not only for their physical bodies but for their souls also:

> "Come to Me, all you who labor and are heavy laden, and I will give you rest. Take My yoke upon you and learn from Me, for I am gentle and lowly in heart, and you will find rest for your souls." (Matthew 11:28–29)

Just as God rested from His re-creation work after six days (Genesis 1:3, 2:3), taking the seventh day as a Sabbath, there remains such a Sabbath for all Believers. Therefore, to realize this rest, there has to be a cessation of work here on earth, just as there was for our Lord Jesus and the saints who have gone on before. To enter into this rest, there has to be a judgment (qualifying factor or selection process) just as the children of Israel had to qualify to enter the Promised Land. For this dispensation, your qualifying factor is that you must believe in and accept the finished work of Jesus Christ on the cross at Calvary.

Here is a word of admonition: this is the surest and safest way out. Don't die without Jesus Christ being your Lord. Bear in mind that your judgment can come when and if you die before Christ comes again. So don't wait until you hear He is coming and then try to accept Him as your Lord. Accept Him now and enjoy the benefits of the Kingdom for the remainder of your life here on earth. No man knows when Jesus is coming again, not even Jesus Himself (Matthew 24:36; 1 Thessalonians 5:2).

The Seventh Millennium

Knowing that this repose is on the Sabbath (the seventh day), it can be assumed then that this event is near at hand. Here are some points that may support this proposition:

- The literal Sabbath today (a week or seven days) is a type of the Sabbath God used during the re-creation.
- With the Lord, one day is as a thousand years and a thousand years as one day (2 Peter 3:8).
- We are on the sixth day as the Jewish calendar is at year 5781. So there are some 219 more years in which to finish the sixth day, assuming that the Jewish philosopher Maimonides is correct. Note here that the Gregorian calendar records the current year as 2021. Consideration must be given to the fact that Jesus rose from the dead "early on the third day." We are in the early stages of the third millennium since His resurrection.
- Historically, according to the book of Revelation, we are in the seventh seal at the seventh trumpet—waiting.

The statements above are all speculations. Anyone who gives a time of Christ's coming can be considered a fool (not prudent) and should not be given any attention.

Reaping the Earth's Harvest

The Son of Man is coming again but on the cloud as prophesied (vv. 14–20). Jesus spoke of this, foretelling the beginning of the end-time (Matthew 24:29–31; Luke 21:25–28). Jesus is coming back the same way He left—on a cloud. An angel also spoke of this in Acts 1:9–11.

A cloud is a visible collection of particles of water or ice suspended in the air usually at an elevation above the earth's surface.[11] The substance is such that one can see it, feel the effects of it, an airplane can fly through it, but neither a human being nor a bird can sit on it. A white cloud in the natural means a clear day with good weather. A white/bright cloud is a symbol of the divine presence of God, His Shechinah glory (Exodus 16:10, 33:9–10; Numbers 11:25; 1 Kings 8:10–11; Matthew 17:5).

Clouds cover. They are temporary and do not last long. They block the sunrays from hitting the earth and they block humans from seeing into the heavens. Even though they are not transparent, they are not solid and, therefore, not able to sustain any weight. Yet God uses them throughout His operations. Spirits have no weight; therefore, they can maneuver about the clouds at will.

When Jesus returns to reap, He will be wearing a "golden crown" and holding a sharp sickle. During His first time on earth, He wore a "crown of thorns." He came the first time as the King of kings to establish a kingdom that will last forever not just until the end of this age (Isaiah 9:6–7). A crown of gold was synonymous with royal honor (Esther 2:17). Wearing gold typified lavish adornment and worldly luxury. Gold is the most mentioned metal in the Old Testament. It is a precious yellow metal found mostly in Arabia and Egypt in the old days and was first mentioned in Genesis 2:11–12. It was used for treasure, jewelry, decorating objects, and the making of implements because it does not rust or decay. Refined gold represents earthly riches.[12] If the elders around the throne could wear a golden crown, then Jesus can wear one also.

In His hand is a sharp sickle—not a sword or some modern-day military weapon, such as the Glock or laser. This is not like the battle of Armageddon in chapter 20. It's harvest time, the time to bring in the sanctified ones. This day has been foretold many times by numerous prophets (Matthew 3:11–12; 1 Thessalonians 4:16–17).

When the season is right there is harvest time. At this time Jesus is not coming to fight but to receive those belonging to Him. You (and everyone else) will have to give an account of your stewardship. When you go to your yard/farm, you do not go to <u>fight</u> the crops and weeds, you simply deal with them. Jesus is Lord of the harvest (Matthew 13:24–30; Luke 10:1–3). Jesus will do the judging at the end-time (John 5:22–24; Acts 17:31; Romans 2:16).

Two more angels to go, one is a harvester and the other has power over fire. This might explain firstly why some cultures have a god for this and a god for that, and secondly why Jehovah is known as the God who answers by fire. Meanwhile, another of Isaiah's prophecies is being fulfilled, Isaiah 63:1–6.

CHAPTER 15

Revelation 15 and 16—the Bowls of the Wrath of God

C LEARLY, AN ERA has ended, now a new dispensation begins—judgment. The harvesting or separation has already taken place (see 14:14–20). The saints who overcame are now in Heaven standing around the throne playing harps and singing. Those who are left on the earth are those whose names are not written in the Lamb's Book of Life and have given themselves over to the kingdom of darkness. These are followers of the antichrist and the enemies of the church of Jesus Christ.

Angels will carry out the wrath of God. Our gracious and loving Father God has wrath. Is this the One who so loved the world that He gave His only Son? Yes! When you reject Jesus Christ, you are rejecting God's provision for your salvation.

> "And as Moses lifted up the serpent in the wilderness, even so must the Son of Man be lifted up, that whoever believes in Him should not perish but have eternal life. For God so loved the world that He gave His only begotten Son, that whoever believes in Him should not perish but have everlasting life. For God did not send His Son into the world to condemn the world, but that the world through Him might be saved." (John 3:14–17)

God is not only love, He is also just, holy, and righteous. The doors for mercy and grace have been shut at this time. The Grace Dispensation is now over (John 1:14–17). God has to keep His word; remember He is just (Numbers 23:19; Ezekiel 18:20–21; Romans 6:23). When you work, you must be paid; otherwise, it is not justice.

Bear in mind that it is God who created evil, and He will use it for His purposes. When Jehovah says that He will destroy a nation or a people, He does so by using His own devices and power. Jehovah told Prophet Isaiah that "I form the light and create darkness, I make peace and create calamity (evil, adversity, affliction, wickedness); I, the Lord, do all these things" (Isaiah 45:7). Not all calamities are of Satan. Yes, God gave man the wisdom to make deadly viruses, swords, guns, bombs, and killer drugs (Isaiah 54:16).

The Wrath of God

The "wrath of God" is the "violent passion (ire, or [justifiable] abhorrence); by implication punishment; anger; indignation or vengeance physically expressed."[1] It is the righteous indignation released from the Creator against the willful and deliberate wickedness of mankind towards Him. It is the natural expression of His justice and holiness towards sin, rebellion (1 Samuel 15:23). To put it simply, the wrath of God is the reward of the wicked (Deuteronomy 29:24–28). As dear as the children of Israel were to Him, He punished them (Psalms 107).

The "wrath of mankind" is "passion (as if breathing hard): fierceness; indignation and wrath."[2] A mild example of this would be King Xerxes towards Vashti. The wrath of man is unjustifiable and can be avoided. It is grossly expressed in the senseless killings you see today in hate crimes, revenge, greed, jealousy, etc. To express the love of God, you must control your response when dealing with persons who offend you.

"Be angry, and do not sin": do not let the sun go down on your wrath, nor give place to the devil. (Ephesians 4:26–27)
See also Romans 12:19–21; James 1:19–20.

There are many warnings of the wrath of God to come. Everything and everyone will be judged. Every prophecy God gave must be fulfilled (Zephaniah 1:14–18; Matthew 3:7–10; Luke 21:22–23). The wrath of God is coming. If you don't have Jesus Christ, then you have the wrath of God.

"He who believes in the Son has everlasting life; and he who does not believe the Son shall not see life, but the wrath of God abides on him." (John 3:36)
See also Romans 1:18–19; 2 Thessalonians 1:7–10.

The wrath of God is revealed already. It's for the unbeliever, the ungodly, and the unrighteous. Your judgment is based on how you dealt with Jesus Christ and not on how you kept the laws or how good you have been. Other gods have no influence at this time, only Jesus Christ. The wrath of God is for everyone, no partiality whatsoever. The Jews and so-called Christians get no special favors. God's wrath is not released on Believers in Christ Jesus, neither is it for those who remain steadfast in the faith (overcomers). But it is released on the sons of disobedience, sinners, and the unsaved. This wrath is against all those who innocently, ignorantly, or intentionally hampered, discredited, resisted, negated, discouraged, perverted, persecuted, blasphemed, or opposed the Kingdom of Heaven in any form or fashion (Matthew 18:2–6, 23:13). You can avoid the wrath of God.

But to those who are self-seeking and do not obey the truth, but obey unrighteousness—indignation and wrath, tribulation and anguish, on every soul of man who does evil, of the Jew first and also of the Greek; but glory, honor, and peace to everyone who works what is good, to the Jew first and also to the Greek. For there is no partiality with God. (Romans 2:8–11)

See also 1 Thessalonians 5:9–10; Colossians 3:5–7.

The Temple in Heaven Was Opened

The temple of the tabernacle of testimony (witness) in Heaven is now open (15:5). John is familiar with the Tabernacle of Moses and the Temple of Solomon because he was a Jew and acquainted with the religious culture. A tabernacle can be a hut, tent, or dwelling place with the ability to be moved.[3] A temple is a sacred building, an edifice or place dedicated to the service or worship of a deity.[4] Amazingly, there is a temple in Heaven with the Ark of the Covenant and other artifacts in it. Earth had a replica of it as a tabernacle and as a temple. God gave Moses specific measurements and materials to use when constructing the tabernacle (Exodus 26). The idea was to replicate something here on earth that represents the one in Heaven. The instruments, furniture, and articles of the earthly temple are in the heavenly temple. The allusion here is that along with the earthly tabernacle there is a heavenly (celestial) tabernacle, one not made with hands (Acts 17:24; Hebrews 9:11, 24).

In the tabernacle of testimony on earth, the high priest made intercession on behalf of the saints. The blood of bulls and lambs was used to cover sins. The Father is about to answer their prayers which were offered by their High Priest. Where the saints are now, there is no more fear whatsoever of the enemy.

Out of the temple (in Heaven) come seven angels dressed in pure white linen and girded with gold bands/sashes across their chest. The fine linen is the righteous act of the saints (Revelation

19:8). They were about to do "dirty work" yet were dressed in white and not expected to get dirty. Just as the priests in Moses's tabernacle wore clothing which had significance because of the color, shape, material, etc., so it is here also, if only to highlight the presence of organized structure, uniformity, and oneness (Leviticus 16:3–4). The priests' regalia were for "glory and beauty" (Exodus 28:2–4).

Each one of the angels is bearing a plague (15:6). The seven plagues were already determined and prepared for execution, but it would have been too intense to administer them at one time (in one shot). The release of the plagues is the answer to the prayers of the saints. The angels are given golden bowls which are full of the wrath of God.

In the earthly temple, there were strict protocols and procedures for entering the temple. Certain people could not enter at all while other people could only access specific areas. The priests needed blood and incense (artificial cloud/smoke) to enter. A sense of dread accompanied anyone who went in there. Nowadays, because of what Jesus did in becoming the Passover Lamb, anybody can go into the temple of God. Jesus calls it "the House of Prayer"; therefore, He had to clean it out. It is cleansed, so it is now open.

> "Also the sons of the foreigner
> Who join themselves to the Lord, to serve Him,
> And to love the name of the Lord, to be His servants—
> Everyone who keeps from defiling the Sabbath,
> And holds fast My covenant—
> Even them I will bring to My holy mountain,
> And make them joyful in My house of prayer.
> Their burnt offerings and their sacrifices
> Will be accepted on My altar;
> For My house shall be called a house of prayer for all nations."
> (Isaiah 56:6–7, emphasis added)

See also Matthew 21:12–13.

The Shechinah presence is now in the temple, but nobody can enter until the plagues are completely administered (performed, concluded). This is a reminder of what happened with Moses and King Solomon. The presence of the Lord (holiness, righteousness, justice, and truth) is not easy to deal with. When His glory fills the place, nothing can stand in God's presence.

> Then the cloud covered the tabernacle of meeting, and the glory of the Lord filled the tabernacle. And Moses was not able to enter the tabernacle of meeting, because the cloud rested above it, and the glory of the Lord filled the tabernacle. (Exodus 40:34–35)
> See also 2 Chronicles 5:11–14.

Pouring out the Seven Bowls

The Dispensation of Grace is clearly over (16:1). The time for repentance is gone. Forgiveness has been given to those who asked, mercy is no longer available, all the decisions have been made, and now it is time to receive rewards for work done in the flesh. The Judgment Dispensation has begun. By this time, every soul has already chosen (by his lifestyle) which kingdom he wants to dwell in.

The pouring out (sprawling or gushing out) of wrath is to begin. Each of the seven angels has a bowl or vial containing what is to be released upon the earth. A bowl or vial is a vessel that holds anointing oil in the temple; it's a broad, shallow cup. But there is no anointing oil in the angels' bowls, just the opposite. These can be the same bowls which collected the prayers of the saints (Revelation 5:8). The earth will begin to see how defenseless it is against the power of the Almighty. The people will find themselves in the same position as the serpent did when Jehovah passed judgment on him in the Garden of Eden—helpless and bewildered with neither strength nor ammunition to counterattack. Now the left-behinders have to accept what's served to them. "To pour out" suggests that there is a supply of these items stored somewhere and held back until this day, the Day of Judgment.

> The Lord has opened His armory, and has brought out the weapons of His indignation; for this is the work of the Lord God of hosts in the land of the Chaldeans. Come against her from the farthest border; open her storehouses; cast her up as heaps of ruins, and destroy her utterly; let nothing of her be left. Slay all her bulls, let them go down to the slaughter. Woe to them! For their day has come, the time of their punishment. The voice of those who flee and escape from the land of Babylon declares in Zion the vengeance of the Lord our God, the vengeance of His temple. (Jeremiah 50:25–28)

This day is the "appointed time" for the release of the vials. When being cast out, demons would insist it is not their time (occasion, set or proper time, season) (Matthew 8:29, 11:22–24, 12:36–37). This is now their time.

> But the heavens and the earth which are now preserved by the same word, are reserved for fire until the day of judgment and perdition of ungodly men. (2 Peter 3:7)

The pouring out of God's wrath is nothing new. This was prophesied many times by His prophets. This wrath is not only for heathens but for rebellious Israel and backslidden Christians, all unbelievers (Psalms 79:5–7; Isaiah 24:21–23; Jeremiah 10:24–25; Ezekiel 21:28–32; Hosea 5:10). God has withheld His wrath in times past (Ezekiel 20:6–9), but He is a God of judgment.

The heavenly Father wants to pour out good and blessings on you also. He is not an angry God, looking for somewhere to vent His power.

> "And it shall come to pass afterward
> That I will pour out My Spirit on all flesh;
> Your sons and your daughters shall prophesy,
> Your old men shall dream dreams,
> Your young men shall see visions.
> And also on My menservants and on My maidservants
> I will pour out My Spirit in those days."
> (Joel 2:28–29)
> See also Proverbs 1:23–27; Acts 2:17–18.

The Plagues Poured Out

These are some of the same plagues released on Egypt in the days of Moses (16:2ff). The judgments during that time were to bring about repentance. This judgment is for "an eternal reward." Some theologians say that while the plagues may be literal, the people and institutions they affect are symbolic. This may be true in some cases. Barnes says that the plagues are symbolic and have already been administered. He also claims that "this noisome and grievous sore would well represent the moral corruption, the pollution, the infidelity, the atheism, the general dissolution of society, that preceded and accompanied the French Revolution (1789–1799); for that was a universal breaking out of loathsome internal disease—of corruption at the center—and in its general features might be represented as a universal plague-spot on society, extending over the countries where the beast and his image were principally worshipped."[5] This is a true preterist's approach.

In late 2019 a virus, which was labeled COVID-19, was maliciously released on the earth by man. By early 2020 the entire world was infected. Almost everything in every nation came to a halt for months. The health and life of everyone were put in jeopardy. The effects were devastating on individuals, families, health institutions, food supplies, churches, schools, businesses, economies, and governments locally, nationally, and internationally. People and things died as the virus made its way across oceans and skies. Not only did businesses, dreams, and plans die, but hope also. To survive the plague, one's entire way of life had to be revised, radically altered. One "plague" brought all this physical death and socio-economic destruction; imagine the global effects if there were six more to follow.

First Bowl poured out upon the earth and causes loathsome sores upon those who received the mark, pain and agony but no death. Supposing that Barnes is correct, then that explains why the continual moral decay and growth in atheistic behaviors are present in our societies globally. However, Barnes's symbolic explanation involving his French Revolution theory does not hold true for the effects of the other bowls.

Second Bowl poured out upon the sea. It takes on the appearance of a dead man's blood, and every soul dies. In the trumpet stage of wraths (Revelation 8:8), the passage says that "the sea became blood," but here the passage says that "it became as the blood of a dead man." A suggestion can be that a massive, very catastrophic military conflict, a blood-related disease, or an explosion involving many people took place on the seas, and there were no survivors. No mention was made of marine life as with the trumpet stage.

Third Bowl poured out upon all the other waters. Everything turns to blood, which those left behind have to drink as retribution for the blood of saints that was shed innocently. All the sources for regular drinking water produce blood instead;

the water became blood. This appears to be a replay of the meeting between Moses and Pharaoh in Egypt, as such an event has not yet happened (been reported) on the earth. Here a preterist would say that this, too, is symbolic because of the unlikeliness of water everywhere becoming blood.

The next two plagues are in the heavens. Satan's kingdom is presently in the air above the earth in the first heaven. He will eventually end up <u>on</u> the earth or <u>in</u> the earth. Satan's kingdom will continue to fall lower and lower.

> And you He made alive, who were dead in trespasses and sins, in which you once walked according to the course of this world, according to <u>the prince of the power of the air</u>, the spirit who now works in the sons of disobedience. (Ephesians 2:2, emphasis added)
> See also Ephesians 6:12; Revelation 9:1–2, 12:7–9.

<u>Fourth Bowl</u> poured out upon the sun (causing an intense global warming). Men are scorched with fire. The gruesome pain and prolonged discomfort they must endure cause them to retaliate with all they have—talks. Rather than repentance or submission being the outcome, they blaspheme God. They speak impiously (lacking reverence) because their hearts are already fixed in rebellion mode, and they know that the period for repentance is over. Their behavior clearly suggests that they are proud of the stand they took but upset about their bad decision and God's faithfulness.

<u>Fifth Bowl</u> poured out upon the throne of the beast resulting in darkness and more pain. There is no mention of the plagues previously released having been recalled or stopped. The beast's kingdom is one of darkness. However, this darkness took away every visible thing, leaving the left-behinders completely obscured (hidden, confused, and blind) (Exodus 10:21–23). They used self-inflicted pain in an attempt to comfort

themselves from the pain of the plagues. Still no remorse from them; instead, only more verbal insults and profanities.

Sixth Bowl poured out upon the great Euphrates River. It dried up, making the entire globe accessible by foot (for groundworks as with the children of Israel leaving Egypt). Is this really a plague if only the river dries up? Let's see:

o   The water supply is dried up causing a national panic and displacement of people because there is no water for drinking and bathing and no seafood, etc.

o   People have to settle all their problems in the flesh with money, witchcraft, deception, and aggression. They are thinking: "This is just another problem that needs fixing."

o   The people are now ready to fight against Jehovah. "Let's go put a stop to this foolishness!" Satan, the carnal military powers, and the counterfeit church powers (magicians and sorcerers) will now join forces to fight for control of the earth. They think that the earth is theirs and not the Lord's. However, the Lord has already promised it to "the righteous" and "the meek" (Psalms 24:1–2, 37:29, 37:34–36; Matthew 5:5).

The wicked in their sinful nature and religious indifferences have hardened their hearts to challenge the Creator for His earth. They want to continue their sins without accountability to and interference from the righteous Judge.

The coming of the lawless one is according to the working of Satan, with all power, signs, and lying wonders, and with all unrighteous deception among those who perish, because they did not receive the love of the truth, that they might be saved. And for this reason God will send them strong delusion, that they should believe the lie, that they all may be condemned who did not believe the truth but had pleasure in unrighteousness. (2 Thessalonians 2:9–12)

Frogs as Demons

"Three unclean spirits like frogs" (16:13), having been classified as demons, will perform signs and wonders as they try to replicate Jehovah. The first time that frogs are mentioned in the Scriptures is in Egypt when Moses was trying to get Pharaoh to let the children of Israel go (Exodus 8:5–8). We hear no more about frogs until now. These demonic religious spirits represent:

- the dragon (paganism) and have nothing to do with Jesus Christ;
- the beast (Roman Catholicism), who wants to take the place of Jesus Christ; and
- the false prophet (diluted Christianity) which consists of pagan practices, backsliders, hypocrites, the unfaithful, false doctrines, a form of godliness, and those fascinated by evil and paranormal activities.

Deception is one of Satan's power weapons, causing kings and people to continue to put their trust in him. They think he can deliver them from the wrath of God. Expect the pope and others to begin working make-believe miracles and lying wonders. Consider that seducers are more deadly than persecutors (2 Corinthians 11:13–15).

Jesus Is Coming!

Out of the blue, a quote by Jesus is placed in the middle of the script. He says, "Behold, I am coming as a thief. Blessed is he who watches, and keeps his garments [on], lest he walk [about] naked and they see his shame" (16:15). This is not prophetic but simply information and wisdom. He has said on numerous occasions, and this was repeated by His disciples, that He is coming again to the earth "as a thief" or as one who steals (Matthew 24:42–44; 1 Thessalonians 5:2; 2 Peter 3:10; Revelation 3:3). When is He coming? I don't know. He Himself does not know. This much is known: as a thief comes prepared to steal from you, He is coming when you least expect Him. Therefore, you have to be on your guard always. Remember the ten virgins of Matthew 25:1–13.

> "But of that day and hour *[instant, season, time]* <u>no one knows</u>, not even the angels of heaven, but <u>My Father only.</u>"
> (Matthew 24:36, emphasis added)
> See also Acts 3:20–21.

Prominent Signs of Jesus's Coming

There is an element of surprise here. With all your intelligence and apocalyptic knowledge, you will not be able to figure out the exact time of His coming. Whatever time you have concluded as the time of His coming is definitely the time He is not coming. However, there are some telltale signs you can look for first. As all of these signs are not yet present, there is still more time to wait.

- The sun will be darkened while it is daytime just as when He was crucified:

> "Immediately after the tribulation of those days the sun will be darkened, and the moon will not give its light; the stars will fall from heaven, and <u>the powers of the heavens will be shaken.</u> *[What are these powers?]* <u>Then the sign of the Son of Man will appear in heaven</u>, and then all the tribes

of the earth will mourn, and they will see the Son of Man coming on the clouds of heaven with power and great glory." (Matthew 24:29–30, emphasis added)

(Some scholars say that the darkening of the sun and the moon, and the falling of the stars are not literal but an attempt to picture how drastic and devastating the times will be.)[6]

- There will be a noticeable falling away of saints from the kingdom, a general apostasy. This can come in the form of a subtle departure from sound doctrine—from preaching Jesus Christ and the Kingdom of Heaven to mixing paganism with Christianity, honoring other gods or having more than one god, etc.,—and not so much as a lot of people leaving the church. Simply present an all-inclusive gospel and the church stays full. Today it is common to find lodge members, witchcraft workers and their clients, gamblers, corrupt business people, adulterers, homosexuals, the sexually immoral, and the like either leading a local church or heading a department therein. The membership will know of these ill-repute characters and still sit in that congregation. Therefore, a falling away of saints from the kingdom may not be as noticeable as expected.

The church has some things right, but there are some wrong things also as far as Jesus is concerned. This was made clear in Revelation 2 and 3 when Jesus addressed the various churches, stating their credits and what they must change if they want to be relevant to His Kingdom. Today some churches have become social clubs, business or economic empowerment centers, status symbols, and everything else except an embassy of the Kingdom of Heaven.

The influence of spiritism (deception, lies, signs, and wonders) and the spirits of devils are busy at work in the churches. These worked on Eve and Adam causing them to deliberately disobey God. The victims (or participants) of spiritism seem bewitched as they would do very unbecoming things and make strange decisions.

> Now, brethren, concerning the coming of our Lord Jesus Christ and our gathering together to Him, we ask you, not to be soon shaken in mind or troubled, either by spirit or by word or by letter, as if from us, as though the day of Christ had come. Let no one deceive you by any means; for that Day will not come <u>unless the falling away comes first</u>, and <u>the man of sin is revealed</u>, the son of perdition, who opposes and exalts himself above all that is called God or that is worshiped, so that he sits as God in the temple of God, showing himself that he is God. (2 Thessalonians 2:1–4, emphasis added)

- The man of sin is revealed. The Antichrist will reveal himself as "the hope" the world is waiting for. He will sit as God and offer himself as the savior.

The Lord Is Coming, Be Patient!

> Therefore be patient, brethren, <u>until the coming of the Lord</u>. See how the farmer waits for the precious fruit of the earth, waiting patiently for it until it receives the early and latter rain. You also be patient. Establish your hearts, for the coming of the Lord is at hand. (James 5:7–8, emphasis added)

Naked and Unashamed

There was a time when being seen naked (with no clothes on) by a stranger brought shame to that naked person. The only time it did not matter being seen naked was if you were crazy (mentally deranged). Adam and Eve, who were in sin, understood that distinction (Genesis 3:7–10). However, nowadays with all the perversion and new cultural and art expressions, being naked publicly seems to be the new normal. Obviously, the naked person's senses and morals have been seared if the individual is naked in public and comfortable.

Assembling for the Great Battle at Megiddo (Armageddon)

This end-time battle at Megiddo (Hebrew *Armageddon*) is the fulfillment of the prophecy by Zechariah:

> "In that day there shall be a great mourning in Jerusalem, like the mourning at Hadad Rimmon in the plain of Megiddo." (Zechariah 12:11)

This is the place where the final battle between "The Christ and the Antichrist" will take place, the place where all disputes of every kind concerning mankind will be settled once and for all (Revelation 19:11–16). Satan is no match for Jesus Christ, the Lion of the tribe of Judah. The Gospel of Matthew's account (4:1–11) of the temptation of Jesus in the wilderness tells us that Jesus has already defeated Satan. Jesus can do it again (Ephesians 1:19–21; Luke 10:17–19). This battle will mark the end of civilization as we know it. This method of physical combat for land is not strange at all. Land disputes are usually settled by wars (e.g., King David and the Philistines). Military and economic supremacy are settled by wars. Acquisition of rights and privileges is by wars. The natural resources are in the land; therefore, land is a must-have. A king must have land to set up his kingdom and establish his sphere of control. Every kingdom has invested in military concerns somewhere along the line.

To get rid of your enemy, you must destroy him or enter a league with him. Invasions are accomplished by military strength and not through passivity. Battles are how nations take spoils, increase their wealth, gain global influence, and promote their agenda. The Egyptians, the Babylonians, the Greeks, the Romans and others conquered the world by initiating warfare. Confrontation must take place to establish authority.

Megiddo ("a place of troops") is the place specifically named for the battle. For this prophecy to be fulfilled, the battle must take place here. Therefore, if no battle has taken place here, then this stage of the end-times has not yet come. Megiddo was originally a royal Canaanite city. The plain or valley of Megiddo was part of the south-western plain of Esdraelon, overlooking the valley of Jezreel, the great battlefield of Palestine. It extends from the Mediterranean Sea to the Jordan River between Carmel and Samaria to Galilee.[7] Yes, Megiddo is a real place:

- Joshua conquered the king there and gave it to Manasseh (Joshua 12:21).
- Judge Deborah and Barak defeated General Sisera there (Judges 5:19).
- King Solomon built a wall around it (1 Kings 9:15).
- Judah's King Ahaziah died there (2 Kings 9:27).
- Pharaoh Neco killed Judah's King Josiah there (2 Kings 23:29–30).

The Seventh Bowl Is Poured Out

Seventh Bowl poured out into the air. The angel poured the bowl into the atmosphere. This was not localized like the others but global (affecting the air, land, and seas) as the winds carried it, covering the entire earth's atmosphere instead of a particular location.[8] What was in that bowl? This brings to mind the modern-day chemical warfare and biological weapons where poison (bacteria, viruses, spawns, etc.) is pumped into the water (air) that will carry a menace to the masses. The earth was utterly shaken with noises, thunder, lightning, and a massive earthquake. Whatever was the nature of the substance, it triggered many things in the atmosphere. It affected the weather, the heavens, the terrestrial landscape, the foundation of cities, and activated the armory of Heaven. This was topped off by a great plague of hail (twelve-inch or thirty-centimeter ice balls)[9] which fell from heaven upon the men. Are these ice balls symbolic or literal?

As a result of these catastrophic "natural" disasters, which God initiated, the people blamed God because they knew that He had a hand in causing them. Thus, they wanted to fight to get "their" earth back so that they could continue to live as they wished. But the pouring out of the seventh bowl had killed many of them already.

Cities of other nations fell with special attention to Babylon to give her a special dose of His wrath. No nation was spared, every world system fell, and every political, economic, social, academic, religious, cultural, and civic institution fell. The global catastrophe was followed by fear and panic.

The islands were covered up by water as if they had sunk and the mountains became a plain as if they had been flattened. This act took away all the hiding places and shadows to expose everything in the open (Isaiah 28:17; Job 38:22–23).[10] The land will disappear—maybe because of "climate change"—as a result of the fourth bowl being poured out or the effect of the great earthquake.

Even though the people are assembled for battle—and a lot of them have died already—the combat does not take place until later.

CHAPTER 16

Revelation 17—the Scarlet Woman and the Beast

THE STAGE FOR this scene is the earth. Here you will see the judgment of the pagan religious system which has been dominating the earth since civilization began and the counterfeit religions which have been perpetuating its work. These religions are so old and very much accepted that they have been institutionalized. You will also see the fall and disintegration of the political, cultural, and economic systems which have been sustaining the counterfeit religions.

Who Is the Harlot?

"Harlot" in Hebrew is the word *zanah* (zaw-naw'), which means one who commits adultery (usually of the female, and less often of simple fornication, rarely of involuntary ravishment); to commit idolatry; commit fornication continually, play the whore, whoredom, go a-whoring, whorish; a prostitute. The Greek for harlot is *porne* (por'-nay), a strumpet, an idolater, whore.[1] Harlots have been around since the early fathers (see the story of Judah and Tamar) and have always played a role in the history of Israel (see stories of Rahab, Gomer, and Samson's wife). Some harlots repented of their lifestyle while others remained in their sinful state. The ones who repented entered the Kingdom of God (Matthew 21:31–32).

In the Old Testament the nations of Israel and Judah are referred to as harlots because according to Jehovah, they slept with or worshipped other gods. Since one cannot be faithful to more than one partner (or one god), persons who had more than one partner were considered harlots (Leviticus 17:7; Jeremiah 3:1). Adultery and idolatry were put in the same category and treated the same way because they both gave worship to the wrong entity (Hosea 4:17–18). God hates them both.

> "Nevertheless I have a few things against you, because you allow <u>that woman Jezebel</u>, who calls herself a prophetess, to teach and seduce My servants to commit sexual immorality and eat things sacrificed to idols. And I gave her time to repent of her sexual immorality, and she did not repent." (Revelation 2:20–21, emphasis added)

The harlot's job is to get you to go after the wrong things. She is still employing the same tricks used on Adam and Eve and throughout the ages—deception, easy way out, outright lies, half-truths, disbelief, the satisfaction of the flesh, lust for power, wealth, and long life. Satan tried some of these enticements on Jesus to no avail (Matthew 4:1–11).

Many theologians who have written on the end-time have classified the Roman Catholic Church or Papal Rome, a very old worldwide religious order as the harlot.[2] The word "catholic" means "universal." Therefore, that church can be called the "Roman Universal Church."

On October 31, 1517, Martin Luther posted his *95 Theses* on the door of the All Saints' Church in Wittenberg, Germany.[3] He was not the first to openly challenge the RCC, but his protest was the foundation for what was to be called the Protestant Reformation. His document protested against clerical abuses, especially nepotism (favoritism, bias), simony (profit from selling of sacred things), usury (lending money at exorbitant rates), pluralism (entertaining more than one standard), and the sale of indulgences (the remission of the temporal punishment still due to sin after it has been forgiven). These abuses were practiced without regard for the written Word of God (the Holy Bible). For this, the RCC was known as "a pagan church."

The Roman Catholic Church presents a counterfeit religion.[4] Whereas the first Babylon was built by Nimrod to replace Jehovah (see Revelation 14), the RCC keeps her people away from worshipping Jehovah. She does this by requiring them to pray to and worship idols, statues, dead saints, and man-made doctrines and to practice witchcraft.

There are other apostate churches today (1 Timothy 4:1–2). Jehovah's Witnesses (JW), Latter-Day Saints (LDS), Unity Church, Christian Science (CS), cults, and seeker-friendly churches are a few of them. All these are harlots. Do not focus on the RCC alone for leading its members astray. Any church that denies Jesus of Nazareth as the Christ or has the spirit of the antichrist can fit in this category (1 John 2:22, 4:2–3).

> But know this, that in the last days perilous times will come: For men will be lovers of themselves, lovers of money, boasters, proud, blasphemers, disobedient to parents, unthankful, unholy, unloving, unforgiving, slanderers, without self-control, brutal, despisers of good, traitors, headstrong, haughty, lovers of pleasure rather than lovers of God, having a form of godliness but denying its power. And from such people turn away! For of this sort are those who creep into households and make captives of gullible women loaded down with sins, led away by various lusts, always learning and never able to come to the knowledge of the truth. (2 Timothy 3:1–7, 13–15)

The Harlot Sits on a Beast

John is carried away in the Spirit into the wilderness—not into the city, but to a solitary place, a desolate place in the desert—so he can see the judgment of the great harlot. The harlot is seated (comfortably placed, riding) on many waters (peoples, multitudes, nations, and tongues). She has a seat on (has great influence over) the United Nations and the European bloc as one would sit while riding a horse, having full control. She is not only interested in individuals and families but nations. Between the RCC and the leaders of nations, there has been an inordinate relationship, fornication. With her false doctrines, immoral practices, lies, deceptive policies, outright wickedness, sexual abominations, and witchcraft, she has caused the nations to be drunk, senseless, and unable to make proper decisions. As a drunk man does not make sound judgments, so are the nations which are controlled by the harlot (Proverbs 20:1; Isaiah 28:7–8).

The name written on the woman's forehead—"MYSTERY, BABYLON THE GREAT, THE MOTHER OF HARLOTS AND OF THE ABOMINATIONS OF THE EARTH"—is so derogatory even though it describes her perfectly (v. 5). A person usually gives herself a name that would encourage others to think well of her. But because she is evil and proud of her destructive accomplishments, she wears the repulsive name gladly and with honor. According to where her name is displayed, she is boasting, flaunting who she is and what role she played in the earth all these centuries. She was a mystery to a lot of unsuspecting people, especially those who faithfully followed her despite being made aware of her evil practices and false doctrines. The harlot can only be a mystery to those who didn't believe the Holy Bible or didn't go to the heavenly Father for themselves.

Mystery

A mystery is a truth undiscoverable except by revelation; long hid, now made manifest (Colossians 1:26–27). It is that which needs to be explained or cannot be understood by finite intelligence. There are a few organizations which identify themselves as reflecting mystery or doing mysterious deeds. Some of them are freemasonry, lodges, KKK, Illuminati, fraternities, and sororities, those who hide from the public and work in darkness.[5]

Some say that Jesus used mysteries in His ministry when He spoke in parables. However, there are other opinions. A parable is an earthly story with a spiritual significance. Parables are not meant to hide but to reveal that which is hidden. Jesus did a lot of teachings in parables so as not to confuse the listeners or hide truths from them. He wanted to provoke them to examine and understand His teachings so that their lives would be dramatically changed for the better (Isaiah 6:9–10; Matthew 13:11–17; Mark 4:10–12). As a believer, you are supposed to know the secrets of the Kingdom.

> He reveals deep and secret things; He knows what is in the darkness, and light dwells with Him. (Daniel 2:22)
> See also Isaiah 45:11.

When truth is hidden from you, the intent is to deceive you or to keep you in darkness. When a mystery is hidden from you, it should provoke you to be diligent and search for answers. According to Daniel, a dream can be classified as a mystery. Only the Creator can reveal mysteries. The kings of Babylon experienced this (Daniel 2:2–22).

The Scarlet Beast

The scarlet beast is similar to the leopard in Revelation 12 but is not the same. This beast (a power-wielder who is most likely connected to the RCC) was prominent in one season but disappeared from the scene for a while. He will come out of the bottomless pit (the abyss) and have an authoritative spell again but will eventually end up in perdition (eternal damnation, destruction, the final state of the wicked). Because he comes out of the bottomless pit you know that he is evil.

"The waters" is the United Nations. Smith says it is the United States of America.[6] This beast is not from Asia, Africa, or Europe but from a place not known to the world at that time, thus "the waters" or overseas. The Western world came into being in the fifteenth century and the UN was organized in the 1940s.[7] Therefore, most of the eschatologists before the sixteenth century would not have correctly factored the UN or the USA as this beast.

The woman (the harlot) arrayed in purple and scarlet is the RCC, whose dominant colors are purple and scarlet worn by the pope and the cardinals respectively.[8] In his day, Apostle Peter referred to Rome as "Babylon" (1 Peter 5:13).

"And the woman whom you saw is that great city which
reigns over the kings of the earth," (Revelation 17:18)
See also Revelation 17:15–17.

Scarlet (worm, an artificial color)—even though it is proudly worn by people of status in religious and political circles—is called by God the color of sin.

"Come now, and let us reason together,"
Says the Lord,
"Though your sins are like scarlet,
They shall be as white as snow;

Though they are red like crimson,
They shall be as wool.
(Isaiah1:18)

Persons to be honored by a king were robed in scarlet. A scarlet robe,[9] representing royalty, was mockingly placed on Jesus by the Romans after He was stripped of His seamless robe (Matthew 27:27–29; John 19:23). This robe symbolized the reality that Jesus was temporarily clothed in sin. The Old Testament priests wore blue, purple, and scarlet. Thus, the RCC, in trying to replicate the early temple, chose to wear these colors also.

Purple also is an artificial color; its dye was costly to make and therefore rare. This made it hard to come by and highly valued by the Jewish people (Exodus 26:1; 27:16; Luke 16:19). Thus, it was reserved mostly for religious ceremonial purposes.[10] The RCC pope and all the cardinals also wear expensive jewelry about their necks and fingers.

The golden cup full of abominations is the accomplishment of her efforts to deceive nations and pollute the earth with perversion and rebels who adamantly oppose anything righteous, just as the nation of Rome did before it was conquered and destroyed. The golden cup should have had purity and truth in it, but instead it was filled with wickedness (the filth of her fornication).[11] Jesus, as the Messiah, has a cup also. In contrast, His cup has His own blood, which is represented by the fruit of the vine. It is not real blood like the harlot has in her cup.

Then He took the cup, and gave thanks, and gave it to them, saying, "Drink from it, all of you. For this is My blood of the new covenant, which is shed for many for the remission of sins. But I say to you, I will not drink of this fruit of the vine from now on until that day when I drink it new with you in My Father's kingdom." (Matthew 26:27–29, emphasis added)

John Marveled in Amazement

She had so much of the blood of the martyrs of Jesus and had gained it so easily that she could have drunk it all day long; she had enough to be stupefied by its excess and consumption. John was amazed because he saw what was supposed to be the Church (the RCC, which professes to be for Jesus Christ) actually leading the war against Christians and the Kingdom of God. He was amazed by who the harlot actually is, a great deception all along. Babylon was known for high levels of moral corruption and as the mecca for idolatry and sorcery, anything that is anti-God.[12]

The left-behinders will marvel because they thought they were doing the right thing. Their high level of sincerity and commitment to the Church, and its leaders (not to God and His Word) made them believe their names were in the Book. Know that you can be very sincere about what you are doing and still be sincerely wrong. Their amazement will heighten when they see who it was that deceived them: someone and the institutions they so deeply trusted (Acts 17:11–12; 2 Timothy 2:15).

Seven Heads, Seven Mountains

This matter is not easily understood by the natural mind (v. 9). Therefore, interpretation from the Creator Himself—Holy Spirit—is necessary for true understanding (Daniel 5:11–12).

John gives an understanding of who the woman is and what she is doing. The woman here is the second woman mentioned in this book. The first was "the true church" with new saints as her baby (Revelation 12:1–2). The other woman (the harlot) is sitting on—ruling over, having under her full control—the seven seats of power in society. She is "the counterfeit church," which is also identified as Papal Rome or the Roman Catholic Church. The seven spheres (mountains) of influence in any society or throughout the earth generally are the media and communication, business and finance, arts and entertainment, religion, education, government, and the family. Whoever controls these spheres also controls the nation or the world. (See chapter 11 for an earlier discussion.)

The seven mountains are seven domains or avenues from which to wield power. Seven, being the number of completion or perfection, alludes to the magnitude of its control and universal strength and influence. "The beast that was and is not" is not the same creature identified in Revelation 13:11–17. A power (institution) that was defeated earlier will rise again and take control as it did before. The civil nation of Rome was defeated, utterly destroyed, but the spiritual nation (the RCC) still lives on and will rise again to take control through the seven mountains of society. Italy is a member of the G7 and Rome is in Italy, making Rome the eighth yet one of the seven. Papal Rome will rise again to a high and lofty position and have great influence throughout the earth.[13] There is no need to fear the pope and the RCC because the saints are already taken out. Yes, they will wreak havoc like before but only for a short time. The end of the story and the good news is that "they are going to perdition."

The Ten Horns

A king represents a foundation of power, a sovereign. For the explanation of the ten kings with no kingdom, see chapter 12. Using their power in their various capacities, they are able to bring nations under subjection to the beast. A movement known as the New World Order (NWO) started in the late twentieth century, whose intention is to replace sovereign nation-states and set up an authoritarian world government. Here is an overview of the NWO:

> The common theme in conspiracy theories about a New World Order is that a secretive power elite with a globalist agenda is conspiring to eventually rule the world through an authoritarian world government – which will replace sovereign nation-states – and an all-encompassing propaganda whose ideology hails the establishment of the New World Order as the culmination of history's progress. Many influential historical and contemporary figures have therefore been alleged to be part of a cabal that operates through many front organizations to orchestrate significant political and financial events, ranging from causing systemic crises to pushing through controversial policies, at both national and international levels, as steps in an ongoing plot to achieve world domination.[14]

These world influencers get to be kings for one hour and are completely under the influence of the beast. "One hour" is a definite short season, an era. This is not sixty seconds, but it is not forever, not even a long period as there are only twelve hours in a "day". "They will make war with the Lamb" tells you what side they support, and it is definitely not the Kingdom of God's side. Therefore, when the NWO comes into your country, they are not there for your overall good but to give glory to the beast. They will persecute or try to destroy any nation that refuses to comply with their demands.

The NWO agenda is at work already on the earth. Who do you think is forcing governments around the world to promote the homosexual agenda and gender equality, to remove the middle class, to stop capital punishment, to decriminalize acts which were deemed immoral or destructive to society, to enslave and abuse the very people they said they wanted to represent – their own? Who is forcing governments to promote other religions, to encourage abortions, to increase taxes, to cause shortages in food and other goods thereby depopulating the earth, to do anything that is contrary to the Word of God (Genesis 1:28)? They will oppose the progress of Christianity. However, their campaign will not last too long. The Lamb will overcome them.

Who can stop the Lord Almighty?

The Chosen

Everybody in the Kingdom of God has been chosen (Isaiah 41:9; 1 Peter 2:9). Nobody got in by chance or error. Abraham and Joseph were chosen. The Levites were chosen (Deuteronomy 18:5). King David was chosen (1 Samuel 16:8–13). The nation of Israel was chosen. The city of Jerusalem was chosen (1 Kings 11:32). Jesus's disciples were chosen. The saints are referred to as "the elect." You are that special to God!

Change of Heart towards the RCC

The tentacles of the RCC are truly universal, touching every nation, social status, age group, academic level, rich and poor. Those who once faithfully and intentionally supported the RCC will turn against her and destroy her. This change of attitude may come in response to finding out how she had deceived and used them. After coming into the knowledge of the truth and unveiling her deception, they will see her wickedness then despise her doctrines, rituals, and practices. They will restructure their policies against her and will strip her (the pope also) of all the influence and power she once had around the world.

To "eat her flesh" (v. 16) is to take away every support and authority given. They will take away (consume) her wealth, glory, fame, beauty, and everything else that made her attractive. Her devastation will be so great that the multitudes that once believed in her will be very disappointed and will abandon her. The "burning with fire" (v. 16) is the method employed to remove every trace of her with the intent of bringing total destruction and eradication. When something is completely burned with fire, only the ashes remain, not even the bones. Nothing that remains is recognizable. Getting rid of the RCC will lead one to think that all the evil is gone. However, the antichrist is still around waiting to make his grand entrance as "the only hope for mankind."

To Be of One Mind

The church of Jesus Christ must be of one mind even as the world strives towards unity. The church must be of one mind before Christ returns. A living body cannot be divided and still function effectively. Just as the kingdom of darkness is unified, so will be the church:

> "that they all may be one, as You, Father, are in Me, and I in You; that they also may be one in Us, that the world may believe that You sent Me. And the glory which You gave Me I have given them, that they may be one just as We are one." (John 17:21–22)
> See also Acts 2:1; Galatians 3:28; Ephesians 4:3–6, 12–13.

There has to be a universal move starting in the near future which will tear down all denominational walls and unify the body of Christ. The church did not start by being fragmented and denominated. The practice of maintaining denominations is one of the divisive measures Satan is promoting to weaken the church; the divide and conquer technique. The Lord's delay may be partially because the church is still divided:

that He may send Jesus Christ, who was preached to you before, whom heaven must receive <u>until the times of restoration of all things</u>, which God has spoken by the mouth of all His holy prophets since the world began. (Acts 3:20–21, emphasis added)

God will <u>allow</u> a lot of things "until His purposes and His Word are fulfilled." Noah preached for 120 years until the time was fulfilled. The children of Israel lived in slavery for 430 years until . . . The children of Israel wandered in the wilderness until . . . The children of Israel lived in Babylon for 70 years until . . . Jesus Christ is not coming back until . . .

Yes, everything can change, no matter how long they have been in existence.

CHAPTER 17

Revelation 18—the Fall of Babylon

I N CASE YOU missed the first announcement in Revelation 14, the message is released again, "Babylon the great is fallen!" The only place that can house these eerie-looking, wicked elements is a place where there are creatures who are just like them in spirit and in lifestyle. The leaders of the RCC are among them.

Babylon the Great Is Fallen!

Here we see the overthrow of the wicked. As powerful and influential as it was, Babylon was still overthrown. The wicked will fall and their entire life efforts will come to naught. It was revealed in chapter 14 that she is Papal Rome or the RCC. Its fall is the same announcement made in Revelation 14:8 by a lower-ranked angel flying in the midst of Heaven. This was a part of "the everlasting gospel" which was preached by the three angels (in a loud voice and to those who dwell on earth). The announcement made in Revelation 14 was made from the air, not from the earth, and was a prophecy or a warning, letting the people know that if they were to side with Babylon, they would be on the losing side and destined for damnation and suffering. When the first announcement was made the city was still structurally intact and saints were still living in it. What took place in Revelation 17:15–18 brought about the desolation and destruction of Babylon, the self-proclaimed "mother of harlots."

David, Isaiah, Jeremiah, and Daniel prophesied the fall of the physical city of Babylon, which actually took place about 500 years before John the Revelator was born[1] (Isaiah 13:19–22, 47:1–3; Jeremiah 25:12–14, 51:6–8). Therefore, this is not the physical city of Babylon in a discussion here in the book of Revelation as the actual city was conquered and destroyed by the Medes. This is a spiritual city, a symbol of the world's system, lived out under the guise of the RCC. This announcement (the second one) is reporting what has taken place already. John does not tell of the time lapse between the two announcements, but they are two distinct publications.

At this point, this angel is on earth shining and with great authority. The city is still somewhat structurally intact because it has now become a dwelling place for demons. This city is real because there are physical pieces of evidence of its emptiness and destruction. It is now a dwelling place for demons, a prison for every foul spirit, and a cage for every unclean and hated bird. It is amazing that people still chose to live in the city with these eerie elements; someone must tell them to get out. People become so accustomed to tolerating evil that they do not know when to quit.

Come out of That Counterfeit Church!

From what is left of the devastation, another voice is calling from Heaven for the people to get out of the shambles of that counterfeit and Christ-less religious system, to "come out from among that wicked city" just as Lot and his family had to come out of Sodom. As those who stayed in Sodom perished with it, so will those who remain in Babylon (the counterfeit church) perish. Judgment has been set against the counterfeit church (Genesis 19:12–17).

People who have a sincere heart for God are still in these counterfeit churches. There are some genuine and good people in these spiritually dead assemblies. Some of them are there to preach to the others, represent the Kingdom of Heaven, keep a light shining like a ray of hope, and give guidance to the lost leaders when requested. Noah had a purpose in the land, Lot in Sodom, Joseph for being in Egypt, Daniel in Babylon, and Jesus in Jerusalem. If you are a member of a dead church, make sure you have a purpose for being there and that you are fulfilling it. Do not be there ignorantly. Otherwise you will get what the folks of Sodom and Gomorrah got – destroyed for lack of knowledge or for not taking corrective action (Luke 17:28–33).

The counterfeit church is not the church which Jesus Christ instituted with Apostle Peter on the day of Pentecost, just the opposite. The counterfeit church has pagan worship and celebrations, recognition of strange gods and idols, acceptance of ungodly practices, activities which are contrary to the Word of God, witchcraft and sorcery, man-made feast days or holidays, and tolerance for sin and anything that will demonstrate rebellion against Jehovah. The counterfeit church is a body of people and a religious system whose practices closely resemble that of Jesus Christ and Christians but want nothing to do with the Holy Spirit, righteousness, holiness, truth, and light. This church has not only moved away from Jesus Christ but has purposely intended to lead others away also (2 Timothy 3:1–5).

Most of the denominations that came out of the RCC brought with them some doctrine or error picked up or adopted from that church. Their coming out was to do away with her pagan practices and to reform themselves so that they can get back to the original church. However, a lot of the RCC's rituals, pomp, and style of worship were copied and implemented in the so-called reformed denominations. Thus, they operated just like the RCC but without the papal power structure. Some of these denominations are the Anglican, Lutheran, and Methodist.

Do Not Share in Her Sins

The entire world system is against the church of Jesus Christ and the Kingdom of Heaven. This includes every facet of the world's system with no exception. Don't expect any kind of agreement between the Kingdom and the world; they are irreconcilable (Genesis 3:15). Meanwhile, the righteous will have to live amongst the sinners on the earth until the time of harvest, the rapture (Matthew 13:24–30).

> Then God said, "Let there be light"; and there was light. And God saw the light, that it was good; and God divided *[separated; distinguished; put a difference between]* the light from the darkness. (Genesis 1:3–4, emphasis added)

There is still an opportunity to disassociate with sin and sinners. Those who were blinded before by ignorance and loyalty will be able to see the obvious wickedness and flee. This present world is not your home. You are a sojourner passing through. You are not here in the flesh forever (1 Chronicles 29:15; John 15:18–19, 17:14–19).

The city of Babel's sins also reached into Heaven and God did something about it (Genesis 11:5). However, God does not have to remember your sins (iniquities) (Psalms 25:7, 79:8–9; Isaiah 43:25–26; Hebrews 10:16–18; 1 John 1:9). The heavenly Father wants you to get rid of your sins; that is why He has given you all these opportunities to confess them and repent. Babylon will neither confess nor repent, thus destruction (2 Corinthians

5:10). When God remembers your sins, He will do something about them. The consequences are doubled for the wicked.

> They are deeply corrupted, as in the days of Gibeah. He will remember their iniquity; He will punish their sins. (Hosea 9:9)
> See also Isaiah 59:2; Matthew 16:27; Romans 2:4–9, 6:23.

Because of the abundance of wealth, good health, favors, influence, authority, power, and good times she was enjoying every day, she thought she would never have a bad day. But the contrary is true; everything and everyone will be judged by the Creator. She was wealthy because she had made the people receive "the mark of the beast" so that they can do business. Now the tide has turned and the harlot must be paid for her wickedness. She has to pay double. The level of punishment is based on the level of wickedness.

The World Mourns the Fall of the Wicked

Numerous people will weep and wail because of Babylon's downfall. They will mourn not for the city itself but for their loss of future benefits from the city. The national leaders who took part in her immoral acts and enjoyed her favors will weep. Political leaders who increased their wealth by capitalizing on her immorality and luxuries will weep. Merchants who are saddened by their loss of business will miss the abundance of easy money they used to make from trading with her. Gold, silver, precious stones, ivory, etc., are not wares for the common man but for that class of people who can afford them. Wealthy people who can appreciate the costly things in life will weep. Captains, sailors, and rank-and-file workers will lose employment. People who trade in "the bodies and souls of men" will go out of business (Ezekiel 13:20–21). Slavery, human sacrifices, human trafficking, prostitution, and entertainment (Christians thrown to the lions, gladiator contests, etc.) will cease.

Today, the more in debt (mortgage, credit notes, loans) you are, the greater slave you are to the system. Your enslavement is because you want a higher standard of living or more luxuries and you don't have the money to pay for them. Slavery can also come about because of lust and appetite, cravings (inordinate desires) for inappropriate things (Romans 1:20–27).

People are heaping up worldly treasures in the last days. They are busy chasing money and fame. This is their entire agenda, not to live abundantly but to acquire wealth and fame. They mourn because they lost money, not for the devastation their associates suffered. Be careful that you do not do this because you cannot carry money with you when you leave this world. "Get rich quick or die trying" describes a popular attitude nowadays. The saying means that you will do anything to get money. If you have a gift to make money, then use the gift to bless yourself. Also use your wealth to be a blessing to the less fortunate (Proverbs 8:20–21, 10:2–3; Matthew 6:19–21; 2 Timothy 3:1–5; James 5:1–3).

> Jesus said to him, "If you want to be perfect, go, sell what you have and give to the poor, and you will have treasure in heaven; and come, follow Me." But when the young man heard that saying, he went away sorrowful, for he had great possessions. (Matthew 19:21–22)

The sympathizing spectators will not get close at all but will mourn from a distance because her devastation will be very great and will negatively affect them. They are amazed that such a well-established and powerful city could fall when everything seemed so right about it (Proverbs 16:25). They don't want to share in her judgment and destruction. These are not religious people but rather political and business associates. No church people will mourn for her because of her gross wickedness. The mourners never thought that the "good times" will ever come to an end.

On September 11, 2001, some Muslims thought that if they destroyed Wall Street in New York, USA, America would fall. The devastation took place in one hour as the whole world watched. Wall Street is the financial center and a hub for economic influence in the United States. Even though mass destruction took place in the city, it did not fall as expected. It was not God's judgment but man's. Babylon's judgment will come and be executed quickly within one hour. The lamentation is great because nothing of her wealth is saved; all these precious things are destroyed with the city. She was amassing physical wealth instead of spiritual growth or godly wisdom.

> "For what will it profit a man if he gains the whole world, and loses his own soul? Or what will a man give in exchange for his soul?" (Mark 8:36–37)

The saints can now rejoice over Babylon's downfall and calamities. They were not allowed to rejoice over another's misfortune until now. They are commanded to rejoice over her fall. This is the first sign of celebration by the saints after a long silence. They are celebrating that justice has been done, not that the wicked have been destroyed (Romans 12:17–21). The celebration continues into Revelation 19.

> "Say to them: 'As I live,' says the Lord GOD, 'I have no pleasure in the death of the wicked, but that the wicked turn from his way and live. Turn, turn from your evil ways! For why should you die, O house of Israel?' (Ezekiel 33:11)

The Conclusion of Babylon

This marks the end of the counterfeit religion. No physical trace of the city (organization) will remain. Its entire headquarters, home base, and center of operations will be sunk in the sea after the burning. There will be no more parties, weddings, celebrations, and merrymaking like carnival (bacchanal) and Mardi Gras. There will be utter darkness like there was in Genesis 1:2. There will be no more social, cultural, economic, and political activities. There will be no more satanic religious activities—no more sorcery, obeah, witchcraft—to cause deception among the people. The evil coming through the religious order will be completely removed—no more bogus church or false religion.

> For thus says the LORD of hosts, the God of Israel: "Behold, I will cause to cease from this place, before your eyes and in your days, the voice of mirth and the voice of gladness, the voice of the bridegroom and the voice of the bride." (Jeremiah 16:9)

One thing of note was found in the ruins, it was the blood of the prophets and saints (as if they were clearly marked as such and put somewhere for safekeeping). Maybe their blood cried out from the ground like Abel's (Genesis 4:10–11). Innocent blood had been shed starting with the old prophets, then with Christ, His disciples, and throughout the Dark Ages and the Inquisitions, right up to today. The various periods of the counterfeit church (even from Old Testament times) are responsible for their deaths and had to be held accountable. This is the generation that will be judged.

> "Therefore, indeed, I send you prophets, wise men, and scribes: some of them you will kill and crucify, and some of them you will scourge in your synagogues and persecute

from city to city, that on you may come all the righteous blood shed on the earth, from the blood of righteous Abel to the blood of Zechariah, son of Berechiah, whom you murdered between the temple and the altar. Assuredly, I say to you, all these things will come upon this generation." (Matthew 23:34–36)

We are continually told to pray to the heavenly Father. He has collected the prayers of the saints over the centuries and is now ready to execute judgment or revenge on behalf of His people. The destruction of Babylon is the answer to the prayers of the saints (Revelation 5:8, 8:3–5). God answers prayers in His time because He has a master global plan; you are only concerned about yourself.

What will happen to the present Babylonian structure is what was prophesied of the former Babylon. The former Babylon was destroyed but not sunk. John's recording coincides with Prophet Jeremiah's clear word. Read Jeremiah 51:59–64 for a clear picture.

CHAPTER 18

Revelation 19—Rejoicing and the Marriage

WHILE THE PEOPLE of the world lament Babylon's destruction by the Kingdom of Heaven, after a long silence, finally the multitude begins to rejoice. The rejoicing continues from Revelation 18:20. After a long absence from Heaven because he was reporting on the activities on earth, Apostle John now returns to update on what's happening up there. The celebration of the events on earth has extended to Heaven, where high praises are being offered to Jehovah, who is referred to as "the Lord Our God." He is complimented and worshipped for having "true and righteous judgments." After a gracious display of His grace, mercy, and long-suffering, He finally judges the harlot (the counterfeit church), who had many reasons and opportunities to repent but refused to do so. God has rewarded the wicked harlot for her deeds (Proverbs 11:5; Romans 2:2–11, 6:23).

The many voices (including Jesus's, the voice of many waters) are saying that Jehovah, the Almighty One, is the "all-powerful One" and He reigns; they are giving Him the highest praise. Jesus has always been reigning in the heavens and the earth. The questions were asked, "Had Christ stopped reigning at some stage?" No! He was always King of kings and Lord of lords. "Was evil reigning in His place?" Maybe evil was reigning in your life or in certain circumstances but not overall. From the time Jesus left earth, He was reigning on His throne at the right hand of the Father, waiting (Acts 3:21).

> He said to them, "How then does David in the Spirit call Him 'Lord,' saying:
> 'The LORD said to my Lord,
> "Sit at My right hand,
> Till I make Your enemies Your footstool"'?
> (Matthew 22:43–44)
> See also Mark 16:19; Acts 2:32–36; Hebrews 12:2.

The Marriage of the Lamb Has Come

It's time to rejoice and celebrate because the wedding between the Lamb (not the Lion) and the called-out ones is about to take place. Who is this bride? She is the church, the body of saints who were received into Heaven. She is the church which Jesus started after Peter testified of His Sonship (Matthew 16:18). Christ was held in Heaven until all things were restored (made ready)—as a Bridegroom awaiting His Bride. The restoration of all things to the church means that the Bride is <u>now</u> mature and ready. Jesus had a hand in her preparations. She has been washed, cleansed, and perfected, and is now of full age. According to Dr. Bill Hamon, Bishop of Christian International, a perfect church is one where every member is in his place playing his part and not necessarily where everybody is sinless and perfect in everyday living.[1]

> And He Himself gave some to be apostles, some prophets, some evangelists, and some pastors and teachers, for the equipping of the saints for the work of ministry, for the edifying of the body of Christ, till we all come to the unity of the faith and of the knowledge of the Son of God, <u>to a perfect man</u>, to <u>the measure of the stature of the fullness</u>

of Christ; that we should <u>no longer be children</u>, tossed to and fro and carried about with every wind of doctrine, by the trickery of men, in the cunning craftiness of deceitful plotting. (Ephesians 4:11–14, emphasis added)
See also Hebrews 10:12–14.

His Bride Has Made Herself Ready

The church has to make herself ready for this great wedding. She has to do some things on her own without the groom's assistance. He wants to marry someone compatible with Himself as He cannot be unequally yoked. She is to wear fine linen, white, clean, and bright, signifying purity and righteousness. She has to take care of herself.

Christ will do anything and has done a whole lot already for His Bride to help her get ready.

- He gave her His love (John 15:9; Romans 8:35–39).
- He gave His life for her (Romans 5:8; John 15:13).
- He gave her His Spirit (Acts 2:1–4).
- He gave her commandments (Mark 12:29–31).
- He gave her gifts (Ephesians. 4:11–13).
- He gave her keys (Matthew 16:19).
- He gave her authority (Matthew 28:18–20; Luke 10:18–19) and His name.
- He forgave her of all sins and cleansed her of all unrighteousness whenever she asked (Matthew 6:14; Mark 2:10; 1 John 1:9).
- He sent ministering spirits to assist her (Hebrews 1:7).
- He disciplines her in love (Matthew 16:23; Hebrews 12:5–6).
- He gives her all things (Romans 8:31–32).

The Bride conforms to the Groom and is subjected to Him. The Groom does not do as the Bride wishes; on the contrary, she conforms to the Groom. The popular secular cliché "Happy wife is happy life" is not practiced here. That is the policy for the seeker-friendly church. The Bride does not do what she wants and has Jesus sanction it. The wife submits to her own husband. She does not have the last say, but her husband does, just as Christ has the last say in His Church. The guidelines and protocol for the relationship between Christ and His Church have already been established and made known. As part of the Church, you either submit to His guidelines or you have your own way in your own church, just as the RCC and others do. Hence, you will then be recognized as a counterfeit church and not qualified to be the Bride.

Jesus would say that if your church does not meet His established specifications, then your church is not His Church or of His kingdom. That is why the Church has to "mature" to make herself ready.

> Wives, submit *[to subordinate, be under obedience, in subjection]* to your own husbands, as to the Lord. For the husband is head of the wife, as also Christ is head of the church; and He is the Savior of the body. Therefore, just as the church is subject to Christ, so let the wives be to their own husbands in everything. (Ephesians 5:22–24, emphasis added)

He Presents Her to Himself

Reading Ephesians 5:22–33 without an understanding of Jewish culture could lead one to think that the marriage between Christ and His Church has already taken place. But the clause "that He might present her to Himself" suggests that the wedding is yet to come. Jesus is not going to marry an immature bride. She has to be perfected first.

> that He might present her to Himself a glorious church, not having spot or wrinkle or any such thing, but that she should be holy and without blemish. (Ephesians 5:27)
> See also 2 Corinthians 11:2.

She is not "glorious" (splendid, noble, gorgeous, honorable) yet as she is in preparation mode in the way Esther was for King Ahasuerus. She is, however, presently espoused (engaged, spoken for) as Mary was to Joseph (Matthew 1:18–19).

You Are Blessed If You Attend the Marriage Supper

Why are you blessed (happy, fortunate) to be at the marriage supper? To have made it this far after going through all those tribulations, persecutions, and setbacks, you are definitely blessed. You are among the "called" or invited and have accepted the invitation. You are getting the best wine and a grand reception for accepting and being ready for the feast, a truly long-awaited celebration. A wedding feast is usually joyful, celebrative, rich, and free. This is a royal wedding, so this should last for at least seven days. The music and entertainment here (praise and worship to the Lord) should not bore you but be rather festive and inspirational.

I Fell at His Feet to Worship Him

Angels (ministering spirits; all ministers of God) do not receive worship from a man. This is the proper protocol of Heaven. A fellow servant does not do obeisance to another, regardless of status. Kissing another man's ring or finger is not permitted in the Kingdom of Heaven even though it is commonly practiced here on earth.² There are many other ways to acknowledge or show respect to someone you regard as important in your life. A man with an ungodly spirit, like Nebuchadnezzar, will demand such bowing and other physical forms of worship. A demon will receive worship at any time from anybody. Satan tried to get our Lord to worship him, but he got rebuked instead.

> And he said to Him, "All these things I will give You if You will fall down and worship me." Then Jesus said to him, "Away with you, Satan! For it is written, 'You shall worship the Lord your God, and Him only you shall serve.'" Then the devil left Him, and behold, angels came and ministered to Him. (Matthew 4:9–11)

There is only one genuine object of worship on the earth. That is the Lord God Jehovah. His instructions concerning worship are clearly established (Exodus 20:3–6). The word "worship" in Greek is the word *proskuneo* (pros-koo-neh'-o). It means "to kiss, like a dog licking his master's hand, to fawn or crouch to, to prostrate oneself in homage (do reverence to, adore)."³ Be careful of folks who demand or accept false worship. Calling someone "holy father," "high potentate," "most worshipful," "illustrious one," etc., is pure blasphemy. The person who receives such worship puts himself on the level of Jehovah, or at least above other men. Doing so is contrary to the Kingdom of Heaven. Jesus Christ, the Son, came to serve (John 13:5–8, 14–15).

> Do not call anyone on earth your father; for One is your Father, He who is in heaven. And do not be called teachers; for One is your Teacher, the Christ. But he who is greatest among you shall be your servant. And whoever exalts himself

will be humbled, and he who humbles himself will be exalted. (Matthew 23:9–12)

The Spirit of Prophecy

The testimony of Jesus is the spirit of prophecy (prediction, scriptural, or other). The design of prophecy is to bear testimony to Jesus. It is not only the design but the end result. Do not expect to find Jesus Christ in every prophecy, but some prophecies do point to Him. All the saints have the testimony of Jesus. I say the greatest prophetic word is "He is coming again to rule and reign as Lord and King over the entire earth." All the Scriptures are a testimony to Jesus Christ.

The Rider on a White Horse

The scene remains in Heaven. Here, John sees a white horse with the rider called "Faithful and True" (v. 11). He is ready to judge and make war. John does not say the rider's written name, but He is called "The Word of God." John describes Him, somewhat. His eyes were like a flame of fire, and on His head were many crowns. He was clothed with a robe dipped in blood. On His robe and on His thigh a name was written, KING OF KINGS AND LORD OF LORDS. And right behind Him are the armies of Heaven, clothed in fine linen, white and clean, following Him on white horses. *(What kind of weaponry are these soldiers carrying?)* Out of His mouth comes not verbal commands as an earthly general would give for his soldiers to perform but a sharp sword that with it He should strike the nations (Hebrews 4:12; Revelation 1:16). The Rider Himself judged, ruled, and trampled down the enemy with the fierceness and wrath of Almighty God.

His army is still sitting on their horses and arrayed in their white, beautiful, and clean robes. They are dressed like this because they came to attend a marriage feast. The Rider Himself will slay the enemy with the Words that come out of His mouth (a sharp two-edged sword). If Jesus can raise the dead, multiply fish and bread molecules, and change the composition of water with His words, then He can also defeat any opposition with His words. Since the earth was recreated with words then words can do whatever else He deems necessary.

Looking down on earth, John relates the events in real-time, "Then I saw an angel standing in the sun, and he cried with a loud voice, saying to all the birds that fly in the midst of heaven, 'Come and gather together for the supper of the great God, that you may eat the flesh of kings, the flesh of captains, the flesh of mighty men, the flesh of horses and of those who sit on them, and the flesh of all people, free and slave, both small and great'" (vv. 17–18). Scavenger birds will be used to clean up the bloody mess after the quick lop-sided battle. Satan's army had been arrayed for battle at Armageddon since the pouring out of the sixth bowl. The beast, the kings of the earth, and their armies are on the ground waiting for the war to begin. Right away the beast and the false prophet are captured and cast alive into the lake of fire burning with brimstone. Everybody else was killed with the sword (Word of God). Only two were taken captive, and the birds had a party with the rest of the bodies of horses and men.

How quickly the battle is over! How easily your enemies were defeated! There was no contest. The army dressed in white never got a chance to get their robes dirty. The battle is not yours, it's the Lord's. When you put your trust in the Lord, your enemies will be conquered and destroyed (Exodus 14:13-14).

And he said, "Listen, all you of Judah and you inhabitants of Jerusalem, and you, King Jehoshaphat! Thus says the Lord to you: 'Do not be afraid nor dismayed because of this great multitude, for the battle is not yours, but God's . . . You will not need to fight in this battle. Position yourselves, stand still and see the salvation of the Lord, who is with you, O Judah and Jerusalem!' Do not fear or be dismayed; tomorrow go out against them, for the Lord is with you." (2 Chronicles 20:15, 17)

CHAPTER 19

Revelation 20—the Pit and the Millennial Reign

JOHN DOES NOT paint a picture of a long intensive battle, some kind of fierce competition, a showdown of some sort, a challenge where at some stage both sides appear to be winning before the angel takes hold of the dragon. The angel used strength to seize Satan and bind him in chains. (The dragon, the serpent of old, the devil, and Satan are one and the same.) He is bound because it is time for his judgment. Satan was never known to be a challenge when it involved Jesus and angels. If he can be physically bound or cast down, then he has a physical body, meaning that he is limited to time and space. Therefore, he cannot be omnipresent. If he is bound, not even by the King but by an angel, then he cannot be omnipotent.

Satan is finally apprehended. He was a bad bully running around loosely. Evil was allowed so much freedom for so long. Consider that he was not given this freedom to do evil but took it. Everybody has this freedom. You are free to do good or evil whenever you want (Genesis 3:22; Matthew 11:12; Luke 6:45; Acts 10:38; 1 Corinthians 14:12). Satan has the freedom to do his bidding where saints or God allow it (Job 1:6–7; Matthew 13:24–30; 1 Peter 5:8).

> "Assuredly, I say to you, whatever you bind on earth will be bound in heaven, and whatever you loose on earth will be loosed in heaven." (Matthew 18:18)

Satan moves about freely because he is the ruler (prince) of this world (John 14:30). However, he can be beaten, bound, rebuked, and resisted (Zechariah 3:2; Matthew 4:10; 1 Peter 5:9). When you submit to God, then you can resist the devil and he will flee from you (James 4:7).

The Millennial Reign

When is the beginning of this thousand years? Is it literally 365,250 days as per the present Gregorian calendar? Which calendar will be used to determine the time—Julian, Roman, Hebrew, Mayan, lunar, or solar? Is a "year" considered prophetically as a "day" is marked (Psalms 90:4; 2 Peter 3:8)? Or is it "in the fullness of time"? Remember that

1. God is outside of time (Genesis 1:1); and
2. man was originally designed to live forever (Genesis 1:26, 2:15–17).

The Bottomless Pit

Is this pit literal or symbolic? Is the New Jerusalem physical or spiritual? These are both physical places identified in the end-time that will be inhabited by people. The bottomless pit (abyss) is the abode of demons or evil spirits (see Luke 8:30–31 and Revelation 9). It is the prison for spirits who rebelled, a place different from the place of "fire and brimstone" (the place of final punishment) (Revelation 19:20). See chapter 9 for further discussion.

Key and chain, are these literal or symbolic? Today, as in millennia past, keys and chains are used to physically bind criminals and unwelcomed elements in society. But if Satan is fully/only spirit, how can he be physically bound? Remember,

Satan has a physical form just like Jesus. Verse 2 says that Satan is the devil, the serpent, and the dragon. He was put (locked up, stopped) into the pit so that he should not deceive the nations anymore, a thousand-year sentence. Why doesn't Satan flee from the impending ruin, judgment, prison? He knows the end of the story, why doesn't he repent? Because of the hardness of the heart, he has purposed to be evil in nature.

Why bind Satan in a pit? At this time, the saints are in Heaven beyond his sphere of influence and the wicked are in their grave, already deceived and punished. He is already deactivated from his evil ministry. He is considered bound because the people are beyond his reach and he can't influence them anymore. Maybe his powers are stripped, or he is immobilized physically.

The First Resurrection

The dead in Christ will live and reign with Him for a thousand years while the wicked will remain dead for that period. Only the righteous dead will be resurrected at this time. Everyone will be given a new (sinless) body which will last forever (1 Corinthians 15:50–53; Philippians 3:20–21).

> So also is the resurrection of the dead. The body is sown in corruption, it is raised in incorruption. It is sown in dishonor, it is raised in glory. It is sown in weakness, it is raised in power. It is sown a natural body, it is raised a spiritual body. There is a natural body, and there is a spiritual body. And so it is written, "The first man Adam became a living being." The last Adam became a life-giving spirit. (1 Corinthians15:42–45, 20–24, emphasis added)
> See also Psalms 16:9–10.

"Resurrection," according to the Greek understanding, is "a standing up again, a (moral) recovery (of spiritual truth): raised to life again, rise from the dead, rising again."[1] This is a New Testament word that was first used concerning Jesus Christ. One can regard the above passage as a prophecy concerning the resurrection of Christ. However, those in Christ will enjoy the same benefit. Apostle Paul gives a clear understanding of this benefit in his letter to the Romans.

> Now if we died with Christ, we believe that we shall also live with Him, knowing that Christ, having been raised from the dead, dies no more. Death no longer has dominion over Him. (Romans 6:8–9)

Your flesh-and-blood body is only good for this realm, to interact with the earth (Genesis 2:7). After the earth has been destroyed (or revamped), there will no longer be a need for the physical body as we presently know it. The righteous and the unrighteous will be given a new body. You will need a spiritual body to use for eternity.

> And many of those who sleep in the dust of the earth shall awake, some to everlasting life, some to shame and everlasting contempt. (Daniel 12:2)
> See also John 5:28–29.

The righteous will have only one resurrection, then they will live forever enjoying that which was promised by Jesus Christ—eternal life. This is why the righteous are reckoned as "blessed" (Matthew 5:2–12). The "holy" comes into play because they are "cut and set apart" for the Lord's pleasure. Eternal life was promised by Christ to His disciples.

> For God so loved the world, that he gave his only begotten Son, that whosoever believeth in him should not perish, but have everlasting life. (John 3:16)
> See also John 14:1–3.

Born Once, Die Twice or Born Twice, Die Once

This is the core message of the kingdom of God; you have to be born again (have a spiritual birth) into God's kingdom if you want to reign or have a relationship with Him. You cannot even enter His Kingdom if you don't have this second birth. When you enter God's Kingdom, you die only once. On the contrary, if you do not have the second birth, then you will die twice: once in the natural and again in the final judgment, along with Death and Hades. The second birth gets your name written in the Book of Life (vv. 13–15).

> Jesus answered and said to him, "Most assuredly, I say to you, unless one is born again, he cannot see the kingdom of God." . . . Jesus answered, "Most assuredly, I say to you, unless one is born of water and the Spirit, he cannot enter the kingdom of God. That which is born of the flesh is flesh, and that which is born of the Spirit is spirit." (John 3:3, 5–6)

Your second birth gives you eternal life through Jesus Christ. It is of the spirit and spirits cannot die. As a Believer, you are also born of God (John 1:12–13). Your belief while here on earth determines your afterlife. If you believe in Jesus Christ, making Him your personal Lord and Savior, you shall never die.

> Jesus said to her, "I am the resurrection and the life. He who believes in Me, though he may die, he shall live. And whoever lives and believes in Me shall never die. Do you believe this?" (John 11:25–26, emphasis added)
> See also John 3:18.

The Second Death

Jesus promised the saints of the Smyrna Church that if they hear and receive what the Spirit says to the Church and they overcome, they shall not be hurt by the second death (Revelation 2:11).

> "But the cowardly, unbelieving, abominable, murderers, sexually immoral, sorcerers, idolaters, and all liars shall have their part in the lake which burns with fire and brimstone, which is the second death." (Revelation 21:8)

Jesus knew no sin; therefore, He could not die (2 Corinthians 5:21). For Him to die He had to take on our sins. My belief is that death is the effect of sin and not a "debt of nature" (Genesis 2:16–17). It is but once in the natural, universal and necessary. Physical death (of the flesh) is natural, even with animals and plants. Spiritual death is not your portion if you are with God (Romans 6:23).

> And as it is appointed for men to die once, but after this the judgment, so Christ was offered once to bear the sins of many. To those who eagerly wait for Him He will appear a second time, apart from sin, for salvation. (Hebrews 9:27–28)

Satan's Second Army Destroyed by Fire

When his thousand-year prison sentence has expired, Satan will be released from the bottomless pit (vv. 2–3). He will form another army. His deception again will play a major role on the gullible pagans, using numbers (maybe three-to-one or four-to-one). Where did these people come from to form this army since the judgment and sentencing have already taken place? The unrighteous dead will be resurrected at this time (v. 5).

Gog and Magog, what are these? According to Prophet Ezekiel, Gog was a pagan prince from the land of Magog in the far north who was to bring destruction to Israel (Ezekiel 38:1–6). Some theologians say that this prophecy occurred in 168 BC when the Maccabees, Chaldeans, and Turks were overthrown by Gog's great army. Unprotected, Israel was to be invaded next, but the hand of the Lord destroyed Gog's great army by self-inflicting damage and from hailstones, while the land of Magog was destroyed by fire from Heaven.[2] However, John wrote this prophecy in AD 95, which is 263 years <u>after</u> Gog's defeat. Prophecy is history revealed <u>before</u> it happens. This means that this particular event that John wrote about has not yet happened. Apparently, John is saying that in the same manner that Gog and Magog were destroyed, God has prepared similar destruction for Satan and his great army.

There was a camp for the saints in the beloved city (Jerusalem). Satan's plan was to surround it and take it. He was confident because he had the numbers. He did not factor in fire coming down from Heaven to devour his army as it did of Gog in Magog. Jehovah is the God who answers by fire. Satan, who was recently released from prison, is now cast into the lake of fire and brimstone. He joins the beast and the false prophet, where they will be tormented day and night forever.

> But the day of the Lord will come as a thief in the night, in which the heavens will pass away with a great noise, and the elements will melt with fervent heat; both the earth and the works that are in it will be burned up. Therefore, since all these things will be dissolved, what manner of persons ought you to be in holy conduct and godliness, looking for and hastening the coming of the day of God, because of which the heavens will be dissolved, being on fire, and the elements will melt with fervent heat? Nevertheless we, according to

His promise, look for new heavens and a new earth in which righteousness dwells. (2 Peter 3:10–13)

The Great White Throne Judgment

The Lord is going to establish (comfort, strengthen, uphold) <u>His throne</u> on earth.

> Of the increase of His government and peace there will be no end, upon the throne of David and over His kingdom, to order it and <u>establish it with judgment and justice</u> from that time forward, even forever. The zeal of the Lᴏʀᴅ of hosts will perform this. (Isaiah 9:7, emphasis added)
> See also Isaiah 16:5; Matthew 25:31–34.

John finally got a better perspective of the One who sits on the great white throne, but he did not describe what he saw, except to say that His face was so awesome that everything fled from it. Moses had a similar effect on the children of Israel when he came down from the presence of the Lord (Exodus 34:29–30). Who can stand in the presence of the Lord? Death (a spirit) and Hades (hell), a holding place for the dead—both are personified—gave up the dead people who were in them (Revelation 6:8). Thus, all the dead, from all over, were now summoned before God and all the books were opened, including the Book of Life (John 5:28–29; 1 Thessalonians 4:13). The entries in these books are what will be the basis for judging and rewarding.

As part of the judgment, anyone whose name was not found in the Book of Life was cast into the lake of fire. Even Death and Hades are judged and sentenced. They were cast into the lake of fire, which is the second death. Because Death, who was a servant of God, is now destroyed, there is no longer anybody or anything to kill you; therefore, you cannot die again. (Death was activated by Adam and Eve when they disobeyed God in the garden. Before that act, there was no death.) After this judgment, mankind—those who are with Christ—will live forever without fear.

> For He must reign till He has put all enemies under His feet. The last enemy that will be destroyed is death. (1 Corinthians 15:25–26)
> "I am the God of Abraham, the God of Isaac, and the God of Jacob. God is not the God of the dead, but of the living." (Matthew 22:32).

Some global and natural signs of the end-time will not be easily discernible to all because of previous events which would have left people in a state of shock, fear, confusion, pandemonium, along with high levels of deception and sorcery, chaos, lawlessness, panic, and dismay from a reality check— "Is this actually happening?" Another event would make no difference to them.

CHAPTER 20

Revelation 21 and 22—a New Heaven and a New Earth

WHILE WALKING THE earth, Jesus instructed His disciples to pray in this manner, "Thy will be done on earth as it is in heaven" (Matthew 6:10). The end will be just like it was in the beginning with Adam with a spot of Heaven (the Garden of Eden) on earth and God dwelling with man as originally intended. There will be all the bliss but without Satan (rebellion, evil, sorcery, counterfeits, etc.), a real utopia, nirvana; genuine love, peace, rest, abundance, respect for others; and all the good stuff you have longed for.

Death and Hades are cast into the lake of fire. Satan, the beasts, and the false prophet are cast into the lake of fire. The dead whose names are not written in the Book of life are cast into the lake of fire. They all will be tormented day and night forever and ever. This puts an end to all the enemies of the saints. Evil is removed from the earth (Matthew 13:24–30).

How Long Is "For Ever and Ever?"

Today one would say "nothing lasts forever." Throughout the book of Revelation, there are many references to the phrase "forever and ever." How long is this period? How long is everlasting life (John 3:16)? According to the text, the Greek word *aionios* (ahee-o-nee-os) is used to equate the word *everlasting.* It means "perpetual, past and future as well, eternal, for ever, world."[1] The Greek word *aion* (ahee-ohn) is translated as "ever," meaning "an age, course, perpetuity, the world present and future, eternal, without end."[2] Therefore, those who have everlasting life will be living until eternity—that is a very long, long time. Similarly, those who have been sentenced to the lake of fire will be tormented for the rest of their existence. Remember that God is outside of time. Also there is no biblical reference as to how long (in years) it was between Adam's creation and the making of Eve. Neither is there time reference as to Adam and Eve living in the Garden before the Fall. Adam and Eve could have been on this planet eons *(aeons)* before their disobedience to God.

In the beginning, before all this chaos and confusion involving mankind was upon the earth, God recreated everything, and it was "very good" (Genesis 1:31). "The first heaven and the first earth" refers to the present heaven and earth and not the different levels. While there are three heavens, there is only one earth. The earth today is the same earth which was recreated in Genesis chapter 1. The recreation was necessary because the earth <u>became</u> "without form, and void; and darkness was on the face of the deep. And the Spirit of God was hovering over the face of the waters" (Genesis 1:2). The Creator then put everything in its place to make it habitable for mankind.

This earth deteriorated again because of Adam's disobedience (Genesis 2:15–17). Evil (rebellion, wickedness, mischief, wrong, adversity) had a significant influence on mankind. The ground was cursed when Adam sinned and the whole earth was made subject to corruption. During this event, Satan was on the earth and in the Garden of Eden, the spot God had set aside for mankind to dwell forever. As sin abounds, the earth and everything in it worsened, along with the life expectancy of mankind. Animals attacked man, trees didn't bear fruits, weeds grew anywhere, the weather worked contrary to mankind, the earth quaked often, demons and diseases ran rampant while man lived an increasingly shorter life span (Psalms 82:5; Romans 6:23).

About fifteen hundred years after the Fall, God saw that mankind intended to do evil (Genesis 6:5–7), so He used Noah and the "great flood" to give the earth a fresh start. However, man went directly back to the same fallen state as Adam, that of entertaining evil. What exist today are the continuation and escalation of what started after the flood. The earth has gone through a lot of physical trauma (Psalms 102:25–26; Isaiah 24:1–6). The effects of all the earthquakes, floods, hailstorms, fires, hurricanes, man-made bombs, mining, man's greed and carelessness, oil spills, global warming, improper waste disposal, and other geographical disasters have taken their toll (Isaiah 24:19–23). What about all the blood running through the streets and battlefields? It's crying out. What about the depletion of natural resources and the extinction of animal species, both of which negatively affect the global and local ecosystems? What about those heavenly bodies slamming into the earth and the air pollution? With the evil now gone, it is time for a new planet.

> "For behold, I create new heavens and a new earth;
> And the former shall not be remembered or come to mind.
> But be glad and rejoice forever in what I create;
> For behold, I create Jerusalem as a rejoicing,
> And her people a joy.
> I will rejoice in Jerusalem,
> And joy in My people;
> The voice of weeping shall no longer be heard in her,
> Nor the voice of crying."
> (Isaiah 65:17–19, emphasis added)

There Was No More Sea

The water from around the planet is gone. This is an indication of or a result of the major transformation which took place. The earth and Heaven were shifting before the great white throne judgment started (Revelation 16:12, 20, 20:11). The mountains and islands are all rearranged. The islands are gone because there is no more sea to surround them. Can you imagine, no more Nassau grouper, conch, and crawfish? Oh no! Presently, three-quarters of the earth's surface is seas. The seas caused a separation of the nations and cultures. What exists now will be unnecessary for God's purposes. Man will have a new body; therefore, he would not need the same resources.

> Are You not the One who dried up the sea,
> The waters of the great deep;
> That made the depths of the sea a road
> For the redeemed to cross over?
> So the ransomed of the Lord shall return,
> And come to Zion with singing,
> With everlasting joy on their heads.
> They shall obtain joy and gladness;
> Sorrow and sighing shall flee away.
> (Isaiah 51:10–11)
> "Assuredly, I say to you, this generation *[age, period of time]* will by no means pass away till all these things take place. Heaven and earth will pass away, but My words will by no means pass away." (Matthew 24:34–35, emphasis added)

A New Jerusalem Coming Down

You may see these words on a product "NEW and IMPROVED." They mean that the product is similar to but different from yet better than its former model. The product is not "the first one ever" but the "recently released or the last one," the latest output or the most recent model. Whether symbolic or literal, there is going to be a major change in the heavens and the earth after the final judgment, making them much different from what now exists. Apostle Peter tells us what to expect, "Nevertheless we, according to His promise, look for new heavens and a new earth in which righteousness dwells" (2 Peter 3:13). The present earth will be severely burnt, not only for the destruction of the wicked but for purification of the righteous even as gold is refined in the fire.

Along with a new earth, there will also be a New Jerusalem. The reference is to both the city (place) and the inhabitants thereof. This one is coming down from Heaven, as the former will be replaced. The old one will not be renovated. The idea is to get things back to the way they were before the Fall. There are so many changes and modifications that this one appears to be "new"—identifiable but never seen before with lots of improvements. It will be the place of abode for the saints (the Church of Jesus Christ). It is the new home of the Bride. Mankind will not be living in Heaven but here on earth (Exodus 25:8–9).

> "Let not your heart be troubled; you believe in God, believe also in Me. In My Father's house are many mansions; if it were not so, I would have told you. I go to prepare a place for you. And if I go and prepare a place for you, I will come again and receive you to Myself; that where I am, there you may be also." (John 14:1–3)

God Is with Man

Of the whole creation, why did God choose the earth to dwell at this time? Earth will be different than before; maybe it will resemble the Garden of Eden. Heaven is now coming to earth because we have been praying for it. This should not be strange because the Holy City (New Jerusalem) will be here. Is the Father leaving His present abode in Heaven to move permanently here on earth? It is possible. The Son will be here because this is where His Bride is. Dwelling with man is what the Father originally intended from the time of the Garden (Genesis 3:8, Leviticus 26:11–12; Ezekiel 37:26–28; Zechariah 2:10–11).

> "In this manner, therefore, pray: Our Father in heaven, hallowed be Your name. Your kingdom come. Your will be done <u>on earth as it is in heaven.</u>" (Matthew 6:9–10, emphasis added)

> "All the way around shall be eighteen thousand cubits; and the name of the city from that day shall be: THE LORD IS THERE." (Ezekiel 48:35)

Consider this, "when you run from God, you will have to embrace who is around you—the devil."

God Will Wipe Away Every Tear

Why are the people in a heaven-like atmosphere crying when they should be rejoicing? Formerly, they were persecuted, had to wait patiently, had sorrows and misfortunes, lost loved ones, etc. Like a good father, God would take care of and comfort His children (Matthew 5:4). This is one of the benefits of being in the Kingdom—being an overcomer. He will remove all the causes for tears; therefore, there will be no more death, sorrow, crying, and pain. The causes for all of these will pass away.

> But be glad and rejoice forever in what I create;
> For behold, I create Jerusalem as a rejoicing,

And her people a joy.
I will rejoice in Jerusalem,
And joy in My people;
The voice of weeping shall no longer be heard in her,
Nor the voice of crying.
(Isaiah 65:18–19)
See also 2 Corinthians 1:3–4.

I Make All Things New

The earthly tabernacle, temple, city of Zion, and Ark of the Covenant were all replicas of the real which are in Heaven (Hebrews 8:5). If the earthly tabernacle is a copy or shadow, then there has to be a real one somewhere. Therefore, the New Jerusalem is physical. Furthermore, it <u>replaces</u> the old one. Jesus did say, "Behold, <u>I make all things new</u>" (Revelation 21:5, emphasis added).

Thus says the Lord, your Redeemer,
The Holy One of Israel . . .
"Do not remember the former things,
Nor consider the things of old.
Behold, I will do a new thing,
Now it shall spring forth;
Shall you not know it?
I will even make a road in the wilderness
And rivers in the desert.
(Isaiah 43:14a, 18–19)

The One on the throne has the authority and power and needs no permission or help. He is basically promising to give everything a different perspective, a fresh condition to whatever was before to bring everything to a permanent spiritual state. The global fire will have purged everything that they will need to be replaced to be useful. Pollution, perversion, contamination, satanic interference, imperfection, weakness, and corruption have to be removed from everything. God is looking for purity all around.

You will still be you, but you will have a new body (1 Corinthians 15:40–45, 51–54). Spirits cannot die. They are immortal. Everything you can see in the natural is temporary and cannot last. You will see it again, but it will be different then (2 Corinthians 4:18). There is a life stage between the first death and eternity. The body you will need for life in the eternal realm is not this one because this one is corruptible; it is of flesh and blood.

Expect More New Stuff

"For behold, I create new heavens and a new earth;
and the former shall not be remembered or come to mind.
(Isaiah 65:17)
See also Isaiah 48:6–7, 66:22–24.

Some new stuff is coming that no man has ever seen before. If your divine inheritance is incorruptible, then you will need an incorruptible body or be in an immortal state to fully appreciate your inheritance.

Blessed be the God and Father of our Lord Jesus Christ, who according to His abundant mercy has begotten us again to a living hope through the resurrection of Jesus Christ from the dead, to an inheritance incorruptible and undefiled and that does not fade away, reserved in heaven for you, who are kept by the power of God through faith for salvation ready to be revealed in the last time. (1 Peter 1:3–5)

It Is Done!

What is done? All that the Father said He would do is done. Every word He gave is from the start to the finish, everything concerning sin, Satan, and the wicked. Everything He spoke of (prophesied or written) has been accomplished at this time. "The Alpha and the Omega", when used together, is the name applied to Christ, the only Being who has referred to Himself as both. Fraternities and sororities incorporate one or the other of these names to identify themselves with hopes of luring unsuspected folks into their organization as the Greek names sound spiritual. But the title Alpha and the Omega is used only in the book of Revelation. It is used four times—twice at the beginning and twice at the end of the book (1:8, 1:11, 21:6, 22:13)—and the name is explained each time. Verse 6 is not in red letter denoting words of Jesus as are the other three references. Some scholars say that this omission is a printer's error while others say that it is not a direct quote. On closer examination, one notices that it is not Jesus Christ speaking but "He that sat upon the throne," the Father.

The Fountain of the Water of Life

There are some thirsty people around and the Father is willing to give them a drink freely. There is a tree, a book, a light, and a fountain of the water of life in the Kingdom. The intention was for mankind to live forever being sustained by provisions of the Kingdom (Ezekiel 47:1–2; Matthew 5:6; John 7:37–39). A drink from this well gives everlasting life, and the drinker will never thirst again. The woman at the well in Samaria had some.

Jesus answered and said to her, "Whoever drinks of this water will thirst again, but whoever drinks of the water that I shall give him will never thirst. But the water that I shall give him will become in him a fountain of water springing up into everlasting life." (John 4:13–14)

No Entry for Cowards and Others

'But the cowardly, unbelieving, abominable, murderers, sexually immoral, sorcerers, idolaters, and all liars shall have their part in the lake which burns with fire and brimstone, which is the second death.' (Revelation 21:8)

This passage needs no explanation; either you accept it as it is, or you reject it. The list of people who will be sentenced to the lake of fire is longer than this but this one specifically addresses certain sins (lifestyles, characters, practices, or preferences) which God considers abominable. Perpetrators of these sins will not get into His Kingdom.

The one who commits sin continually will not share in the Kingdom of God. If you before time practiced these sins and you stopped (repented), that exclusion does not refer to you. There are many persons who have repented and will enjoy the presence of Jesus Christ, people such as Rahab the harlot, Mary Magdalene, the thief on the cross with Jesus, and Apostle Paul. If a person repents of his sins, he shall live. Not repenting leads to judgment (Ezekiel 33:14–16; Romans 2:1–11; 2 Peter 3:9; 1 John 1:9, 3:8). Here are categories of sinners who will NOT ENTER the New Jerusalem:

- dogs (unbelievers, base characters, hounds, male prostitutes [Philippians 3:2])

- sorcerers (magicians, warlocks, witch doctors, voodoo priests, psychics, practitioners of all the black arts, obeah workers and their clients, Chaldeans, etc.)
- sexually immoral people (whoremongers, adulterers, fornicators, lesbians, homosexuals, transgenders, rapists, persons who practice bestiality, prostitutes, persons who practice incest)
- murderers (hard-core criminals, people who intentionally touch God's image/creation, shedding innocent blood)
- idolaters (worshippers of false gods, Satanists, everyone who does not worship Jehovah)
- whoever loves and practices a lie (everyone who does not have the truth in him, those who disagree with God, the deceitful, and the wicked [John 8:44]).

Do you not know that the unrighteous will not inherit the kingdom of God? Do not be deceived. Neither fornicators, nor idolaters, nor adulterers, nor homosexuals, nor sodomites, nor thieves, nor covetous, nor drunkards, nor revilers, nor extortioners will inherit the kingdom of God. And such were some of you. But you were washed, but you were sanctified, but you were justified in the name of the Lord Jesus and by the Spirit of our God. (1 Corinthians 6:9–11)

The Lamb's Wife

"Come, I will show you the bride, the Lamb's wife" (v. 9b). The Bride is the city of New Jerusalem with the collection of the called-out as its inhabitants. She is neither a person nor a group of persons but a city. She was just sitting up there suspended in the heavens and now is being lowered to the earth like a giant spaceship making its landing. The entire city has the glory of God. A prophecy by Isaiah alludes to this city being the Bride,

"For thy Maker is thine husband" (Isaiah 54:5, KJV). The city has its own light that is like a most precious stone, jasper.

> JASPER—"A precious stone. It was the last of the twelve inserted in the high priest's breastplate, Exodus 28:20; 39:13, and the first of the twelve used in the foundations of the New Jerusalem. Revelation 21:19. The characteristics of the stone as far as they are specified in Scripture, Revelation 21:11, are that it "was most precious," and "like crystal"; we may also infer from Revelation 4:3, that it was a stone of brilliant and transparent light. The stone which we name "jasper" does not accord with this description. There can be no doubt that the diamond would more adequately answer to the description in the Book of Revelation." Note: diamonds were not known in the first century. Also, jasper is known today to be an opaque stone.[3]

The wall with the gates is described by Prophet Ezekiel (Ezekiel 48:30–35). John gives an exterior description of what he sees. The walls and gates were built when the city was in Heaven; it came to earth just as it was in Heaven. These are rather high walls and the gates are guarded by angels, making the city very secure. This security is rather strange because these gates shall not be shut at all (21:25). The length and breadth of the city are 12,000 furlongs, and the wall is 144 cubits high.

8 furlongs = 1 mile; thus 12,000 furlongs = 1,500 miles or 2,414 kilometers

1 cubit = 1.5 feet; thus 144 cubits = 216 feet or 72 yards or 66 meters.[4]

The foundations of the wall of the city were adorned with twelve layers of all kinds of precious stones. These are basically the same stones used on the breastplate of the high priest. They were placed three in a row with four rows (Exodus 28:15–21). These precious stones were not used simply for using sake; they have significance. Just as gold was instructed to be placed in the temple and on the Ark of the Covenant and precious stones to be placed on the high priest's chest, these stones in the foundation of the Holy City have particular meaning and serve a specific purpose. Today you use white dirt (quarry) to build your foundations because this is the cheapest fill you can find; whereas God's Holy City uses the most expensive stones known on the earth. Various stones are used as healing agents while diamonds are used for lasers. Imagine what the natural layer of the foundation would be worth!

The first foundation of the wall was jasper, the second sapphire, the third chalcedony, the fourth emerald, the fifth sardonyx, the sixth sardius, the seventh chrysolite, the eighth beryl, the ninth topaz, the tenth chrysoprase, the eleventh jacinth, and the twelfth amethyst. The twelve gates were twelve pearls; each individual gate was of one pearl. And the street of the city was pure gold like transparent glass (vv. 19–21).

I Saw No Temple and No Sun

John is now taken on a tour of the inside of the city. He doesn't see a physical temple building. For Christians, church buildings (the edifice, physical structure) were not constructed until the fourth century. Roman Emperor Constantine began the construction of church buildings to appease the Christians. Before that time, believers met from house to house because they were not allowed to preach or teach Jesus Christ in the synagogues. Furthermore, they were being persecuted for making their beliefs public. There is no need for a physical temple because God has said that "you are the temple of the living God . . . I will dwell in them and walk among them" (2 Corinthians 6:16; 1 Corinthians 3:16–17).

There is no need for the sun. The Lamb (Jesus Christ) is its light (Genesis 1:3–4; Psalms 119:105; Matthew 17:1–2).

Then Jesus spoke to them again, saying, "I am the light of the world. He who follows Me shall not walk in darkness, but have the light of life." (John 8:12)

The nations will bring their glory into the city. Nations will be distinguished and recognized separately. Nations will still be recognized, and people will be recognized by their nations. The saints will enter the New Jerusalem by nations. Its gates shall not be shut, but they will still be guarded by angels. There is no more enemy moving about because they are all in the lake of fire and brimstone. There is no more night; the sun, moon, and stars have fled away since the judgment (Revelation 20:11).

The Holy City shall be just that, holy, meaning, pure, morally blameless, sanctified, consecrated. Nothing profane shall enter it, only those whose names are written in the Lamb's Book of Life.

The Lamb's Book of Life

When you receive salvation (enter the Kingdom of Heaven) your name is written in the Lamb's Book of Life, which is in Heaven. The Book is a register of all the saints even the ones gone before. As long as you remain faithful to your confession of Jesus Christ, your name remains in the Book. There is the possibility of your name being removed for not overcoming or for your being unrighteous (Revelation 3:5; Ezekiel 18:24, 33:18–19). The doctrine of "once saved always saved" does not hold true based on the above references. You will be held accountable for your lifestyle after accepting Jesus Christ as Lord. This Book will be used on Judgment Day to determine your fate according to your works (Psalms 69:28; Luke 10:20; Revelation 2:23, 14:13).

And I saw the dead, small and great, standing before God, and books were opened. And another book was opened, which is the Book of Life. And the dead were judged according to their works, by the things which were written in the books. And anyone not found written in the Book of Life was cast into the lake of fire. (Revelation 20:12–15)

From here onward, you will see the continued restoration of all things as they were in the Garden of Eden, just as the heavenly Father originally intended in the beginning with Adam—Eve came on the scene afterward. There are no women (females) in Heaven, only spirits who are referred to in the masculine gender (Matthew 22:29–30; Galatians 3:28).

The River of Life

The angel still has John on a tour of the city. The water of life was discussed in Revelation 21:6 where it was referred to as a fountain (source or supply). Now it is referred to as a river (a current, running water) of life. I should like to think this river of life is in the Bahamas or the Caribbean for the water is fresh and crystal clear, not muddy or cloudy with debris or strong undertow. The flow begins from the throne of God and goes into the street. There was a similar river in the Garden of Eden (Genesis 2:10). The Father's and the Lamb's thrones are in the New Jerusalem. He did say that He would dwell among His people (v. 3).

The Tree of Life

The street and both sides of the river are all lined with the tree of life (Genesis 2:9). In the New Jerusalem, there are many such trees. This is not a symbolic tree but a literal one, just like the one in the Garden of Eden that was there in the beginning. That tree in Eden was taken away from mankind because of sin and is now restored. It seems there was only one tree back then, but now there are many trees, enough for everybody to live on forever.

The tree of life is a plant which was created by God to give eternal life to man. It's a tree that will preserve life and give mankind immortality (Genesis 3:22-23). Even though this tree sustains life and Jesus gives everlasting life, this tree is not Jesus; it is simply a tree and not a being. Eternal life is one of the innate benefits given to mankind since the beginning of creation. Originally, man was not supposed to die because he was created in the image and likeness of God (Elohiym). Note that Adam's physical death took 930 years. In his first created state (Genesis 1:26–27), had he eaten of this tree before he disobeyed God, he would have been immortal.

Eternal life is not in man himself but in the God who created him. In this natural world, there is nothing a man can do of himself to live forever as he will die at some stage for one reason or another. Special foods, medicated concoctions or supplements, stem cell implants, cosmetic surgery, organ implants or transplants—none of these can cause man to live forever (Psalms 89:48; Hebrews 9:27; 1 John 5:11–13). If God is your eternal Father and you want eternal life, then the only place you can go to get this eternal life is the Father. Jesus the Son of God says that He is the only way to the Father. Jesus at the same time declares that He is the life also (John 1:4–5, 3:14–17, 6:33–35, 11:25–26).

> Jesus said to him, "I am the way, the truth, and the life. No one comes to the Father except through Me." (John 14:6, emphasis added)

There is a symbolic tree of life; it is known as "wisdom." She (wisdom) is a tree of life to those who take hold of her, and happy are all who retain her (Proverbs 3:18). It was originally intended for man to live forever. The heavenly Father did not want man to live forever in sin. Now that sin is removed, man can live eternally in holiness and in fellowship with Him. Therefore, man can now eat freely of all the trees with no restrictions (Genesis 1:11, 3:22–24,).

The leaves of the tree are for the healing of the nations. If a tree could bestow immortality, then it should be able to heal also (Ezekiel 47:12). This should not be hard to accept because ordinary plants nourish the physical body right now and the drugs (alcohol, cocaine, marijuana) which are made from plants do influence the soul and spirit, not just the body.

No More Curses

There shall be no more cursing (calling down or invoking evil upon a person). There is nothing evil, wicked, or from the kingdom of darkness there as Satan and his agents will not be there. Satan will not be able to come before God as in past times (Job 1:6–7). Curses were released after Adam disobeyed God. The serpent and the ground were execrated (Genesis 3:14, 17–18). These curses will be broken so that the earth can return to the state it was before the Fall. However, the New Jerusalem, the place where God dwells, will never have a curse in it because it is tranquil and glorious.

They Shall See His Face

Finally! The people in Heaven now get to see the Father's face. This is in keeping with a promise made by Jesus (Matthew

5:8). Before the Fall, Adam used to walk and talk with Him in the cool of the day (Genesis 3:8). Throughout the ages, men have been asking the Father to see His face but to no avail (Exodus 33:18–23).

> As for me, I will see Your face in righteousness; I shall be satisfied when I awake in Your likeness. (Psalms 17:15)

His Name on Their Foreheads

The most forward and pronounced part of the human body is the forehead. That is why oil is applied there, representing the Holy Spirit's presence. Marking the forehead is for separation, sanctification, and identification. When other religions apply a mark to the forehead, it usually means devotion to a deity. The marking on the forehead is originally God's idea (Exodus 28:36–38; Deuteronomy 6:6–9; Ezekiel 9:4–6). The enemy has counterfeited what God has established.

No Night There

The darkness that was on the face of the deep at the beginning (Genesis 1:2) is now in the bottomless pit. There is no more sun to mark the starting of the day; therefore, there is no night. This means that there is no more sunrise and sunset. The need for sleep, apparently, is also taken away. Does a spirit need rest, sleep, or time?

They Shall Reign Forever

This is where one age will end and the next age begins. After the judgment and the separation, eternity begins. The prophecy is finished. Now John is exhorting the reader. The phrase "These words are faithful and true" has been quoted many times. This prophecy must be true because it was revealed by Jesus and spoken of by other persons before and after Him (Matthew 24:34–35; Revelation 1:1).

"They will take place shortly" means that the events herein will begin to unfold in the near future, starting even in John's days. When they happen, they will happen quickly and altogether. Even though this prophecy was written almost 2,000 years ago, "shortly" can mean "in the fullness of time." Take this book of prophecies very seriously. You will be blessed if you do (Revelation 1:3).

Do Not Seal This Book, It's for the Now

"And he said to me, 'Do not seal the words of the prophecy of this book, for the time is at hand'" (Revelation 22:10). He was unlike Prophet Daniel who was given a similar prophecy and told to withhold it (Daniel 12:4), John is told to make the contents of this book available right away to those who search for the truth. In obedience, John wrote and published what was given to him. This revelation was given as a gift. The idea was never to hide its contents. The best gifts come wrapped, not to hide them but to protect them from the wrong eyes and hands. Then it must be opened and enjoyed. Holy Spirit will reveal its contents to the one who digs for treasure. Treasures are not easily attained (Psalms 119:162; Matthew 13:44–46). God wants you to know what the end looks like so that you may govern yourself as one with knowledge and not like a fool (Proverbs 1:7; Job 28:27–28; Psalms 14:1).

David, Isaiah, Jeremiah, Ezekiel, Daniel, Jesus, and other prophets all spoke of the end-time, but John is saying that the end is about to begin. Truth be told, partial fulfillment of this book has taken place already. Some folks believe we are now in the last trumpet sound. In any event, this disclosure is for the present time. Further still, time is shorter than it used to be. The preterist believes that these things have already happened. Remember that the entire book of Revelation is a prophecy. Therefore, it has:

o   timing (futuristic)
o   condition(s) to be met
o   the unknown, the unseen, and the unheard-of
o   elements of its manifestation and
o   the person who gave it (God) with the ability to fulfill it.

As You Were in Your Lifetime, You Remain

After your death in the flesh, you will remain how you were when you died. He who was unjust in life, let him be unjust after death. Whatever you are upon death of your flesh or on Judgment Day, that is what you will remain. The time will be gone to change or repent. There will be no new opportunity for redemption or reconsideration at that point. So hold fast to what you believe. Persevere! The story Jesus told about the rich man and Lazarus (Luke 16:19–31) was not a parable but a true event. There will be no crossing over after you die. Your decision about eternity must be made while you are still living. After you die there is no "Now that I have seen all this, now I believe" (John 3:15–17, 20:29–30).

The Difference between "Righteous" and "Holy"

The opposite of "unjust" (do wrong, offend) is "righteous" and the opposite of "filthy" (to soil, to become dirty) is "holy." There is a difference between "righteous" and "holy." Do not confuse the two; they are as different as "blue" and "hard." Blue is a color while hard is a texture; they describe different features of the same thing.

> I speak in human terms because of the weakness of your flesh. For just as you presented your members as slaves of uncleanness, and of lawlessness leading to more lawlessness, so now present your members as <u>slaves of righteousness for holiness</u>. (Romans 6:19, emphasis added)
> See also Luke 1:74–75.

Righteous—*dikaioo* (dik-ah-yo'-o) in Greek means to render (i.e., show or regard as) just or innocent, free, justify (-ier).[5] It has different but related meanings:

o the state of him who is such as he ought to be;
o the inner desire to do or be right;
  - the will to do right;
  - something may be right at different times and under different circumstances (laws may change [e.g., the sale of alcohol was once illegal] or Jews do not eat cheeseburgers, yet they eat cheese and beef at different times);
  - doing a good thing on the wrong day makes it unrighteous (Matthew 12:10–14). This could be influenced by customs and the social order.

> "For I say to you, that unless your righteousness exceeds the righteousness of the scribes and Pharisees, you will by no means enter the kingdom of heaven." (Matthew 5:20)

You can <u>appear</u> to be righteous by following your so-called moral convictions when all the while you were motivated by your fear of the consequences of violating a custom or law. The fact that a potential criminal did not break the law does not mean he was righteous if his heart was not pure from the beginning, and it was truly fear that helped him to stay in line. A righteous person does not need fear to govern him; he is governed by his heart. Hence, a righteous man is one who does what is godly without being externally prompted to do so. Here is an example:

> Then Joseph her husband, being a just *[righteous]* man, and not wanting to make her a public example, was minded to put her away secretly. (Matthew 1:19, emphasis added)
> See also Leviticus 20:10; Deuteronomy 24:1.

> Righteousness comes out of a pure heart.

> Who may ascend into the hill of the Lord? Or who may stand in His holy place? He who has clean hands and a pure heart, who has not lifted up his soul to an idol, nor sworn deceitfully. He shall receive blessing from the Lord, and righteousness from the God of his salvation. (Psalms 24:3–5)
> See also 2 Timothy 2:22.

The righteous one lives differently from the unjust; he lives by faith in God and not by his own understanding or feelings. Living by your own righteousness is ungodly.

> For in it the righteousness of God is revealed from faith to faith; as it is written, "The just *[righteous]* shall live by faith." (Romans 1:17, emphasis added)
> In those days there was no king in Israel; everyone did what was right *[straight, convenient, equitable]* in his own eyes. (Judges 21:25, emphasis added)

Holy—Greek *hagios* (hag'-ee-os) from *hagos* (an awful thing), sacred (physically, pure, morally blameless or religious, ceremonially, consecrated), saint.[6]

To be holy is an innate attribute that is ascribed to God (Jehovah) alone. Holiness expresses His pure supreme divinity. A person or thing is considered holy when it is cut and separated unto God like a tailor preparing to make a suit. Nothing is holy of itself. It becomes holy after it is cut and separated to God. The separation is to keep you free from contamination and distraction and from other uses. A person or thing is holy because it is consecrated to God's service.

> And they were calling to one another: "Holy, holy, holy is the Lord Almighty; the whole earth is full of his glory." (Isaiah 6:3, NIV)
> But as He who called you is holy, you also be holy in all your conduct, because it is written, "Be holy, for I am holy." (1 Peter 1:15–16)
> See also Leviticus 11:44–45.

Being holy is different from person to person. You going to a barber does not make you unholy or reduce your anointing, yet it was so for Samson.

> "For behold, you shall conceive and bear a son. And no razor shall come upon his head, for the child shall be a Nazirite to God from the womb; and he shall begin to deliver Israel out of the hand of the Philistines." (Judges 13:5)

Jeremiah, Samson, John the Baptist, Jesus were all different with different assignments and anointing, yet they were all holy men. Jesus drank wine but Samson and John the Baptist could not. The qualifications for a bishop and a deacon are different. Are not bishops and deacons all cut and set apart? See 1 Timothy 3:1–13.

Jesus Christ was righteous because He did exactly as His Father expected of Him every time. He was holy because He was set apart for God from the womb.

Everyone Gets His Just Reward

Jesus gives an assurance of what is to happen. He is coming quickly, suddenly, by surprise, and that will be soon. He is bringing with Him rewards, pay for services good or bad, your wages (Psalms 62:12; Isaiah 40:10; Matthew 16:27; 2 Corinthians 5:10). The righteous (those who overcome) will receive eternal life (be comforted, Revelation 21:4) while the wicked will get the lake of fire with eternal death and torment. Everybody in hell (Satan, the two beasts, the false prophet, the fallen angels, the unrighteous) gets the lake of fire, which burns forever.

You are either in the New Jerusalem where you get to eat of the tree of life, or you are outside with the dogs. The reference here to dogs is not to pets (animals) but to the base or worthless character of man. Here the dog's nature is grouped with evil workers and is disallowed entry to the new city. There is not only exclusion from Heaven but also condemnation (Matthew 13:49–50; Luke 16:24).

There will be different levels of reward for Heaven. Everybody will get something glorious and everlasting (Matthew 5:11; 1 Corinthians 9:24–25). The twenty-four elders have received their golden crowns already. Apostle Paul is expecting the crown of righteousness, Prophet Isaiah and Apostle Peter each the crown of glory, the seven thousand and others who have not bowed to Baal the crown of life (Revelation 2:10; James 1:12). Jesus Himself had many crowns (Revelation 19:12).

Sitting on His throne next to the Father, Jesus has the first and the last say. There is no higher court or court of appeal. All His decisions are final. He is the just God (Isaiah 43:11).

Who Is Jesus Christ?

Jesus Christ is the root and shoot of King David even though He is the Messiah (Psalms 110:1; Isaiah 11:1–2; Matthew 22:41–45). A lot of people will miss the Christ because they don't know how to identify Him. Here is how others and Jesus described Himself in the book of Revelation. There are twenty-four references:

- the Faithful Witness (1:5)
- the Firstborn from the dead (1:5)
- Ruler over the kings of the earth (1:5)
- the Alpha and the Omega (1:11,17; 22:13)
- the Son of Man (1:13)
- the Holder of the keys for Hades and Death (1:18)
- He who holds the seven stars (2:1)
- the First and the Last (2:8; 22:13)
- He who was dead and is alive (2:8)
- He who has the sharp double-edged sword (2:12)
- the Son of God (2:18)
- He who has the seven Spirits of God and the seven Stars (3:1)
- He who is holy and true (3:7)
- The Faithful and True Witness (3:14; 19:11)
- The Beginning of the Creation of God (3:14)
- the Lion of the tribe of Judah (5:5)
- the Root of David (5:5)
- The Lamb (5:6)
- Lord of lords (17:14; 19:16)
- King of kings (17:14; 19:16)
- The Lord our God (19:1)
- The Beginning and the End (22:13)
- The Root and Offspring of David (22:16)
- The Bright and Morning Star (22:16)

An Open Invitation to You

The Holy Spirit and the Church say, "Come!" Come into the Kingdom of Heaven. Come, receive Jesus Christ as your personal Lord and Savior. The Kingdom and the living water are free. You are still alive and have an opportunity to choose, so make the right choice. This is an open, universal invitation (Matthew 22:8–10).

> "So that servant came and reported these things to his master. Then the master of the house, being angry, said to his servant, 'Go out quickly into the streets and lanes of the city, and bring in here the poor and the maimed and the lame and the blind.' And the servant said, 'Master, it is done as you commanded, and still there is room.' Then the master said to the servant, 'Go out into the highways and hedges, and <u>compel *(force, oblige)* them</u> to come in, that my house may be filled. For I say to you that none of those men who were invited shall taste my supper.'" (Luke 14:21–24, emphasis added)

> *The burden is on you to choose.*
> For God so loved the world that He gave His only begotten Son, that <u>whoever believes in Him</u> should not perish but have everlasting life. For God did not send His Son into the world to condemn the world, but that the world through Him might be saved. (John 3:16–17, emphasis added)
> See also Ezekiel 33:11, John 4:13–14; 2 Peter 3:9.

If you are reading this book and the last trumpet has not sounded, then you are still in the Grace Dispensation. There is still time for repentance and forgiveness of sins.

The Dispensations

Below are the eight biblical dispensations, their covenants, and the periods they cover, according to Bishop Bill Hamon.[7]

DISPENSATION	COVENANT	PERIOD
Innocence	Edenic	From the Creation to the Fall, no sin
Conscience	Adamic	From the Fall to the Great Flood, deliberate sin
Human Government	Noahic	From the Great Flood to the call of Abraham
Promise	Abrahamic	From Abraham until the law given at Mt. Sinai
Law	Mosaic	From Mt. Sinai to the first coming of Christ
Grace	Church	From the Crucifixion to the Second Coming of Christ
Millennial	Kingdom	From Christ's Second Coming to the end of the Millennial Reign
Universal	Everlasting	End of Millennial into Eternity

Time to Move Forward

If religion (sacrifices, rituals, and laws, Exodus 29:36–46) could have saved, healed, and delivered mankind, there would be no need for Jesus the Messiah. Even after Christ came to the earth, mankind still held onto religion (to no avail). How ironic? Yet people pray religiously as Jesus taught His disciples, "Your kingdom come. Your will be done on earth as it is in heaven" (Matthew 6:10). They make the Word of God of no effect by their traditions and hardheartedness (Mark 7:13). Nonetheless, they want Christ to come quickly. It's time to leave the old method of doing church and adopt what John the Baptist and Jesus started, preach and live the Kingdom of Heaven.

Don't Alter this Book of Prophecy

There is a strong warning about tampering with this book (Revelation 22:18–19). The phrase "this book" cannot correctly be applied to all sixty-six books of the Bible. It is specifically meant for the book of Revelation written by John. But wisdom says not to touch any of them (Proverbs 30:5–6). Persons who, nonetheless, tamper with this book suffer plagues, their names are omitted from the Book of Life, and they are prevented from entering the New Jerusalem. Don't be one of those persons.

Errors can be made during translation between languages. Even when such an error is unintentional, it still qualifies as an alteration. Translators should be Spirit-led. In recent times there has been an increase in new versions of the Holy Bible in the English language, some with intentional omissions and additions yet claiming to be the truth. Be careful of these. However, there are some English versions that basically say what the original manuscripts say. For the most part, the better versions are produced by scholars who have a very good command of the Hebrew, Aramaic, and Greek languages, and are using the Dead Sea Scrolls as an additional source of reference. Mankind can still receive further revelation about the end-time from Holy Spirit, but he cannot make those revelations a part of the Holy Bible.

Come, Lord Jesus!

If your life is anchored in Christ and you are doing your assignment of advancing the Kingdom of Heaven, you can join with the writer and call for the coming of the Savior, "Come, Lord Jesus!" (Revelation 22:20) The Church or people undergoing persecution will eagerly pray this way because they know of the wonderful end results of the entire matter. Time is the major factor in realizing their change. The Word of God is faithful and true; that is why you are continually told "to overcome." When you are suffering a great deal and you are tired and weary, you pray either "Jesus, come in now" or "Lord, take me out." You would be like the folks in Revelation 6:10, asking, "How long, O Lord, holy and true, until You judge and avenge our blood on those who dwell on the earth?" Do not lose hope because God is faithful and His Word is true. Remember that Christ is not coming "until the times of restoration of all things, which God has spoken by the mouth of all His holy prophets since the world began" (Acts 3:21). Also, when He comes, He is coming on the clouds and every nation shall see Him (Matthew 24:30, 26:64).

Until Christ comes, as a Believer you are required to stay strong and overcome:

Finally, my brethren, be strong in the Lord and in the power of His might. Put on the whole armor of God, that you may be able to stand [continue; hold up; stanch] against the wiles of the devil. For we do not wrestle against flesh and blood, but against principalities, against powers, against the rulers of the darkness of this age, against spiritual hosts of wickedness in the heavenly places. Therefore take up the whole armor of God, that you may be able to withstand in the evil day, and having done all, to stand. (Ephesians 6:10–13, emphasis added)

See also Zechariah 4:6; Hebrews 12:2.

My Grace Is Sufficient for You

To endure in these last days, you will need God's grace more than before. You will need God's divine influence upon your heart and its reflection in your life. You will need His divine enablement and His undeserving favor or kindness given to you not based on your perceived value (John 1:17; 2 Corinthians 12:8–9; Ephesians 4:7; Hebrews 4:16).

The grace of our Lord Jesus Christ be with you all. Amen. Amen!

CONCLUSION

The ultimate measure of a man is not where he stands in
moments of comfort and convenience, but where he stands
at times of challenge and controversy.
—Martin Luther King Jr.

WHILE LIVING FOREVER with the Lord in a
place where there is no more stress of any kind, no
sickness, no lack, no pain, no fear, and no regrets sound like
a very good idea; the reality is that it comes with a price. The
only place where you can find true bliss is in the Kingdom of
Heaven. Nothing in life is free, not even salvation. Salvation will
cost you your sins (you have to give them up) and a change of
mind. It will cost you something, but the sacrifice is worth it.
Whatever you give up for the Kingdom of God, it is worth it.

Dealing with kingdoms, power, freedom, and peace is never
a casual matter because they all call for wisdom, knowledge, a
belief system, inner strength, and the ability to sustain whatever
you decide on. You have to choose the world you want to live
in and how you want to live in it. The outcome all depends on
the choices you make. Bear in mind that the best things are not
free or easy to achieve; they require diligent effort on your part.

Just as Elohiym invaded the darkness and void to establish
His new domain on earth (to have a new place to reign) and Jesus
conquered death and Hell (so you could live forever with Him), you
are required to overcome something to get into God's Kingdom.
The seven churches all had to overcome something to be rewarded.

While the kingdom is free and open to all, you don't just
walk in and it's over. You have to earn your stripes. You have
to prove to yourself that this is where you want to be. Tests,

trials, and temptations will come your way so that you could be[8] promoted or at least remain in school. You have to know that this is what you want. Everything is prepared for you and you are given promises to be secured and guidelines (the Holy Bible of laws, beatitudes, prophecies, and admonitions) to help you operate by the established rules. When you abide by the rules, you win in the end. If you mess up along the way, there are chances to correct your mistakes. Better still, you are given a personal coach to make sure you win—Holy Spirit.

> And from the days of John the Baptist until now the kingdom of heaven suffers violence *[allows for, is pressed into],* and the violent take it by force. (Matthew 11:12, emphasis added)

It seems whatever the persecution, hard time, or discomfort you go through in life, it has the potential to groom you to become a better Kingdom citizen. The Hall of Famers in Hebrews 11 all had to please God by using their faith to overcome whatever their challenge was. The good news is that you are created and designed to win and dominate this earth. You can live for 34ever with Christ.

The only thing that matters is how you dealt with Jesus Christ and His Kingdom (John 3:16–18; Acts 16:31). King Solomon, the man who is known for wisdom, topped everything off with these words:

> Let us hear the conclusion of the whole matter: "Fear God and keep His commandments, for this is man's all. For God will bring every work into judgment, including every secret thing, whether good or evil." (Ecclesiastes 12:13–14, emphasis added)

NOTES

Chapter 1

[1] "AD 95," *Matthew Henry Complete Bible Commentary*, Biblesoft. "AD 96," *Thompson Chain-Reference Bible.*

[2] International Standard Bible Encyclopaedia (ISBE) Electronic Database, Biblesoft.

[3] Ibid.

[4] en.wikipedia.org>wiki>Maya_civilization.

[5] Nelson's Illustrated Bible Dictionary, PC Study Bible, Biblesoft.

[6] Ibid.

[7] ISBE.

Chapter 3

[1] ISBE.

[2] *Easton's Bible Dictionary*, PC Study Bible formatted electronic database, Biblesoft.

[3] https://www.donquijote.org/Spanish History.

[4] https://forums.anglican.net/threads/sydney-anglican-archbishop-tells-same-sex-marriage-supporters-to-leave-the-anglican-church-virtueo.3831/.

[5] https://en.wikipedia.org/wiki/Mary_Baker_Eddy.

[6] https://en.wikipedia.org/wiki/Shakers.

[7] https://www.britannica.com/topic/Shakers.

[8] https://www.adventist.org/church/what-do-seventh-day-adventists-believe/history-of-seventh-day-adventists/

[9] https://www.jw.org/en/

[10] https://www.yelp.com/search?find_desc=Gay+Church&find_loc=Atlanta%2C+GA

[11] ISBE.

[12] Ibid.

[13] Ibid.

Chapter 4

[1] ISBE.
[2] *Nelson's Illustrated Bible Dictionary.*
[3] "atmospheres," *BNESNC.*
[4] "throne," *BNESNC.*
[5] *Easton's Bible Dictionary.*
[6] "sardius color," *BNESNC.*
[7] "face," *BNESNC.*
[8] "Iris," *BNESNC.*
[9] en.wikipedia.org/wiki/LGBT
[10] "crown," *BNESNC.*
[11] "elder," *BNESNC.*
[12] McLean, page 51.
[13] "holy," *BNESNC.*
[14] "holy," *ISBE.*
[15] *The Timechart of Biblical History.*
[16] *Nelson's Illustrated Bible Dictionary.*

Chapter 5

[1] ISBE.
[2] IVP Bible Background, Biblesoft.
[3] ISBE.
[4] *The Timechart of Biblical History.*
[5] *Nelson's Illustrated Bible Dictionary.*

Chapter 6

[1] Barnes' Notes, Biblesoft.
[2] Smith, p. 391.
[3] en.wikipedia.org/wiki/Parthian_Empire#Military
[4] "The Beginning of Catholicism."
[5] ISBE.
[6] *Nelson's Illustrated Bible Dictionary.*
[7] Ibid.
[8] Smith, p. 395.
[9] *Easton's Bible Dictionary.*
[10] www.populationmatters.org/population.
[11] Smith, p. 402.

[12] Ibid. pp. 402–412.

[13] en.wikipedia.org/wiki/predictions and claims for the second coming of Christ

Chapter 7

[1] en.wikipedia.org>wiki>Effects of Hurricane Dorian in the Bahamas www.thenassauguardian.com>Hurricane Dorian the aftermath – September 4, 2019.

[2] www.wipo.int>about-ip.

[3] www.theatlantic.com>technology>archive>2018/09>how-i-learned

[4] Spanish Inquisition.

[5] HEWD.

[6] Luther, Thomas, et al.

Chapter 8

[1] "trumpet," Easton's Bible Dictionary.

[2] en.wikipedia,org>wiki>2019-California-wildfires.

[3] cnbc.com/2020/02/01/australias-capital-braces-as-hot-windy-conditions.html.

[4] "wormwood," *BNESNC.*

[5] en.wikipedia.org/wiki/Branch-Davidians.

[6] Barnes' Notes.

Chapter 9

[1] "star," BNESNC.

[2] "abyss," *BNESNC.*

[3] "sheol," *BNESNC.*

[4] "key," *Easton's Bible Dictionary.*

[5] Smith, pp. 459–461.

[6] Barnes' Notes.

[7] Smith, p. 471.

[8] Adam Clarke Commentary, Electronic Database, Biblesoft.

[9] https://en.wikipedia.org>wiki>Euphrates.

[10] Clarke Commentary.

[11] Smith, p. 465.

[12] Ibid, p. 476.

[13] https://www.newscientist.com/article/mg22730313-500-semen-has-controlling-power-over-female-genes-and-behaviour/ 07-22-2015.

Chapter 10

[1] "voice," BNESNC.
[2] Smith, p. 477.
[3] A prophetic "time" is "one year." *BNESNC*, OT:5732 (Aramaic) D*u! `iddan *id-dawn*`; a set time; technically, a year.
[4] Smith, pp. 479 and 489.

Chapter 11

[1] "measure," BNESNC.
[2] Personal notes from a conference with Dr. Lance Wallnau on "The Seven Mountains."
[3] www.worldometers.info.

Chapter 12

[1] Matthew Henry Commentary.
[2] Information received while attending a conference at Christian International, Santa Rosa, Florida, in October 2015.
[3] Ibid.
[4] Barnes' Notes.
[5] Matthew Henry Commentary.
[6] Clarke Commentary.
[7] en.wikipedia.org/wiki/group-of-seven.
[8] en.wikipedia.org/wiki/group-of-seven.
[9] en.wikipedia.org>wiki>economy-of-china.
[10] en.wikipedia.org>wiki>new-world-order-conspiracy-theory.
[11] *Easton's Bible Dictionary.*
[12] "heaven," *BNESNC.*
[13] Constantine. This war has already occurred.
[14] "persecute," *BNESNC.*
[15] en.wikipedia.org>wiki>islam-in-the-united-kingdom and www.independent.co.uk>life-style>visit-my-mosque-day

Chapter 13

[1] "blasphemy," BNESNC.
[2] "religion," *BNESNC.*
[3] HEWD
[4] Smith, p. 526.
[5] Ibid, p. 115.
[6] en.wikipedia.org>wiki>jim-jones
[7] "mark," *BNESNC.*
[8] cnbc.com/video/2017/07/24/three-square-market-ceo-microchip-technology.html.
[9] Anderson Cooper, CNN.
[10] www.myjewishlearning.com>article>gematria.
[11] www.christianforums.com/threads/emmanuel-macron-is-the-antichrist, and www.prophecyupdate.com/pun111618.html

Chapter 14

[1] "repent," BNESNC.
[2] Barnes' Commentary.
[3] *Easton's Bible Dictionary.*
[4] ISBE.
[5] *Easton's Bible Dictionary.*
[6] *Easton's Bible Dictionary.*
[7] Barnes' Commentary.
[8] *Easton's Bible Dictionary.*
[9] en.wikipedia.org/wiki/Ninety-five Theses.
[10] "abide," *BNESNC.*
[11] HEWD.
[12] ISBE.

Chapter 15

[1] "wrath of God," BNESNC.
[2] Ibid.
[3] Easton's Bible Dictionary.
[4] Ibid.
[5] Barnes' Commentary.
[6] Author unable to recall source but wishes to acknowledge that the work belongs to another.

[7] *Easton's Bible Dictionary.*
[8] Smith, p. 649.
[9] Ibid, p. 651.
[10] Ibid, p. 650.

Chapter 16

[1] "harlot," BNESNC.
[2] Smith, p. 655. *Matthew Henry and Barnes.*
[3] en.wikipedia.org/wiki/Ninety-five Theses.
[4] www.amazon.com>Devils Greatest Counterfeit Church.
[5] en.wikipedia.org/wiki/list of secret societies in popular culture.
[6] Smith, p. 529.
[7] en.wikipedia.org/wiki/History of the United Nations.
[8] Smith, p. 656.
[9] ISBE.
[10] *Nelson's Illustrated Bible Dictionary.*
[11] Smith's Bible Dictionary, p. 657.
[12] www.ancient.eu>babylon.
[13] Smith, p. 658.
[14] en.wikipedia.org/wiki/new_world_order_ (conspiracy theory)

Chapter 17

[1] The Timechart of Biblical History.

Chapter 18

[1] Personal notes from a conference with Dr. Bill Hamon in October 2016.
[2] www.npr.org>2019/03/28>why did the pope refuse to let worshippers kiss his ring.
[3] "worship," *BNESNC.*

Chapter 19

[1] "resurrection," BNESNC.
[2] *Matthew Henry Commentary.*

Chapter 20

[1] "everlasting" BNESNC.

[2] "ever" *BNESNC.*

[3] *Smith's Bible Dictionary.*

[4] www.kylesconverter.com>length>cubits

[5] "righteous," *BNESNC.*

[6] "holy," *BNESNC.*

[7] Bishop Bill Hamon, EC, p. 61.

REFERENCES

Barnes' Notes. Electronic Database Copyright © 2006 by Biblesoft, Inc.

Biblesoft's New Exhaustive Strong's Numbers and Concordance with Expanded Greek-Hebrew Dictionary. Copyright © 1994, 2003, 2006 Biblesoft, Inc. and International Bible Translators, Inc.

"Biblical Prophecies Fulfilled Around The World" – Released: June 27, 2018. https://www.facebook.com/1500184283535607/videos/2075894869297876/?sfnsn=xmmo

The Timechart of Biblical History, New York, USA: Chartwell Books, Inc., (2010). By arrangement with Third Millennium Press Limited, Chippenham England.

Easton's Bible Dictionary, PC Study Bible formatted electronic database Copyright © 2003, 2006 Biblesoft, Inc.

en.wikipedia.org/wiki/list of dates predicted for apocalyptic events

Hamlyn Encyclopedic World Dictionary, London, GB: The Hamlyn Publishing Group Ltd., 1972.

Hamon, Bill, *The Eternal Church*. Shippensburg, PA, USA: Destiny Image Publishers, Inc., 2003.

McLean, Renny, *Eternity Invading Time*, USA: Advantage Books, 2005.

Nelson's Illustrated Bible Dictionary, Copyright © 1986, Thomas Nelson Publishers.

Smith, Uriah, *The Prophecies of Daniel and the Revelation,* USA: Pacific Press Publishing Association, 1944. Revision Copyrighted by the Southern Publishing Association.

"The Dawn of Jesus Christ's Return." End Times Alert: Bible Documentaries.

Lightning Source UK Ltd.
Milton Keynes UK
UKHW040641180821
389030UK00008B/506/J

9 781664 187504